CADOGA

Belize

Introduction	vii
Travel	1
Practical A–Z	7
History	39
Natural Belize	55
Belize City	69
The Cayes	89
The West	121
The South	145
Northern Belize	173
Chronology	189
Language	193
Further Reading	205
Index & Advertising	207

Cadogan Books plc
27–29 Berwick Street,
London W1V 3RF, UK
guides@cadogan.demon.co.uk

Distributed in North America by
The Globe Pequot Press
6 Business Park Road, PO Box 833, Old Saybrook,
Connecticut 06475-0833

Copyright © Natascha Norton 1997
Illustrations © Polly Loxton 1997
Cover design by Animage
Cover photographs: front: Gavin Anderson
back: Sylvia Cordaiy Photo Library/Guy Marks

Maps © Cadogan Guides, drawn by Map Creation Ltd

The right of Natascha Norton to be identified as the author of this book has been asserted by her in accordance with the Copyright, Designs and Patents Act 1988.

Series Editor: Rachel Fielding

Editors: Katrina Burroughs and Samantha Batra
Indexing: Isobel McLean
Production: Book Production Services

A catalogue record for this book is available from the British Library

ISBN 1-86011-087-8

Printed and bound in Great Britain by Redwood Books Ltd.

The author and publishers have made every effort to ensure the accuracy of the information in this book at the time of going to press. However, they cannot accept any responsibility for any loss, injury or inconvenience resulting from the use of information contained in this guide.

Please help us to keep this guide up to date

We have done our best to ensure that the information in this guide is correct at the time of going to press. But places and facilities are constantly changing, and standards and prices in hotels and restaurants fluctuate. We would be delighted to receive any comments concerning existing entries or omissions. Authors of the best letters will receive a copy of the Cadogan Guide of their choice.

All rights reserved. No part of this publication may be reproduced, stored in a retrieval system, or transmitted, in any form or by any means, electronic or mechanical, including photocopying and recording, or by any information storage and retrieval system except as may be expressly permitted by the UK 1988 Copyright Design & Patents Act and the USA 1976 Copyright Act or in writing from the publisher. Requests for permission should be addressed to Cadogan Books plc, 27–29 Berwick Street, London W1V 3RF.

About the Author

Natascha Norton has been coming to Belize since 1990, travelling on foot, by bicycle, canoe and motor-boat, not to mention by pick-ups, landrovers, buses and aircraft. Each time she discovers she likes Belize even better than the last time and each time she marvels at how such a tiny country can have so many things to see and do. This new edition was researched in the company of her young son—once conveniently unborn, once inconveniently walking—and you have her personal assurance that Belize is a great place to travel with children.

Acknowledgements

This guide could not have been researched without the assistance of the Belize Tourist Board and a special thank you must go to Joy Vernon, Michele Longsworth and Valerie Woods Burke, who have greatly assisted me at different times over the years.

Many people have given their time and help (both practical and material) far beyond what was requested and I thank them all, in particular Alfredo Villoria, Chet Schmidt, Rose O'Doherty, Bob Jones, Josie Pollard, Meb Cutlack, Tom Brown, John Masson, Ava Davis, Francis Reid, Malcolm in Dangriga, Tony & Christine Reid, Chadwick & Eleanor Usher, Jennifer Hall, Roger Dinger, Allan Forman, Theresa Parkey, Alex Page, Ceasar Sherrad, Fred Prost, Ray and Vicki Snaddon, and the owners and managers of Discovery Expeditions, Maya Airways, Tropic Air, the Radisson Fort George Hotel, San Ignacio Hotel, Serenity Resort, Tropical Paradise Hotel, The Mayan Princess, St. Charles Inn, Chaleanor Hotel, Manatee Lodge, Bellevue Hotel, Cottage Colony, Tree Top Hotel, Sun Breeze Hotel, Blancaneaux Lodge, Hidden Valley Inn, Maya Mountain Lodge, and Chaa Creek Cottages. Last, but not least, a heartfelt thanks to Bart and Suzi Mickler who were there for us when we needed them. In addition, thanks to Gavin Anderson.

Back in England I would like to thank my husband, Benoit LeBlanc, for his support and forbearance. Thanks also to Samantha Flint of Coral Caye Conservation, Peter Jones of PCD Company, and all those staff at Cadogan who have contributed to the production of this book.

Contents

| Introduction | vii | The Best of Belize | x |

Travel 1–10

Getting to Belize	2	Getting Around	5
By Air	2	By Air	5
By Sea	2	By Boat	5
By Rail	3	By Bus	7
By Road	3	By Car or Motorbike	7
Entry Formalities	4	By Bicycle	8
Passports and Visas	4	Travel Agents and Tour	
Customs	5	Operators	8
Currency	5		

Practical A–Z 11–38

Children	12	National Holidays	23
Climate and When to Go	13	Newspapers and the	
Crime	14	Media	23
Disabled Travellers	14	Packing	24
Drugs	15	Photography	25
Electricity	15	Post Offices	25
Embassies and Consulates	15	Sexual Attitudes	25
Festivals	16	Shopping	26
Food & Drink and Eating		Sports and Activities	27
Out	16	Diving	28
Gay Travellers	18	Telephones	33
Health, Emergencies		Tipping	34
and Insurance	18	Toilets	35
Living and Working in		Tourist Information &	
Belize	20	Travel Bookshops	35
Maps	21	Where to Stay	36
Money	21	Women Travellers	36
Opening Hours	22		

History   39–54

Pre-Independence History	40	Buccaneers and Pirates	48
Prehistory	40	Creole Society	48
The Origin of Agriculture	41	A Controversial Territory	49
Early Societies	42	Independence and	
The Maya	43	Democracy	51
European Discovery and		Towards the Year 2000	52
the Colonial Era	45	Economy	52
Independence from		Modern Society	54
Spanish Rule	47		

Natural Belize   55–68

Wildlife	56	Life on the Reef	62
Birds	57	A Short Note on Reef	
Mammals, Reptiles and		Hazards	64
Insects	59	Ecotourism in Practice	65
Flora	61		

Belize City   69–88

History	72	Eating Out	82
Getting There	72	Entertainment and	
Getting Around	73	Nightlife	83
Belize City Directory	74	Trips From Belize City	84
Around Belize City	78	Nearby Cayes	86
Where to Stay	80		

The Cayes   89–120

Ambergris Caye	92	Lighthouse Reef	116
Caye Caulker	106	Glover's Reef	117
Other Cayes	114	Bluefield Range	119
Turneffe Islands	115	Tobacco Reef	119

The West: Cayo District 121–44

Belmopan	124	San Antonio and Pacbitun	133
San Ignacio	127	Mountain Pine Ridge	
Around San Ignacio	131	and Caracol	134
Branch Mouth	131	Macal River Trip	137
Cahal Pech	131	Caves	138
Xunantunich	132	Jungle Lodges	140
El Pilar, Bullet Tree Falls	132	To Guatemala	143

The South: Stann Creek and Toledo 145–72

Dangriga	151	Punta Gorda	164
Placencia	159	Around Punta Gorda	170
Around Placencia	163		

Northern Belize 173–88

Along the Northern Highway	175	Shipstern	182
Crooked Tree Wildlife Sanctuary	175	Rio Bravo Conservation Area	183
Orange Walk	176	Corozal	185
Lamanai	180		

Chronology, Language, Further Reading 189–206

Index 207

Maps

Belize	*inside front cover*	San Ignacio	129
Belize City	71	Dangriga	155
The Cayes	93	Punta Gorda	167
San Pedro	97	Orange Walk	177
Belmopan	125	Corozal	187

Belize is unique in Central America. Not just because it is mostly English-speaking and traditionally peaceful, but also because there is no other country in this region that is so small and yet offers such a huge variety of experiences, environments and atmospheres. Spending time on any of the country's islands will transport you into an easy-going Caribbean world, where sun, sea and sand entice you

Introduction

from one leisure pursuit to another, and tropical evenings tempt you to saunter along sandy streets in search of fresh seafood and the best music and bars.

Travel around Orange Walk on the mainland, and you could find yourself transported back a few centuries, among traditionalist Mennonites who still use horse-drawn buggies and speak a dialect descended from German. They live in a tightly knit, self-contained community. In the south, meanwhile, you can discover a living and historic tradition that goes back even further. This is where you can explore many of the country's Maya ruins and modern villages.

Head west, and you enter a mysterious world of caves and forests, hidden waterfalls and the most spectacular archaeological sites—this is also in many ways the most exciting part of the country for land-based activities such as hiking, horseback riding, canoeing, cycling and discovering tropical wildlife.

Even the briefest of visits should include a journey to Belize City, which is not the capital any more but certainly still feels like it. Here an urban pace and occasional danger blend in with pockets of faded colonial grandeur and havens of peace and, while it is unlikely to be a destination in itself, the city can be an interesting stepping stone for those who tread carefully.

Belize is a country of little more than 200, 000 people, which is one of the reasons why it has done exceptionally well at protecting its natural heritage on land and underwater. The problems experienced due to population needs and unequal ownership, so familiar elsewhere in Central America, have not been an issue here so far, and large swathes of the country, especially its western forests, have remained relatively undisturbed by human activity. Except for the logging camps that have periodically invaded the forest since the 18th century, few people have settled far from the coast, giving local wildlife, including the jaguar, scarlet macaw, and other rare animals an excellent chance to survive in decent numbers.

Some travellers like to say that the best thing about Belize is underwater. Frankly this is unfair, but it is easy to see why many might think so. The kaleidoscope of fish and coral that hide beneath the shallow waters of the reef are so captivating that few visitors ever succeed in tearing themselves away. That, combined with the indolent pace of tropical life, means the rest of the country remains very much undisturbed, which is excellent for the minority of travellers who venture there. News is getting around fast, though, that Belize has a great deal more to offer than your average Caribbean holiday, and the western district of Cayo

(San Ignacio) is fast becoming a favourite base for exploring inland. One of the best routes into the forest is via its rivers, teeming with brilliant kingfishers, glittering butterflies, and bright green lizards that can walk on water.

The multi-cultural nature of Belizean society is another feature, which makes travel here intriguing. Along the coast and on the islands, you will find the majority of the black population, which is largely characterized by English-speaking Creoles, but also includes a significant number of Garifuna, descendants of the Black Caribs banished from St. Vincent in the 18th century. To the north and west, especially near the Mexican and Guatemalan borders, you will find most of the country's largest ethnic group: Spanish-speaking Mestizos, many of them refugees from El Salvador and Guatemala, but also Mexican descendants that have lived here since the mid 19th century. In the remote south, you will encounter Mopan and Kekchí-speaking Maya in the villages of Stann Creek and Toledo districts, while Yucatec Maya from Mexico can be found in the west and north of Belize.

Finally, living amongst them all are a minority of whites. Some have been here for centuries, descendants of the original British pirates and loggers that settled here. Others are more recent, mostly North American arrivals, many of whom have helped develop some of the country's finest tourist facilities. And there are other groups too, of which several thousand Hong Kong Chinese are the most significant; they are also the most recent arrivals. If you look at a map you will see that Belize is about 300km long, and looks like a large bite out of Guatemala. But the wild Maya Mountains stand as a bulwark against Guatemala's historic claim on its neighbour's territory, and make up almost the entire western border. Never more than 109km wide, Mexico and Guatemala mark the country's northern and southern border respectively, while the east consists of a 288km Caribbean coastline and hundreds of islands dotted off-shore, outcrops of the largest living reef in the world.

Travel around this tiny country is relatively cheap and easy as long as you stick to the main sea and land routes, while those with a little more time and money can really get off the beaten track. Compared to the rest of Central America Belize is an expensive country to visit and many backpackers avoid it for that reason. But consider this: which other country can offer you pristine jungles and wetlands teeming with wildlife, some of the world's most extensive cave systems, archaeological ruins from a major civilisation, the longest barrier reef in the northern hemisphere, and a terrific selection of leisure facilities—all within a short travelling distance? My guess is you won't find one so if you visit this magnificent country, remember your trip encourages Belize to protect the vast natural wealth it possesses.

The Best of Belize

Artefacts: Marine products: San Pedro. Maya: Garcia Sisters in San Antonio/Cayo District
Beach: Placencia
Birdwatching: Chan Chich Lodge and any river trip
Books: *Belize 1798, The Road to Glory*, Emory King
Colonial Architecture: Belize City
Diving: Turneffe Atoll and Glover's Reef
Festivals: St George's Caye Day in San Pedro (10 Sep) and Garifuna Settlement Day in Dangriga (19 Nov)
Hiking: Mountain Pine Ridge and Cockscomb Basin Wildlife Reserve
Island Retreat: International Zoological Expedition Lodge on South Water Caye and Cottage Colony on St George's Caye
Jungle: Rio Bravo Conservation Area
Jungle Lodge: Chaa Creek and Chan Chich Lodge
Lakes: New River Lagoon
Markets: Belize City
Month of the Year: March
Museum: Chaa Creek Natural History Centre
National Park: Cockscomb Basin Wildlife Reserve and Mountain Pine Ridge
Nightlife: San Pedro
Pre-Columbian Ruins: Lamanai and Caracol
Rafting: Cayo district and near Blue Hole National Park
Road: Hummingbird Highway from Belmopan to Dangriga
Shopping: San Pedro and Belize City
Snorkelling: day trips from Caye Caulker

Travel

Getting to Belize	2
By Air	2
By Sea	2
By Rail	3
By Road	3
Entry Formalities	4
Passports and Visas	4
Customs	5
Currency	5
Getting Around	5
By Air	5
By Boat	5
By Bus	7
By Car or Motorbike	7
By Bicycle	8
Travel Agents and Tour Operators	8

Getting to Belize

By Air

Several major airlines operate a service between Europe and Central America via the US or Mexico and the price of a return ticket will probably be between £500 and £600. Fixed date tickets are cheaper than open ones, and travelling during the week also sometimes lowers the price. As always there are seasonal fluctuations in ticket prices. Good places to begin your search for the best deals on offer are the travel classifieds in your national newspaper, especially the weekend editions, as well as magazines carrying travel ads. Some of these offer extremely good deals if you scour their pages.

From the UK

British Airways ✆ (0345) 222111, KLM ✆ (0990) 750900, Iberia ✆ (0171) 830 0011, American Airlines ✆ (0181) 572 5555, and Continental Airlines ✆ (01293) 776464 all offer connections to **Belize City** (Philip Goldson Airport). While there are no direct flights at present, a route is under development and worth asking about when you come to book. For the moment, your best option is to fly via Miami. Slightly cheaper, though more time consuming, is flying to Cancún in Mexico, and then travelling by bus to Belize City, which can be done in one day (5–6 hours to the border, 3–4 hours to Belize City). Unfortunately there is no longer a flight between Cancún and Belize City but you can fly as far as Chetumal, on the border between Mexico and Belize.

From North America

There are daily direct flights between Belize City and Houston and Miami offered by TACA Airlines ✆ (1 800) 535 8780 and American Airlines ✆ (1 800) 433 7300. There are also regular services from Houston offered by Continental Airlines ✆ (1 800) 231 0856, and from New Orleans by TACA Airlines. A connecting flight service is also available from Los Angeles, New York, San Francisco and Washington offered by TACA airlines. Return fares from Miami and Los Angeles are priced at around US$400 but expect to pay twice that if coming from New York and close to US$1000 if coming from Canada. For further information call the Central America Corporation on ✆ (01293) 553330.

By Sea

Finding a space on a ship bound for Central America is a time-consuming and uncertain business. Plenty of cruise ships head there and a great many freighters make their way to the Panamá Canal; however, few of these will be enthusiastic about taking on casual passengers. If you do get lucky the journey by sea takes at least two weeks from Europe or a week from the US. If your heart is set on arriving by boat then your best bet is to work as a crew member on a yacht. Boats heading for Central America leave Gibraltar and the Canary Islands in October and November and are often searching for an extra pair of hands, while in the US you'll just have to search around the large marinas and keep an eye on yacht club notice boards. In the US the best marinas to check out are at Fort Lauderdale in Florida. There are no commercial maritime connections between the US and Belize.

There is a maritime connection between Belize and Guatemala: the twice-weekly ferry between Punta Gorda in southern Belize and Puerto Barrios in Guatemala (Tuesdays and Fridays, journey time approximately 2.5hrs; *see* pp.168 for further details).

By Rail

Belize has no railway at all and none leading to its borders but travellers coming from the US can at least get some of the way to Central America by train, covering the huge expanse between the US border, Mexico City, and further. Reasonably comfortable sleepers operate on this line. However, if you plan to sleep your way out through the boredom then make sure you're absolutely exhausted as the trip takes at least 30 hours, often more. From Mexico City onwards, the journey becomes slow and hot, with delays a regular occurrence.

By Road

Many visitors to Belize come from Cancùn by bus. The overland routes between the **US and Central America** are relatively direct, with good highways covering the main routes, although they do demand a degree of stamina. From Texas the most direct route cuts down the side of the Gulf of Mexico, bypassing the horrors of Mexico City. From California the drive is almost twice as long. By car you should expect to take at least a week to get through Mexico, even if you do use the most direct route. By bus you'll almost certainly have to travel via Mexico City and change buses. If you're sleeping on the bus it's possible to make it through Mexico in four or five days, but don't expect to arrive in a fit state to enjoy yourself.There is one road connecting **Guatemala and Belize**, running from the Petén jungle town of Flores to Belize City, via the Maya Mountains. The road is unpaved at the Guatemalan end and very rough during the rainy season, but with frequent buses (*see* p.74 for more details).

Between **Mexico and Belize**, there are regular daily buses run by the **Batty** and **Venus** companies from Chetumal in the Yucatán Peninsula to Belize City (4 hrs), which charge around BZ$12.

Entry Formalities

All visitors are granted leave to stay for 30 days initially which can be extended at the Immigration Office in Belize City. Please note that all passengers leaving from the international airport in Belize City will be charged a BZ $22.50 exit tax as well as a BZ$7.50 PACT tax. PACT stands for the Protected Areas Conservation Trust, and the money collected is distributed amongst all government and non-government agencies responsible for the country's reserves and national parks. Travellers leaving by land only pay the PACT tax. You must have the appropriate documents before you set off; once your plane touches down in Central America you'll face immigration and customs officials. If you have not got a visa and do not need one you will simply have your passport stamped. The International Airport has banks and you should get hold of some local currency there. If the bank is closed then you should be able to find a taxi driver who will accept US dollars.

Officially you must be in possession of a return flight ticket in order to enter Belize and the airlines will not normally allow you to fly without one.

Passports and Visas

UK, American and Canadian citizens do not need visas for Belize, nor do they need a tourist card (sold by the airlines for US$5). Irish nationals, New Zealanders and Australians will not be allowed into parts of Central America without one, however. Most EU and Commonwealth nationals are also exempt, apart from Austria, Switzerland and some East European countries. If you do need a visa then try and get hold of one before you go, and in every event it is a good idea to contact the relevant embassy or consulate for the latest regulations, which do tend to change periodically.

The official time limit for tourist visits to Belize is one month, with extensions possible for up to six months (*see* p. 77 for immigration office). You may be asked to show you have sufficient funds for your stay, and unless arriving in private transport, an onward flight ticket. As a general rule, US$50 per day is considered enough by the officials. If you have less, you can always bluff, and hope they do not ask you for proof; they often don't. Alternatively, showing a credit card would help.

Customs

You cannot bring any fruit or vegetables into Belize, but otherwise there are no unusual restrictions. Electrical goods may incur duties, refundable on leaving the country. You may be asked where you intend to stay and what you intend to do, but if you have no fixed plans this will not cause any problems.

Currency

The best currency to bring with you is the US dollar, though sterling can also be changed. For safety's sake, you should bring at least half your money in traveller's cheques, which can be cashed at banks, as well as up-market hotels and even selected shops.

The **Belizean currency** is the Belize dollar, whose value is fixed at BZ$2 to US$1. Expect to buy all local currency within Central America; it is hard to get hold of, and nearly impossible to get rid of, elsewhere, except in Miami, where currencies are easily obtained and off-loaded.

Getting Around

By Air

In Belize there are local airports in almost all of the country's main towns and some cayes (reef islands), and getting around by air is easy, if not cheap. Three airlines provide internal flights: **Maya Airways** which has the most flights; **Island Air** and **Tropic Air**. Tickets can be booked at any travel agent. There are airports in Belize City (both international and municipal airports are used for domestic flights), Corozal, Caye Chapel, Caye Caulker, Dangriga, Placencia, Big Creek, Punta Gorda and Ambergris Caye, as well as many small airstrips for private or charter flights. For reputable charter companies ask at the Tourist Board in Belize City.

Flights to and from the municipal airport in Belize City are always cheaper than to the international one. Sample return airfares from the municipal airport are: Ambergris Caye BZ$82; Corozal BZ$87; Caye Chapel BZ$66; Dangriga BZ$104; Placencia BZ$175; Punta Gorda BZ$250. Flights connecting Ambergris Caye and Caye Chapel are around BZ$42 one-way. Children under 12 only get 30% discount on their tickets.

By Boat

Travel to all major destinations on the cayes is possible by plane, though travelling by boat is cheaper and usually more fun, if you have the time. Boat schedules are outlined in the text. However, the main routes are between Belize City, Caye Caulker and San Pedro which operate daily. (This includes boat transport between Caye Caulker and San Pedro. A one-way ticket from Belize City to San Pedro will cost BZ$ 25–30, and the journey will take around one and a half hours.

You can also use boats on these routes to reach Caye Chapel and St. George's Caye, if you make the request prior to departure. Equally, they will come and pick you up from Caye Chapel or St George's Caye if you arrange it by telephone the day before. The smaller islands near Belize City, such as St. George's Caye, Goff's Caye and Sargeant's Caye, can all be reached by water taxi as well, which is surprisingly affordable. (For example a one way fare from Belize City to St George's Caye will cost you around BZ$10). The more distant atolls such as Turneffe Atoll, Glover's Reef and Lighthouse Reef are normally only reached by charter boat. Most of these are live-aboard dive boats that go out on day trips and overnight tours, although increasingly they are also catering to snorkellers. Day trips, including all meals and equipment cost around US$150 per person. Overnight tours cost US $250 per person). *See* pp.99–100. If you book into any of the remote island resort hotels, they can arrange to pick you up in their own boat, for which they will certainly charge you no less than BZ$100 each way. From Dangriga you can easily reach Tobacco Caye and South Water Caye with boats leaving daily from outside the River Cafe. Take a bus to Sittee River from Dangriga, and you can also catch a boat to Glover's Reef Resort every Saturday, which is cheaper than making your own arrangements. (*See* pp.118–119 for info on Glover's Reef resort). A boat also leaves Dangriga every Saturday for Puerto Cortés in Honduras, though you should think twice about using it if the seas are rough. The journey takes at least three hours and you have no protection against the elements, except a plastic sheet.

From Placencia you can catch a boat to the mainland (Mango Creek) without having to return to Dangriga, which is actually more convenient if you are continuing south by bus. (Equally travelling north by bus from Punta Gorda, you can catch a boat to Placencia from Mango Creek, where all buses make a stop en route to Dangriga).

Finally, there is a twice weekly ferry between Punta Gorda and Puerto Barrios in Guatemala (*see* p.168 for details) as well as daily departures run by Julio Requena leaving Punta Gorda at 9am and returning from Puerto Barrios at 2pm. His charter is by speed boat, and takes one hour less than the ferry although the ride can be somewhat wet and bumpy, depending on the weather.

By Bus

This is the standard mode of transport for most travellers, and the pleasure of meeting local people and the beauty of the landscapes provide adequate compensation for the inconveniences and delays.

Getting around Belize by bus is easy. There are regular daily services (greatly reduced on Sundays) to all corners of the country, and fares are cheap. As elsewhere in Central America, the buses tend to be old American school buses, rather uncomfortable for tall people. The main highways are all paved, except the Southern Highway beyond Dangriga, which makes travel in southern Belize slow. Apart from local buses operating out of the major towns, four companies have carved out their specific regions, all with their main terminals in Belize City: **Batty Bus Line** serves western and northern Belize; **Venus Bus Line** also runs a service to the north; **Novelo Bus Service** runs west to the Guatemalan border; and **Z-Line Buses** serve southern Belize.

By Car or Motorbike

In Belize the roads are generally excellent and even the dirt roads in the more rustic south are well maintained. Your own transport will make it easier to visit places away from the main highway. Local buses do serve outlying areas, but not often, and not usually when it will suit you. None of the Maya sites are served by commercial buses, but most have roads leading to them.

The only region where a high-clearance vehicle with four-wheel drive is recommended is in southern Belize. However, the dirt road leading to the remote Maya site of Caracol also requires a tough, four-wheel-drive vehicle, and even then, you can only use it during the dry season from March to May. You also need permission from the local Forestry Commission to enter the Mountain Pine Ridge area.

In Belize you drive on the right hand side of the road, but there is one important rule to remember: when you want to turn left, both traffic behind you and oncoming vehicles have right of way, and the custom is to move to the side of the road, allowing traffic in both directions to pass before turning left. There are only two sets of traffic lights in the entire country, both in Belize City. There are few petrol stations outside the main towns, so always keep an eye on the gauge.

In southern Belize, road signs are almost non-existent and it is easy to get lost. Dirt roads can go on for a very long time before they end at a logging camp, so a road map and regular enquiries from the locals are essential. As one Belizean put it: 'We know where we're going, so what do we need road signs for?' An entertaining book, published locally, is *Emory King's Driver's Guide to Beautiful Belize*, on sale in bookshops and from the Tourist Board office in Belize City.

Car hire is best arranged in Belize City, but there are other towns with local rental agencies too. You will have to reckon on around US$90 a day for a jeep with unlimited mileage, so renting is not cheap. If you rent by the week, you will get a better deal (*see* p.75 for recommended rental agencies).

By Bicycle

Cycling is becoming ever more popular and bicycles are common throughout the country, so basic repairs are no problem but if you can turn your hand to a few repairs, so much the better. Insurance against theft is vital. Unfortunately, few places actually hire out bikes. If you are a serious cyclist, take your own machine and contact the **Cyclist's Touring Club**, 69 Meadow, Godalming, Surrey, ✆ (01483) 417217, ✉ (01483) 426994. In the USA, contact the **Adventure Cycling Association,** ✆ **(**406) 721 1776.

Only in the south, where clouds of dust rise from the dirt road every time a vehicle thunders by, is cycling less pleasant, and you will certainly need a sturdy mountain bike. Don't think of cycling here during the rainy season, though. At any time of year, remember that Belize is very hot and humid, while inland, away from the coastal breeze, cycling along shadeless roads can be arduous. The only place where you will find spares is Belize City and San Ignacio. Not all Belizean buses have roof racks, but if they do, you should have no trouble transporting your bike.

Travel Agents and Specialist Tour Operators

from the UK

Cathy Matos Mexican Tours 215 Chalk Farm Road, Camden Town, London NW1 8AF, ✆ (0171) 284 2550, ✉ (0171) 267 2004: includes trips to Belize.

Cox & Kings St. James's Court, 45 Buckingham Gate, London SW1E 6AF, ✆ (0171) 873 5000, ✉ (0171) 630 6038: covers beach, wildlife and ruins trips.

Exodus Expeditions 9 Weir Road, Balham, London SW12 OLT, ✆ (0181) 675 5550, ✉ (0181) 673 0779: trip featuring Belize as part of La Ruta Maya.

Explore Worldwide, 1 Frederick Street, Aldershot, Hants GU11 1LQ, enquiries ✆ (01252) 344 161, reservations, ✆ (01252) 319448, ✉ (01252) 343 170: specializes in small group exploratory holidays often using local transport, with the emphasis on discovering local cultures and wildlife.

Frontiers International, 18 Albemarle Street, London, W1X 3HA, ✆ (0171) 4930798, ✉ (0171) 4919177: is a fishing holiday specialist.

Global Travel Club, 1 Kiln Shaw, Langdon Hills, Essex, SS16 6LE, ✆ (01268) 541 732, ✉ (01268) 542 275: offers diving as well as guided tours inland.

Hayes and Jarvis (Travel) Ltd, 152 King Street London W6 OQU, ✆ (0181) 748 0088, ✉ (0181) 741 0299: offers a wide variety of trips to Belize.

Journey Latin America, 16 Devonshire Road, Chiswick, London W4 2HD, ✆ (0181) 747 8315, (0181) 747 3108 ✉ (0181) 742 1312: organizes a range of bespoke and package tours including environmental expeditions.

Peregrine Holidays Ltd, Special Interest Tours, 41 South Parade, Summertown, Oxford OX2 7JP, ✆ (01865) 511642, ✉ (01865) 512583.

Reef and Rainforest Tours, Prospect House, Jubilee Road, Totnes, Devon TQ9 5BP, ✆ (01803) 866 965, ✉ (01803) 865 916: arranges tailor-made tours to Belize as well as opportunities to join research programmes, working with dolphins, monkeys, turtles and manatees.

South American Experience, 47 Causton Street, London SWIP 4AT, ✆ (0171) 976 5511, ✉ (0171) 976 6908: offers range of tailor-made packages.

Steamond Latin American Travel, 23 Eccleston Street, London, SW1 W9LX, ✆ (0171) 730 8646, ✉ (0171) 730 3024: provides tailor-made special-interest tours and itineraries including bird-watching, scuba-diving, etc.

Trailfinders, 194–196 Kensington High Street, London, W8 7RG, ✆ (0171) 938 3232; ✉ (0171) 938 3305: Other offices in Birmingham ✆ (0121) 236 1234, Bristol ✆ (0117) 9299000, Glasgow ✆ (0141) 353 2224 and Manchester ✆ (0161) 839 6969.

Trips, 9 Byron Place, Clifton, Bristol, BS8 1JT, ✆ (0117) 987 2626 , ✉ (0117) 987 2627, www.trips.demon.co.uk: organizes tailor-made tours to Belize, and its protected rainforest managed by Programme for Belize.

Wildlife Worldwide, 170 Selsdon Road, South Croydon, Surrey CR2 6PJ ✆ (0181) 667 9158; ✉ (0181) 667 1960: offers a five day bird watching tour to Chan Chich Lodge and a seven-day diving trip to Ambergris Caye.

from the USA

Barbachano Tours 9500 Dadeland Blvd, Miami, FL 33156 ✆ (305) 670 9439; ✉ (305) 670 9695: specializes in Mexico and Belize.

Belize Adventure Tours, 110 Harrison Avenue, San Antonio TX 78209, ✆ (210) 828 3758; ✉ (210) 828 3758: arranges escorted tours as well as independent itineraries.

Close Encounters, P. O. Box 1320, Detroit Lakes MN56502 ✆ (888) 875 1822, (218) 847 4411; ✉ (218) 847 4442: Specialists in trips to Belize, close connections with resorts and also offering discounted airfares.

Council Travel, 35 West 8th Street, New York 10011, ✆ (212) 254 2525, ✉ (212) 822 2600; 2846 Channing Way, Berkeley, CA 92093, ✆ (510) 415 848; 1314 Northeast 43rd Street, Suite 210, Seattle, WA 98105 ✆ (206) 632 244: specialists in a wide range of tours.

International Expeditions Inc., 1 Environs Park, Helena AL 35080, ✆ (205) 428 1700, ✉ (205) 428 1714: offers a full travel service as well as special interest tours for birding, canoeing, fishing, hiking and horseback riding.

International Zoological Expeditions, 210 Washington Street Sherborn MA 01770, ✆ (800) 548 5843, ✉ (508) 655 4445: specializes in educational tours to Belize, mostly for student groups but not exclusively, using either their island resort on South Water Caye or their jungle lodge at Blue Creek.

Sea & Explore, 1809 Carol Sue Avenue, Suite E, Gretna, LA 70056, ✆ (504) 366 9985; ✉ (504) 366 9986: offers combination packages to Belize, including inland and sea activities

Voyagers, Department EC, P O Box 915, Ithaca, NY 14851, ✆ (607) 257 4321, ✉ (607) 273 3873: offers natural history and photography tours to Belize and Costa Rica.

Wildland Adventures Inc., 3516 NE 155th, Seattle, WA 98155, ✆ (800) 345 4453, ✉ (206) 363 6615: specializes in ecotravel.

Children	12
Climate and When to Go	13
Crime	14
Disabled Travellers	14
Drugs	15
Electricity	15
Embassies and Consulates	15
Festivals	16
Food & Drink and Eating Out	16
Gay Travellers	18

Practical A–Z

Health, Emergencies and Insurance	19
Living and Working in Belize	20
Maps	21
Money	21
Opening Hours	22
National Holidays	23
Newspapers and the Media	23
Packing	24
Photography	25
Post Offices	25
Sexual Attitudes	25
Shopping	26
Sports and Activities	27
Diving	28
Telephones	33
Tipping	34
Toilets	35
Tourist Information & Travel Bookshops	35
Where to Stay	36
Women Travellers	36

Children

Travelling with children in Central America is easy, as everyone accepts them wherever you go. There is never a problem of not being able to enter a hotel, bar or restaurant because you have children in tow, and you will not normally be charged extra for accommodation. Transport on the buses is free for any child not using a seat. Your main worries are disease and gastric problems, so do consult your doctor regarding the relevant immunisations and never give your child anything other than bottled water. Nappies and most other infant equipment, including formula milk, is available in any town or city, but not in the villages or remote areas. Sun screen and insect repellent suitable for children is best brought from home.

In the UK specialist advice on vaccinations for tropical countries is available from **The Hospital for Tropical Diseases Helpline** ✆ (0839) 337733 or the Medical Advisory Service for Travellers Abroad (MASTA): ✆ (0891) 224100. Calls cost around 40 pence per minute (50 pence at peak rate). In the USA try the **Travelers Medical Center** ✆ (212) 982 1600, or Travel Medicine, ✆ (1 800) 872 8633. Note that anti-malaria medication for babies is available in the shape of Chloroquin syrup. A large packet of healthy breakfast cereal would not go amiss if your child goes off all other food available during your trip.

For babies remember that hygiene cannot be guaranteed so bring a suitable container (1 litre) and sterilizing tablets for your bottles and feeding equipment. A bottle and teat cleaning brush is useful, as is sticky tape in case nappy tabs fail. Nappy rash cream and medicated talc are good for heat rash. If you're only travelling for a short period, bring nappies and wipes with you as they will probably be cheaper at home. Make sure you have plenty of purified drinking water with you at all times so that you can encourage your child to drink as much as possible.

Your first aid box should include either a rehydration spoon or rehydration sachets, antiseptic disinfectant, teething relief, fever and pain relief medication, thermometer, tweezers, plasters, nail clippers, insect sting relief, adhesive wound dressing, and first aid skin closures for minor cuts.

Sleepsuits are too sweaty in the tropics: use a cotton sleeping bag instead. Baby backpacks are ideal for very young babies but otherwise too exhausting for walking around all day with a heavier child. A sun hat and/or parasol is essential and you can buy both cheaply in Belize. Strollers/buggies are not practical as they cannot be easily manoeuvred on pot-holed streets, dirt tracks and beaches.

The only useful alternative is a specially adapted three-wheeled 'multi-terrain stroller', with high clearance wheels. It will make all the difference to your trip and is very useful for rural walks at home. They are usually lightweight and the wheels come off easily to facilitate travel on buses, cars and planes. In the UK they are sold by PCD Limited PO Box 28, Tavistock, Devon PL 19 9YT ✆ 01822 618077. Their 'Land Rover' model which has detachable wheels is expensive at around £275 but well worth the investment. Another extremely useful item at feeding times is a 'Safe Seat' which is a cleverly designed cotton and velcro gadget that secures your baby or toddler to any type of chair; it is lightweight and folds into the smallest bag. In the UK Boots sell a version, but the best design is sold by The Great Little Trading Company, 134 Lots Road, London SW10 ORJ, ✆ (0990) 673 008 ✉ (0990) 673 010. In the US the same model is marketed as 'Sit'nSecure' from Leachco PO Box 717 Ada Oklahoma 74820, ✆ (1 800) 525 1050.

Climate and When to Go

At any time of year Belize's lowland areas are stiflingly hot; during the rainy season high humidity makes it particularly sticky. Meanwhile up in the highlands it is always pleasantly cool in the shade, although the sun is even sharper. The seasons are simple: it's either raining or it isn't. The rains start around June and ends sometime in December. However things are changing here too, and you can now expect rain to carry on as far as February. The rains can be very heavy, particularly towards the end of the rainy season, but they need not stop you travelling as they

Average Temperature °C and Rainfall (no. of days) in Belize City

	Jan	Feb	Mar	April	May	June	July	Aug	Sept	Oct	Nov	Dec
Max	27	28	29	30	31	31	31	31	31	30	28	27
Min	9	21	22	23	24	24	24	24	23	22	20	20
Days	2	6	4	5	7	13	15	14	15	16	12	14

tend to be in the form of afternoon downpours; you'll just get less of a tan. The best time of year to travel in Belize is between March and September, even though you can expect the rains to begin around June, which is also when the hurricane season begins. You should note that southern Belize receives far more rain than the rest of the country and since this is also where the roads are unpaved, travel is most difficult during the rainy season.

If you travel in March, April or May you can reasonably expect no rain and calm seas, although temperatures will soar, and some might find it too hot. In December, at the end of the rains, Belize experiences the finest weather of the year—fresh, clear and warm, and prompts a few weeks, if not months, of indulgence among local people, who like to take it easy towards the end of the year.

Crime

Perhaps the best way to ensure your safety is to avoid carrying unnecessary valuables and accept the fact that the ones you do bring may be stolen. Most visitors have no real trouble at all, although petty theft and pickpocketing are always a possibility. The best way to avoid it is to keep your wits about you and avoid putting your money in easily accessible pockets. Far more serious and less likely is violent crime. Women should always take taxis when going out at night in Belize City.

Belize is the happy exception to the Central American rule: its defence forces are not notorious for human rights abuses or a high level of corruption. Politically motivated killings or disappearances are unknown here, though Central American refugees and non-English-speaking Belizeans have occasionally suffered abuse from the authorities. The latest arrivals are 5,000 Hong Kong Chinese, whose evident wealth and separate housing estates have inspired deep resentment among ordinary Belizeans. Belize even has its own Human Rights Commission, founded in 1987, which has been responsible for such projects as incorporating human rights into police training courses.

The country's civilian police force is made up of just 500 people and called the Belize Police Force (BPF). The Belize Defence Forces (BDF) were founded in 1980, a year before independence, its army not much larger than the police force. The BDF is trained and, to a large extent, financed by Britain, the United States and Canada. British military officers command them; however, the Belizean government has a programme for replacing the foreign commanding officers.

There are still some British soldiers stationed in Belize though the British troops officially pulled out of Belize in 1993—these days the remaining soldiers seem to spend their time using Belize as a jungle training camp. Guatemala formally recognized Belize in 1991, and the British have at last agreed to honour their promise of building a road from Guatemala City to Belize City (basically the Petén road, via Flores and Benque Viejo), which they made in 1859. Hopefully one of the region's most futile disputes should be over. On the other hand, if you read the Guatemalan press you will see that recognition of Belize may only be temporary.

Disabled Travellers

Travel can be quite rough, and no specific concessions or provisions are made to smooth the way for those with a physical handicap. Unfortunately, due to poverty and malnutrition, many more people suffer from disabilities here than in the West. If you or your travelling companion have special needs, you can make life much easier if you can afford to book organized tours and travel, where all aspects of transport are arranged for you, and provided in comfortable vehicles.

There are quite a few organizations which advise and encourage international travel for disabled people. DIVE (Disabled International Visits and Exchanges), c/o The Central Bureau for Educational Visits and Exchanges, Seymour Mews House, Seymour Mews, London WIH 9PE; SATH (Society for the Advancement of Travel for the Handicapped), International Head Office, Suite 1110, 26 Court Street, Brooklyn, NY 11242, USA.

Specialist guide books or publications include: *Access to the World*, Louise Rice, Facts of File, London (1985); *Disabled Traveller's International Phrasebook*, Ian McNeil, Disability Press, 60 Greenhayes Avenue, Banstead, Surrey; *A List of Guidebooks for Handicapped Travelers*, The President's Committee on Employment of the Handicapped, 1111 20th Street, NW, Washington, DC 20036, USA.

Drugs

Marijuana and crack cocaine are both found in Belize, though less so than they used to be. Concerted efforts by the authorities both Belizean and American in the 1980s and 90s have resulted in a sharp decline in marijuana grown locally. Belize is still, however, a popular stopping off point for drugs en route between South and North America, and many a small airstrip has been used for illicit arrivals and departures. The use of soft drugs is widely tolerated in Belize, although foreigners would be well advised to be discreet. Penalties against drugs are strict, particularly for outsiders.

Electricity

The current runs at 110 volts. This means North Americans can use all their electrical equipment without any problems. Europeans, however, will need adaptors for everything electrical bought in their own countries. Adaptors are not always easy or cheap to find, so do bring your own if you really need one.

Embassies and Consulates

Even though Belmopan is the capital, many offices remain in Belize City, which has always been the commercial and cultural heart of the country.

UK: High Commission, Embassy Square, Belmopan, ✆ 08 22146, ✉ 08 22761 (Mon–Fri, 8–noon and 1.30–4).

USA: 29 Gabourel Lane, Belize City, ✆ 02 77161, ✉ 30802 (Mon–Fri, 8–noon and 1–5).

Canada: 83 North Front Street, Belize City, ✆ 02 31060, ✉ 02 30060 (Mon–Fri, 9–1).

EU: Commission of European Union, 1 Eyre Street, Belize City, ✆ 02 32070. (Mon–Fri, 8–noon and 1.30–4).

In the UK: Belize High Commission, 19a Cavendish Square W1M 9AD ✆ (0171) 499 9728, @ (0171) 491 4139.

In USA: Belize Embassy, 2535 Massachussetts Avenue NW, Washington DC 20008 ✆ (202) 332 9636, @ (202) 332 6888.

In Canada: Consulate General of Belize Suite 094, 1112 West Pender Street, Vancouver V6E 2S1 ✆ (604) 683 4518.

In Australia and New Zealand: contact the British High Commission for limited information on Belize.

Festivals

Belize is not blessed with many festivals, but its Caribbean culture ensures that there is no lack of entertainment, with parties and discos almost every weekend. Reggae music and Punta Rock predominates, but Latin American music is popular.

The main national celebrations are Independence Day (21 September), Columbus Day (12 October) and Garifuna Settlement Day (19 November). The latter is one of the most interesting times to be in Belize because there is a good chance of seeing some traditional Garifuna dancing if you head for Dangriga or any of the Garifuna villages further south. The Garifuna are descendants of African slaves and Carib Indians, and their festivals are rich with African songs and drum rhythms, the dancing a mesmerizing mixture of African and Caribbean.

Another lively festival is the Agriculture and Trade Show, which takes place every other year outside Belmopan in June. Not only is it a good opportunity to sample Belizean cooking and crafts, but also to see all the country's major bands.

Food and Drink and Eating Out

You can find good basic Creole cooking everywhere in Belize and a wonderful variety of fresh seafood particularly in the Cayes. Yet in general standards are not as high as you might expect, and the prices are certainly higher. Imported tinned food is often more popular among locals than home-produced cooking. Burgers, fried chicken and chips predominate, fresh vegetables are a rarity and salads invariably consist of processed coleslaw. The bread is usually white and often tasteless. Whenever you get the chance order 'fried jacks' instead, which are delicious pieces of deep fried dough. Occasionally you come across a Mennonite bakery, which is always a good place to sample interesting bread, as well as wholesome fruit buns.

A popular, filling Creole dish available in most restaurants, is rice and beans or stew beans (a flavoursome mixture of rice and kidney beans enhanced by either chicken, pork or fish). Portions are generous and frequently include a serving of coleslaw and fried plantain with a piece of fruit for good measure. This is almost always the cheapest item on the menu BZ $6–9. If you're staying over in Belize City make sure you sample the stew beans at GG's on King Street, which are undoubtedly the best in the country.

If you are travelling in northern and western Belize, you will find a great many latino snacks (all around BZ$2), such as *chile relleno* (stuffed jalapeno chillies) and *tamales* (ground corn and shredded chicken or pork steamed in a banana leaf). Other tasty snacks are *panades* (deep fried fish or bean pies), *garnaches* (crisp tortillas topped with refried beans, grated cheese and ketchup) or *salbates* which are similar, but also have shredded meat and cabbage on them. A popular soup is *escabeche* (onion and chicken), and Marie Sharpe's hot sauce is liberally applied. Very occasionally, you might also find some Maya dishes which use exotic rainforest meats, such as gibnut, known as *tepezcuintle* in Guatemala. When it was served to the Queen during her last visit the press shrieked 'Queen fed rat in Belize!' but even though gibnut is a member of the rodent family, it looks nothing like a rat. In fact it is more like a small deer and tastes extremely good, a little like venison. If you ever see Bamboo Chicken on the menu, remember that it is not chicken but iguana, and very delicious too.

Garifuna dishes are rarely found on restaurant menus, though typical Garifuna ingredients are used in Creole cuisine. Cooking with coconut milk is common and makes all the difference to boiled rice as well as to seafood stews. Distinctive flavours are created by the addition of ginger, nutmeg or lime. Cinnamon and vanilla spice up puddings made from banana or plantain. Meat dishes often consist of the most unappetising parts of animals, by western standards: pig tails, cowfeet or chicken feet are all standard ingredients in *Garifuna* stews. Even the most voracious carnivores might find these dishes an acquired taste.

A little more accessible to visitors are the huge number of seafood dishes. Top of the list is lobster which you can find in any style you can possibly imagine from barbecued, fried, stewed or cut into sauces for pasta or rice. Naturally, the best places to eat fresh seafood are on the cayes, and the prices are very affordable. Away from the resort hotels, which charge around BZ $30–60 for main courses, you will find lobster dishes cost around BZ$20–30, which is generally the top end of the price scale. Shrimp dishes are a good BZ$5 cheaper, and conch (pronounced 'konk') soup or fritters are cheaper still. Fish dishes are dominated by red snapper, which is usually fried whole. But you can also find grouper, shark and barracuda.

However, please support the country's efforts to preserve its marine stocks by respecting the closed seasons. Do not eat the following seafood during these periods: shrimp 15 April–14 August; conch 1 July-30–September; lobster 15 February–14 June; hickatee turtle 1 May–31 May; marine turtles 1 April–31 October.

Perhaps surprisingly, there is plenty of good Chinese food to be found in Belize particularly in Belize City, so if you're a fan of oriental cuisine, you'll find plenty of choice.

When it comes to drinks, fizzy imports predominate, though you can usually find delicious freshly squeezed juices made from lime, orange, watermelon, papaya, or pineapple amongst others. The strangest Belizean drink is a sickly concoction of sweet seaweed, mixed with milk and cinnamon. Drinking water from the tap is not recommended, although it is claimed that water in Belize City is safe. Unfortunately the water is heavily doused with chlorine Sadly tea or coffee in Belize is usually weak and disappointing, even in the most up-market hotels.

The national beer is Belikin, which is refreshingly watery and cheap (around BZ$4), and also available on draught. Order imported beer, and watch the price rise steeply, while shots of imported vodka or whisky can set you back a good BZ$10. The best local alcohol is rum, produced locally, served in huge measures topped with cola.

Gay Travellers

Homosexuality is as much a part of Belizean society as it is of any other, though it remains confined to a secretive subculture that visitors are unlikely to encounter. Public opinion on the subject is characterized by a mixture of contempt and amusement, so beware of these attitudes. Homosexual and lesbian couples will have no trouble with accommodation arrangements though, since it is very common for travellers of the same sex to share rooms.

Health, Emergencies and Insurance

Medical preparation should begin with a visit to your doctor at least six weeks before you plan to go as he or she will be able to offer the most up-to-date information. The standard vaccinations for the region are yellow fever, rabies, typhoid, tetanus, polio, hepatitis, and hepatitis B. It is not necessary to take malaria pills in cool mountainous regions, but only on the tropical plain and in the jungle. Malaria prophylactic is recommended for Belize, especially if you intend travelling during the rainy season.

The most common complaint is a stomach upset, and it's a good idea to come prepared with medicine. Good medical labs operate in all cities and towns, so help is always easy to find. When it comes to tips on avoiding intestinal problems travellers are divided: some insist that you can eat any street vendor's snack and survive; others prefer to avoid street food and fresh salads in all but the best restaurants. However, there are no hard or fast rules.

Sunburn is another problem, and sun screen is not always on sale so do bring your own. Hats are available cheaply anywhere in the region. Contraceptives, tampons and sanitary towels are all available, though again, it is best to bring your own contraceptives or tampons. (Remember that severe diarrhoea can diminish the effectiveness of the contraceptive pill.) Contact lens soaking and cleaning solutions are also best brought with you, as well as insect repellent. If you intend to do a lot of hiking, remember to bring your own padded foot plasters which make open blisters easier to bear. A basic medical kit should include insect repellent, flea powder, antiseptic, Lomotil for diarrhoea and a rehydration powder like Dioroalyte, antihistamine cream, essential personal medicines, and preferred contraceptive.

Finally, if you would like a detailed, personalized vaccination assessment and up-to-the-minute advice, contact the excellent Medical Advisory Service for Travellers Abroad (MASTA), at the London School of Tropical Medicine ✆ (0891) 224100. In the UK British Airways run clinics at 32 locations from Aberdeen to Plymouth; their phone numbers are obtainable from a recorded message on ✆ (0171) 831 5333. In London, you could also visit Nomad Traveller's Store & Medical Centre, 3–4 Turnpike Lane, London N8, ✆ (0181) 441 7208 (opposite Turnpike Lane Underground Station). In the USA try the Travelers Medical Center, 31 Washington Square, New York, NY 10011 ✆ (212) 982 1600.

Chemists stock most drugs and toiletries you might need, including contraceptives, suntan lotion and mosquito repellent. Outside Belize City, you are unlikely to find tampons, but sanitary towels are readily available. See your embassy or consulate for a list of recommended doctors. If you require outpatient attention at a hospital, it's free. The Belize City Hospital is on Eve Street ✆ 02 31548, although the private Belize Medical Associates on St Thomas Street ✆ 02 30303 has a better record when it comes to diagnosis. *The Cadogan Guide to Healthy Travel Bugs, Bites and Bowels* by Dr Jane Wilson Howarth will give you plenty of additional tips and advice.

Insurance

Travel insurance, available through any travel agent, is always a good idea. Make sure the policy covers both theft and medical expenses and a flight home should you become seriously ill if you're particularly worried about ending up in a local hospital.

Good insurance policies are available through all the main travel operators, including Thomas Cook and American Express (for their customers only). Specialist travel insurance is also offered by Columbus Direct, 17 Devonshire Square, London EC2M 4SQ, ✆ (0171) 375 0011, @ (0171) 375 0022 and Jardine's ✆ (0161) 228 3742. Columbus' prices are marginally cheaper than anyone else's, and they will cover you for individual trips, or offer an annual policy. Children under two years are insured for free, but their names must be stated on the policy. In the USA try Access America ✆ (1 800) 2848300, or Carefree Travel Insurance ✆ (1 800) 323 3149. Finally remember that most water sports require extra cover and are not usually included in ordinary policies, so read the small print carefully.

Living and Working in Belize

This is no easy matter, involving a great deal of paperwork and running around if you want to do it legally. On a casual basis (with no employment rights and minimal pay), however, you would rarely get work in the tourist bars and hotels. Bear in mind that local people need the work much more than many westerners and will certainly work for substantially less. Professional diving instructors and sailing crew might be able to find something in the tourist resort of San Pedro, especially between the months of November and May.

Voluntary work is quite easy to arrange if you have enough time and money to spare: most programmes require a minimum commitment of three weeks to three months and expect you to pay your own way. There are a number of high profile conservation projects that use volunteers, who work alongside professional scientists and archaeologists: Earthwatch, Belsyre Court, 57 Woodstock Rd, Oxford, OX2 6HU, ✆ (01865) 311600. In the USA telephone (617) 926 8200, @ (617) 926 8532. Trekforce Expeditions, ✆ (0171) 824 8890.

One of the most rewarding and exciting opportunities for voluntary conservation work in Belize is with **Coral Caye Conservation**. This charitable trust works with the governments of several tropical countries to help establish efficient coastal management plan, which are intended not only to protect some of the world's reefs but also develop sustainable means by which they can be used economically, both as a food resource and as a tourist destination.

Anyone over 16 years can join a voluntary expedition, lasting from two to twelve weeks and no special knowledge or training is required. In fact this is a great chance for novice divers to get full PADI training and immediately put it to use in some of the most exciting areas of the reef. In Belize the research station is located on the remote Calabash Caye.

An additional bonus of joining a CCC expedition is the opportunity to learn scientific data collection methods, as your main job is surveying the reef daily for fish and plant species. You can also join optional training courses in anything from advanced diving to marine ecology.

Conditions at the research station are basic but adequate, and possibly the hardest aspect of any trip is having to rise at dawn. Volunteers sleep in bunk beds, dormitory fashion, and all camp jobs are shared, including preparing meals and maintenance of equipment. The work is exhausting but time for socialising and relaxation is set aside especially at weekends. Expedition fees begin at £650 (US$995) for two weeks.

Coral Caye Conservation can be contacted in the UK at 154 Clapham Park Road, London SW4 7DE, ✆ (0171) 498 6248, ✉ (0171) 498 8447, e-mail ccc@coralcay.demon.co.uk. In the USA contact them at Suite 124, 230 12th Street Miami Beach FL 33139, ✆ & ✉ (305) 757 2955, e-mail cccoralcay@ aol.com.

The best source of information in Belize, if you want to set up home or in business there, is Emory King's publications, available all over Belize or by written request and enclosing US$12 from Emory King, P.O. Box 107, Belize City.

Maps

Detailed maps of Belize are difficult to get hold of, and the tourist map sold by the Tourist Board is the best you will get in the country itself. Only the main roads and highways are marked, but there are street maps of most of the major towns. Petrol stations are only indicated in the towns.

A trip to your local map shop is highly recommended, as they may have more detailed maps. In England, the best place to go is Stanfords International Map Centre, 12–14 Long Acre, London WC2P 9LP, ✆ (0171) 837 1321. Also worth trying in England is the Overseas Surveys Directorate, which has published maps of Belize to a scale of 1:250 000 and 1:50 000.

In the USA, Rand McNally Map Travel, 444 Michigan Avenue, Chicago, IL 60611 is a useful stop for maps.

Money

The best currency to bring with you is the US dollar, since the region is economically dominated by it and always accepts it as payment. For safety's sake, you should bring at least half your money in traveller's cheques, which can be cashed at banks, as well as up-market hotels and even selected shops.

It's also a good idea to bring some dollar cash for border crossings and emergencies, or even to clinch a bargain. It's always useful in case you need to change money outside banking hours. Dollar cash, and sometimes cheques, can also be changed on the black market, which is widely tolerated but illegal.

Black-market dealers operate in the streets and usually offer a slightly better rate than the banks, although they often indulge in sharp practices and well rehearsed rip-offs. Avoid showing your passport, which could be stolen in the process; don't hand over your cash first; and don't go into an unknown house with a supposed money changer. Up-market hotels usually accept and exchange traveller's cheques, but at a poor rate.

Once in Belize it can be difficult to buy US dollars, and few banks are willing to break down large bills for you, so avoid US$100 notes, unless you really intend to change that amount. Credit cards are only useful at top hotels and shops, travel agents, and car hire agencies but American Express, Diners, and Access are also widely accepted. Mastercard and Visa are the best known here.

A word of advice: do invest in a money pouch that can be discreetly kept under your clothing, and never leave valuables unattended. Most hotels have safes for customers' money and papers, which you should use. The money belt remains the safest place to keep your valuables but is by no means infallible. Everyone knows 'gringos' keep their money around their waist these days, but there is still no need to draw attention to yourself. The best type to use are either a leather belt with a concealed zip, or a wider cotton version that is concealed under your clothing and can fit your money and passport. Pouches can be sewn on to an elasticated armband and worn under clothing for extra safety. Be warned purses, wallets and handbags are a bad idea.

The Belizean currency is the Belize dollar, whose value is fixed at BZ$2 to US$1. It's best to buy your local currency dollars in Belize as you'll find it hard to get hold of elsewhere, with the notable exception of Miami, where currencies are easily obtained—and off-loaded.

Wiring money from abroad is best done via Barclays Bank in Belize City, or by using the American Express office (at Belize Global Travel, 41 Albert Street, ✆ 77363; (*open Mon-Fri 8–noon and 1–4; Sat 8–noon*).

As always, having to wire money can be tedious and time-consuming, so it should be avoided if possible. Credit cards are widely accepted, and certainly essential when hiring a vehicle. Mastercard and Visa are the best known here, but others too are acceptable. There is also a branch of the Belize Bank at the International Airport (*open daily, 8.30–11 and 12.30–4.30*).

Opening Hours

Normal business hours are Mondays to Fridays, 8–5. Commerce and industry hours are Monday–Friday, 8–noon and 1–5. Very few businesses are open on Sundays. Most nature reserves and archaeological sites are open to the public daily, from 8–5, though regulations vary, since you can camp in some reserves, and some Maya sites just have a local guard, but no official hours. Details are given in the guide text. There are very few museums in Belize, so always check information for an individual institution in the relevant town.

National Holidays

In Belize even the public transport comes to a standstill on public holidays, especially outside Belize City. The major holidays are:

New Year's Day	
9 March	Baron Bliss Day
Good Friday	
Easter Saturday to Easter Monday	
1 May	Labour Day
24 May	Commonwealth Day
10 September	St George's Caye Day
21 September	Independence Day
12 October	Columbus Day
13 October	Pan-American Day
19 November	Garifuna Settlement Day
25 December	Christmas Day
26 December	Boxing Day

Newspapers and the Media

English-language newspapers—usually *The Miami Herald* or *International Herald Tribune* or *New York Times*—are sold in Belize, and you can also keep in touch with international news via CNN which is available in up-market hotel rooms throughout the region.

Belize has a large number of publications for such a small country. There are five weekly newspapers, but their reporting is dominated by school functions and personality profiles, with little useful political coverage. *The Reporter* is a business paper, with a heavy bias towards the conservative United Democratic Party (UDP).

Amandala, although basically a sports paper, has the most varied political coverage. *The Beacon* is another mouthpiece for the UDP, and so is the *People's Pulse*. The *Belize Times* serves the interests of the People's United Party (PUP), which is also conservative, though its origins lie in the social democratic tradition.

The left-wing periodical *Spearhead*, published by the research foundation SPEAR, concentrates on long-term issues concerning community development, education and social welfare. *Belize Studies* is published three times a year, and is a forum for Belizean and international research on the country. *Belize Currents*, published by Emory King in Belize City features local creative writing.

An excellent source of tourist information and inspiration for places to visit is *Destination Belize,* the official visitor's magazine published by the private sector Belize Tourism Industry Association. You should find it free in most hotels and at the tourist office. Finally, the best coverage of environmental issues is offered by *ECO (Journal of Environmental Information)*, only available in Belize City.

There are two main radio stations: Belize Radio One broadcasts in English and Spanish; and Radio Krem is under the same ownership as the Amandala paper. National television programming is still in the early stages, and most of what you see are pirated programmes from the United States. A local company, Great Belize Productions, is trying to redress the balance with documentaries and features on local life and culture.

The only towns with cinemas are Belize City, San Ignacio, and Orange Walk, all predictably dominated by the latest US releases.

Packing

Certain items are vital for Latin American travel; however, before you leave home take another look at your luggage. The chances are you have packed too much; many things such as hats and light clothing can be bought cheaply and easily when and if you need them. If you intend to go walking you should bring sturdy footwear as suitable boots are difficult to find in Belize too. You will also need something to ward off the rain, and wind, all of which can strike with a vengeance.

Ideally, use a small rucksack or shoulder bag which can be padlocked. This is no guarantee of security but at least it hinders pickpockets. The advantage of small luggage is that you can keep it with you inside buses.

Always keep with you your passport, vaccination booklet, flight ticket, traveller's cheques, insurance papers, and photocopies of relevant pages in your passport and the counterfoils of your travellers' cheques. Some people find a pocket calculator invaluable for making sense of and assessing prices of goods.

Foot plasters, sun screen and toilet paper are also very useful. Remember that toilet paper is generally not provided in toilets and should always be carried with you.Flip-flops are excellent for dubious showers and for general use. Sunglasses are essential. Also worth remembering are a small alarm clock for those 4am buses, a torch, and a camping knife.

Other things you might want to include are a universal plug and electrical adaptor, water purification tablets, earplugs, writing materials, a simple sewing kit and a water bottle.

Photography

With its tropical islands Belize is a photographer's paradise. Bear in mind that the range of light is enormous, so bring a wide range of film, as anything beyond the 100-400 ASA range is not available here. Standard slide and black and white film is available, although only in Belize City. Colour film is available in most tourist resorts.

Photographing sensitive subjects, including police and soldiers, can easily land you in deep trouble and you should make a point of asking local people if they mind being photographed. Photographing Indian religious ceremonies is deeply offensive, unless you are invited to do so.

Post Offices

Postal services are variable and it's always a good idea to make a point of using main Post Offices. Letters should take around 10 days to reach the USA and 2 weeks to Europe, but it can take a lot longer. Parcels tread a very unpredictable path and are more likely to go missing than letters, particularly if you send them from small, remote post offices.

Postal rates are fixed at BZ$0.60 for letters to the USA, and BZ$0.75 for letters to Europe, taking roughly a week to ten days in both cases. Their business hours are Mon–Fri, 8–noon and 1–5. If you want to send a parcel, you will have to use a cardboard box and take it open to the parcel office in Church Street, Belize City, where it will be checked by customs before you can close it with string.

Receiving post is straightforward: just have it mailed to Poste Restante, The Main Post Office, Belize City, Belize. Letters will be kept for up to three months before being sent back. Remember to take your passport for identification. Alternatively, holders of American Express cards or traveller's cheques could use their office as a postal address: American Express, Belize Global Travel, 41 Albert Street, Belize City, Belize.

Sexual Attitudes

Machismo is still alive and well, and the concept of sexual equality is generally not even paid lip service. The traditional roles of women are defined by their place in the family, even though circumstances force the majority of them to work outside the home as well. Men are considered the natural head of the family, though this is often not the case in practice.

As with many other things you will find Belize exceptional in Central America for the easy going relationship between men and women, characterised by friendly , flirtatious banter, rather than threatening or insulting behaviour. Caribbean rather than Latin American style dominates although topless bathing is not permitted or advised away from the seclusion of private beaches. Women need take no more care than anywhere else, and the only place where solitary excursions at night are dangerous is Belize City. Don't stay in, just take a taxi where you might have taken a bus or walked.

Shopping

> *Gati gati no wanti, an wanti wanti no gati.*
> If you've got it, you don't want it, and if you want it, you can't have it.
>
> Creole proverb

Belize is not the best place in Central America for handicrafts, though plenty of trinkets are made of sea creatures, shells, wood and coconuts. As you browse through jewellery made of tortoiseshell or black coral, it is worth remembering that the former comes from an endangered species, and the latter is banned from export. It is also illegal to import black coral into the United States.

The quality of weaving and embroidery is very primitive compared to Guatemalan standards. The few remaining Maya settlements in southern Belize have entirely lost their artisan knowledge, and are only now trying to relearn it, in order to benefit from tourism. But what you find will be expensive—and Belizean Mayas do not seem to appreciate the art of bargaining either. The best buys are most certainly the wood carvings, which you can buy direct from the artists on roadside stalls. Most commonly you will find them on the approaches to Maya ruins, but also in the tourist centres.

The best selection of shops in Belize is found in San Pedro, where the most original art gallery is owned by 'Iguana Jack', whose ceramic art always includes his iguanas. San Pedro is also a great place to find local painting and craftwork made of anything from wood to slate.

Another good place for shopping especially for jungle remedies, is San Ignacio (Cayo). Some of the most entertaining items available anywhere are T-shirts, which are usually of good quality and covered in local scenes and popular slogans from the latest carnival.

Finally if duty free shopping is your thing, you can shop to your heart's content at the International Airport, which boasts up to 40% lower prices than found in the USA for items ranging from perfumes to alcohol, watches and cigarettes. No doubt you will also find bottles of Marie Sharp's famous Belizean hot sauces, a familiar sight on any restaurant table.

Sports and Activities

Belize is a great destination for outdoor sports and activities and the choices increase each year, as more and more specialist operators set up shop here. For any activity not listed or for more information, contact the operators direct or the Belize Tourist Board. Once in Belize you can also find the latest contact telephone numbers for boat charters and fishing guides in the official visitor's guide handed out free at the Tourist Board in Belize City. *See* p. 75.

Amateur Archaeology

The Maya ruins of Belize offer a fascinating insight into the area's pre-Columbian history. Local tour companies can take you to almost any site you wish to visit, and certainly the major ones, so there is no need to book from home. There are no local tour companies specializing exclusively in Maya ruins. If you would like a professional archaeologist to accompany you, he/she needs to be booked via the specialist tour operators in the USA or UK.

Bird Watching

There are excellent National Parks in Belize. The best bird-watching is at Sarteneja Nature Reserve, Crooked Tree Wildlife Sanctuary, around the Macal and Mopan Rivers near San Ignacio, as well as at the glorious Chan Chich Lodge, where luxury accommodation provides a superb base to search for 300 local bird species in the surrounding forest. Less luxurious but more affordable, is the nearby research station run by **Programme for Belize**, which runs the country's largest protected forest area. Contact Ava Davis for more information: P.O. BOX 749, #2 South Park Street, Belize City, Belize, ✆ 501 2 75616; ℱ 501 2 75635.

Cari Search Ltd is a specialist tour company whose forte is natural history, located on Caye Caulker and offering everything from birdwatching to slide lectures on reef ecology.

Diving

Belize is one of the best places in the western hemisphere for scuba diving. It possesses the world's second largest coral reef, second only to Australia's Great Barrier Reef. And when you include the many little islands and the offshore atolls, there are over 550 kilometres of reef in total.

Diving on the reefs you'll be able to see great forests of deep water gorgoniums, brilliant orange and red sponges, large brain and staghorn corals and a huge variety of fish including Queen and French angels, nassau grouper, squirrelfish, surgeonfish and soldierfish and those popular little sergeant major fish! These are no bigger than the palm of your hand and stripey, like the fish equivalent of bumble bees. Turtles, dolphin, stingrays and shark are at home here; the sharks are likely to be either Caribbean reef or nurse sharks and are not dangerous. The most likely outcome is that they will swim away when they see you!

The only dangers to really watch out for are the stinging corals such as the aptly named fire coral, long spined sea urchins and the extremely well camouflaged scorpionfish, which have poisonous spines along their backs. A 'look, don't touch' philosophy is encouraged so as to preserve the reef and avoid nasty accidents! *See* pp.64–65.

But if you're really observant you might also spot some of the more elusive creatures of the reef such as the rather unusual frogfish, the daddylong legs arrow crab, the endearing sea horse or the beautifully coloured crayfish, known locally as the spiny lobster.

You can dive in Belize all year round although the best time to visit is in the Spring, when the sea is at its calmest and the weather most settled. Expect the underwater visibility to reach anything between 100 and 150 feet at this time. During the winter it can be windy and as a result visibility can be much worse at this time. It is worth noting that from midsummer to late autumn is hurricane season (although Belize is rarely affected).

Belize's barrier reef is located between 15 and 30 kilometres offshore so dive centres tend to be based on the little offshore islands, known as Cayes. *See* pp. 89–120. The most popular and well known Caye, is Ambergris Caye which is also one of the closest Cayes to the mainland. Although the diving is good all along the Barrier Reef, it is even better at the offshore atolls of Glovers, Turneffe, and Lighthouse; they are located well south of Ambergris Caye and considerably further out to sea.

Ambergris Caye has several dive schools and dive centres, most operating from the hotels and resorts on San Pedro. Diving is good here, although the reefs are

by Gavin Anderson

beginning to show a little sign of wear and tear. The area is excellent for novices and seasoned divers alike, though the latter will prefer to head off to the offshore atolls. The best sites are located on the south end of the Caye, and include Tuffy Cut where you can find shallow forest of elkhorn and staghorn coral, and slightly deeper down enormous brain and lettuce corals, and the sites within the Hol Chan Marine reserve. Here there is an incredible diversity of marine life and some spectacularly scenic diving. You can expect to dive in caves through tunnels down mini drop offs and see spectacular coral formations; at Boca Ciega there is even a mini Blue Hole! The highlight of Ambergris Cay has to be Shark Ray Alley, where you can snorkel with stingrays and docile nurse sharks in just 12 feet of water!

Wherever you go diving, ensure that you take your own mask, fins and snorkel with you for the best fit, any additional equipment that you need you can hire.

Ambergris Caye is your best value-for-money option as there is a wide variety of accommodation and dive schools. Expect a one tank dive on the reef to cost around US$40, a 2 hour snorkel trip US$20, while day trips to the Blue Hole will range from US$65 to US$90 for divers and US$50 to US$70 for snorkellers.

Other Cayes along the Barrier Reef worth considering are Caye Caulker and located much further south, South Water Caye, where the Blue Marlin Lodge is the best place to stay.

If you are looking for the very best diving in Belize then you'll need to head for the offshore atolls of Glovers, Turneffe Islands and Lighthouse Reef. They themselves are surrounded by huge areas of reef and some of the most thrilling dives sites in Belize. To reach them you'll need to book a place on a liveaboard dive vessel (the best ones leave from Belize City), or fly and base yourself at one of the many little Cayes that lie within the atolls themselves.

Lighthouse Reef Atoll is probably the most popular of the three, it now has its own runway. It is where you can find Belize's most famous dive site, the Blue Hole. Formed 15,000 years ago in an ice age, it was only made famous by the late Jacques Cousteau, back in 1970. Its quite wide, over 300 metres but it's the sheer vertical walls that plummet to over 150 metres that make it an awesome sight. To appreciate its stunning deep blue colour, it's best viewed from the air.

Other great dive sites include The Half Moon Caye Wall, which starts in just 10 metres and plummets to over a thousand! Dramatic scenery, large shoals of Jackfish, barracuda, brilliant coloured creole wrasse and occasionally the odd turtle will leave you with plenty to write about in your log books.

To dive Half Moon Caye wall you don't necessarily have to be an expert diver, but to dive on Turneffe Islands Atoll's best site you really should be. At the Elbow there can be exceptionally strong currents, and as a result the reef is stunning. You can expect thick forests of deepwater gorgoniums, colourful sponges and large schools of fish, possibly barracuda eagle rays and plenty of shark.

You won't find many wrecks in Belize's waters because the ocean walls are so sheer. But look out for one, the wreck of the *Sayonara*, a cargo boat sunk in 1985. This is an easy wreck dive on the leeward side of the Turneffe island atoll.

The furthest south of the three Atolls, Glovers Reef offers excellent diving for all levels. Shallow elkhorn forests are popular with novices while the dramatic drop-offs along Southwest Caye wall and Long Caye wall are extremely popular with the more experienced diver. This is the least developed of the three atolls and it is best to bring your own equipment.

Fishing

Sport fishing is big business in Belize and the opportunities are terrific. The local fishing seasons are as follows:

Fish	Season	Whereabouts
Blue Marlin	jan–mar, nov–dec	offshore
Sailfish	feb–apr	offshore
White Marlin	jan–apr, nov–dec	offshore
Bonito	jan–dec	offshore
Blackfin Tuna	jan–dec	offshore
Sharks	jan–dec	offshore
Yellowfin Tuna	jan–dec	offshore
Wahoo	jan–feb, nov–dec	offshore
Barracuda	jan–dec	on the reef
Bonefish	jan–apr, nov–dec	on the reef
Grouper	jan–dec	on the reef
Jackfish	jan–dec	on the reef
Snapper	jan–dec	on the reef
Mackerel	jan–dec	on the reef
Kingfish	mar–jun	on the reef
Tarpon	jun–aug	channels & mangroves
Tarpon	feb–jun	rivers
Permit	feb–oct	flats at incoming tide
Snapper	feb–nov	rivers
Snook	feb–jul	rivers

Staying at the Atoll resorts tends to be more expensive than at Ambergris Caye. A week's accommodation and diving will cost between US$1150 and US $1478.

For serious divers the best way to dive Belize is undoubtedly on a liveaboard. Peter Hughes operates the superb Wave Dancer and the Aggressor Fleet operates the Belize Aggressor. They both concentrate on the best dive sites around Turneffe Island and Lighthouse Atolls. Prices for a week's all inclusive diving start at US$ 1642. Although the boats may carry a limited supply of dive equipment for hire, again it is best to bring your own. Firms often only provide cylinder and air without a back-pack or harness. They do provide weightbelts and weights.

Gavin Anderson is a diving expert, underwater photographer and travel writer. He writes for Diving Magazine, Sport Diver and The Scotsman, amongst other publications.

As the saying goes 'if you cannot catch fish in Belize, you cannot catch fish' and a number of specialist hotels, guides and tour operators exist to help you on your way. Two long established fishing lodges are the **Belize River Lodge** ✆ 025 20021, 📧 025 2298 whose luxury yachts will take you wherever you want to go, and the **El Pescador** (✆ & 📧 026 2977), ✆(501) 26 2975; 📧 (501) 26 2398 on the beach of Ambergris Caye, which also has its own tackle shop. Flats fishing is offered by **Turneffe Islands Lodge** (✆ 014 9564, 📧 014 49564 and **Tuneffe Flats Lodge** (✆ 02 30319, 📧 021 2046). Individual guides and tour operators are listed in the BTB's Visitor's Guide available from the main office in Belize City. Whoever you choose to go with, remember that all qualified fishing guides in Belize must have a license bearing their photograph.

The latest information on fishing regulations and license fees can be obtained by contacting the Fisheries Department, at the Ministry of Agriculture and andFisheries, ✆ 08 22241, or any of the lodges mentioned above. Alternatively contact the Belize Tourist Board in Belize City. At present there are no fees for vessels or anglers, but there will be soon. In future tourists will probably have to pay for permits of one week, one month or one year, which will cost around BS$5, BZ$10 and BZ$20 respectively. Although equipment can be hired locally, it is always best to bring your own. A selection of rods and lures will give you enough flexibility.

Hiking

The landscapes of Belize are very tempting to explore on foot, but sadly there are very few opportunities to do so outside some of the national parks and private reserves. There are no recreational long-distance trails and few places to buy provisions in remote places, inside or outside the parks. Excursions are generally limited to day trips or a couple of hours walking short trails, which is great but hardly adventurous. With a bit of extra time and money, though, you could book yourself a local guide at the Cockscomb Basin Jaguar Reserve, and spend five days hiking through jungle to reach the country's highest mountain: Victoria Peak (1120m). That would be a serious challenge and should only be attempted during the dry season(approximately March–June) and if already fit. (Note that you would have to carry all your own food and drink into the reserve). Arrangements can be made via the **Audubon Society** in Belize City ✆ 02 34 987, ◉ 02 34 985. If you really enjoy walking, the ideal place for it is the **Mountain Pine Ridge**, which is also one of the few places where you are allowed to camp (at the forestry station only). Best of all, spend a few days at one of the five lodges scattered around the reserve, and use them as your base. The best lodge for keen walkers is **Hidden Valley Inn**, ✆ 08 23320, ◉ 08 23334, which owns 18 000 acres right in the heart of the Mountain Pine Ridge, and not only boasts some superb trails taking in the best views and waterfalls, but also strategic resting places and barbecue spots.

In all cases the best months for walking are from March–June, when trails should be dry and there are fewer bugs. Take your own lightweight walking boots, long-sleeved cotton trousers and shirts, and insect repellent. A water bottle, camping knife and binoculars are also useful.

Horse Riding

The Mountain Pine Ridge and rainforests around San Ignacio are the only areas in Belize where horse riding is easily arranged. Many of the jungle lodges offer guided day trips for a couple of hours, and some make it their speciality. The leading outfit is **Mountain Equestrian Trails** (✆ 092 3310, ◉ 082 3235), outside San Ignacio, but **Maya Mountain Lodge**, **duPlooy's** and **Chaa Creek** are also highly recommended. For the latest horse-riding tours on offer it is always worth checking the notices at Eva's Bar in San Ignacio. Near Belmopan, you could stay at **Banana Bank Lodge**, which has a magnificent setting, right on the Belize River.

Potholing

The karst limestone that makes up large parts of the Maya Mountains is absolutely riddled with caves and underground rivers, all of which have been used for ceremonial purposes by the Maya for thousands of years. In fact, Belize boasts the largest cave system found in Central America (the Chiquibul caves south west of the Mountain Pine Ridge), which also contains the largest single cave so far found in the Western Hemisphere. The potential for adventurous exploration is therefore huge, and is being exploited more and more. Ideally you would go during the dry season, from March to June, when caves are less likely to be flooded out. In all cases you need to go on a guided tour, which will ensure both your safety and finding some of the most exciting spots, which could reveal anything from gigantic stalactites hundreds of years old, to Maya artefacts left untouched for centuries. Caving trips will often include tubing or rafting the rivers that run through them, which is an added bonus.

In San Ignacio, the best tours are offered by **Pacz Tours** (Pacz Hotel, 4 Far West Street, ✆ 092 2110) but for the most adventurous journeys and for the fit and hardy only—be sure to spend some time with Ian Anderson at his **Caves Branch Jungle Camp** (✆ & ✉ 08 22800) located just off the Hummingbird Highway, near Belmopan. Overlooking the Caves Branch River, the property has over twenty caves and caverns to explore, as well as over 25 miles of jungle trails.

River Rafting and Canoeing

Some of the most exciting river rafting trips are those taken to explore the country's many caves (*see* above). But you can also take more sedate journeys up and down the country's many rivers and in particular the Belize River, the Mopan and Macal, all of which can best be accessed from San Ignacio, in the western Cayo District.

The main tour operator for rafting and canoeing is Pacz Tours (see above), but others are bound to start up and you will find their publicity displayed at Eva's Bar in San Ignacio. Most of the surrounding jungle lodges also hire out canoes, and will even transport them upriver for you to float down. You'll need no expert training and can simply book a day out once you arrive.

Sea Kayaking

This is best done using one of the resort hotels on the cayes as your base. Many hire out kayaks, or even offer them free to guests, giving you an excellent opportunity to slip off and explore those tiny islands and quiet mangrove inlets. As a sport, sea kayaking is very much in its infancy in Belize, but its calm reef waters make it an ideal destination, so there are several North American tour operators offering trips. One of the most experienced is **Slickrock Adventures**, P.O. Box 1400, Moab, Utah 84532 tel ✆ & ✉ (801) 259 6996. An excellent mainland operator in Belize is **Kitty's Place** ✆ 06 23227, ✉ 06 23226 on the beach in Placencia, who offers escorted trips to a small mangrove island six miles off-shore.

Telephones

Phoning to and from Belize is easy and international calls from here are the cheapest in Central America. Public payphones are rare, and your best option is to use either the BTL offices or phones in hotels and restaurants, which usually charge a flat fee. For example, a local call of three minutes officially costs no more than 15 BZ cents; long-distance calls within Belize cost BZ$1.10 for three minutes. Operator assisted international calls cost BZ$12.80 for three minutes to North America and BZ$24 to Europe, and are 25% cheaper if direct dialling is used. The number for the regional operator is 114, for the international operator it is 115. You can also send faxes, telexes, and telegrammes from any BTL office.

Belize Telecommunications (BTL) has offices in all the major towns, normally in the same building as the post office. In Belize City, their office is at 1 King Street, open Mon–Sat, 8–6. If you wish to make an international call, you will be asked for a BZ$30 deposit. Direct dialling is possible and collect calls can be made to the US, Canada, Great Britain, Australia, New Zealand, France, and most Central American and Caribbean countries. To telephone Belize from outside the country the code is 501 followed by the number.

To make a reverse charges call or a collect call ring the operator in the country you are phoning or ask any BTL office to connect you. Collect calls or telephone credit card calls to the US can also be made by accessing AT & T on 555, Sprint Express on 556 or MCI on 557 from any hotel phone. (Dial 1, 4, or 5 respectively, if using a payphone at the International Airport or BTL's central office in Church Street, Belize City). For the UK dial 552 (Belize City hotels only), or 2 from payphones at the International Airport or central BTL office; for Canada dial 558 (Belize City hotels only), or 6 from payphones at the above named locations.

Telephone codes around Belize are: Belize City: 02; Belmopan: 08; Benque Viejo: 93; Caye Caulker: 22; Corozal: 04; Dangriga: 05; Orange Walk: 03; Punta Gorda: 07; San Ignacio: 092; San Pedro/Ambergris Caye: 026.

The emergency number for the police is 911; for the fire department or ambulance it is 90.

The cheapest way to stay in touch is via **e-mail**, but unfortunately this service is not widely available for tourists. Your hotel or lodge might be persuaded to let you use their machine, but don't count on it. Only Belize City and San Ignacio have commercial e-mail sending and receiving facilities. In Belize City head for Angelus Press, 10 Queen Street, (*open Mon–Fri, 7.30–5.30 and Saturday 8–4*). which will charge you BZ$17.25 for one hour's computer time. In San Ignacio head for Eva's Bar & Restaurant, (*open daily, 7.30 –late*), which charges just BZ$3 for sending and BZ$1 for receiving e-mails.

Tipping

Tips are given in hotels and restaurants and to taxi drivers, porters and chambermaids. However, there are no hard and fast rules and you're free to do as you please, responding to each situation as it arises. Generally speaking the staff in more up-market establishments will expect to be tipped, while those in cafés and cheap restaurants may be pleasantly surprised but will appreciate the gesture. Hotels add anything from 5–20% to their bills and it is well worthwhile checking on this before using their services.

The government is planning to introduce VAT at 15% for all accommodation, which is a great worry to smaller businesses who fear they will go bust if forced to charge higher prices. Currently hotel room tax remains at 7%.

Toilets

Public toilets are unheard of in Belize. In general, your best bet is to use the toilets in any restaurant, hotel or bar, which nobody will mind. On the road, you will find petrol stations invariably have clean toilets, which are kept locked for the use of customers only. (Get the key from the attendant or cashier).

Tourist Information

The Tourist Board (BTB) has its main office at 83 North Front Street, Belize City, ✆ 77213/73255; ✉ 77490. If calling from abroad add 011 501 2. (*open Mon–Fri, 8–4; Sat 8–noon*). This is the place to come for maps, books and local publications, as well as information on tours, public transport schedules (maritime and buses) or hotel and car hire rates. There are many tour operators offering everything from sightseeing to sailing charters, and a full list is available from BTB. Strangely, for a country trying hard to promote itself as a tourism destination, there is no official tourist office at its main resort: San Pedro, on Ambergris Caye. Even stranger you will find a brand new BTB office in distant Punta Gorda, which gets the fewest visitors in the country. Wherever you go, however, the local people will be helpful.

International Tourist Information Services

These are very limited and usually performed by consulates. That means tourist information is not their business but they have a few leaflets and brochures. By far the fastest and and most efficient access to information is gained by looking up Belize on the World Wide Web. More and more of the country's accommodation for example now have their own web sites. Try http://www.belizenet.com/ which is endorsed by both the Belize Tourist Board and the Belize Tourism Industry Association.

UK: Belize High Commission, 19 Cavendish Square, London W1M 9AD, ✆ (0171) 499 9728, ✉ (0171) 491 4139. The European Tourism Office for Belize is located in Germany so you could also try Bopserwalderstr. 40G, 70184 Stuttgart, Germany ✆ (0049) 711 233947, ✉ (0049) 711 233954.

US: Belize Tourist Board, 421 Seventh Avenue, New York, New York 10001, © (800) 624 0686 or (212) 563 6011 @ (212) 563 6033.

Canada: Consulate General of Belize, Suite 094, 1112 West Pender Street Vancouver BC V6E 2Sl, © (604) 683 4517, @ (604) 683 4518.

Travel Bookshops

The longest established travel bookshop, which also sells maps, in the UK is Stanfords, 12–14 Long Acre, London WC2, © (0171) 836 1321, or Stanfords, 29 Corn Street, Bristol BS1 1HT © (0117) 929 9966. Apart from the widest selection of guide books, you will also find literary travel books, usefully arranged according to countries. A short walk away you will find The Traveller's Bookshop, 25 Cecil Court, London WC2, © (0171) 836 9132, which also has a travellers' noticeboard.

Other travel specialists include the Travel Bookshop, 13 Blenheim Crescent, London, W11 © (0171) 229 5260 and Nomad Books, 791 Fulham Road, London, © (0171) 736 4000. Finally, a well laid out travel bookstore is Daunt Books for Travellers, 83 Marylebone High Street, London, W1M 3DE, © (0171) 224 2295.

In the USA try Traveller's Bookstore, 22 West 52nd Street, New York, NY 10019, © (212) 664 0995, The Complete Traveler, 4038 Westheimer, Houston, TX 77027 or Travel Merchandise, 1425 K Street NW, Washington, DC 20005, © (202) 371 6656.

Where to Stay

Prices in the book are grouped under four price bands, which refer to the average price of a double room. (As everywhere else, single travellers are generally penalized by having to pay almost the same as couples.) Prices are quoted in US dollars.

luxury	US$110–US$300
expensive	US$50–US$110
moderate	US$20–US$50
cheap	US$10–US$20

If you are travelling on a budget, keep your ear to the travellers' grapevine: the state of places to stay in the inexpensive category changes all the time—and the addition of a (workable) shower, or laundry facilities, can make all the difference. Generally speaking, good value accommodation will be found around bus and train stations, markets, and truckers' stopping places (near petrol stations).

Make sure you also ask if prices that are quoted at the hotel reception are in Belize or US dollars, per room or per person. Children under 12 usually stay for free, if they sleep in their parents' room.

Note that room prices will vary according to the season (high season being November to May); and that it is always worth bargaining about the price, especially if you intend to stay three or more nights. If planning to be around for any of the major festivals, remember to book in advance by fax, telex or registered mail, or make sure you arrive at least two days in advance.

Belize has an enormous variety of tropical luxury hotels, though service standards tend to be a little lax by Western standards. To meet tourists' highest expectations, the Belize Tourism Industry Association is trying to establish training courses for hotel and catering staff, but this programme is in its infancy.

There are hotels and guest houses to suit all pockets, though it has to be said that Belize is expensive compared to the rest of Central America. The cheapest price range for one or two persons per night, is US$10–20. Expensive resort hotels begin at US$115 for a single (which is above the normal price bands generally used in the book, and is always indicated in the text). International reservation procedures are observed by Belizean hotels.

Added to these prices is a 7% government hotel tax, and some places charge up to 15%–20% service tax on top of that. Always make sure you know whether the price quoted included these two taxes or not, as many places do not openly display their charges.

There are no youth hostels in Belize, and camping is forbidden in almost all parts of the country. Two exceptions to this rule are the Cockscomb Basin Wildlife Reserve and Mountain Pine Ridge, though both are difficult to reach without your own transport, and there is no food available in either place.

Both sites are administered by the Audubon Society in Belize City, which can provide up-to-date information and help for organizing visits. Commercial renting of holiday homes is common in all the tourist areas, especially on the Cayes. Contact the Belize Tourist Board for information on long-term lets. Outside the tourist season (May–November), you should have no trouble finding a self-catering apartment or beach house, even if you have not booked in advance.

Women Travellers

Women travellers have nothing to fear in Belize that they don't face in any Western country, though cultural differences should be respected. The Afro-Caribbean culture is relaxed regarding dress codes, and relations between men and women are much more casual than in the other countries of Central America. This leads some female travellers to mistakenly feel more at ease than they should, forgetting that it is not safe to wander about alone at night in Belize City nor on lonely beaches or by remote waterfalls. Note also that there is a 'trade' in sex, especially on Ambergris Caye and Caye Caulker, and some local studs think nothing of slapping their foreign conquests around should they tire of them or think of leaving without a 'gift'.

Altun Ha

History

Pre-Independence History	40
Prehistory	40
The Origin of Agriculture	41
Early Societies	42
The Maya	43
European Discovery and the Colonial Era	45
Independence from Spanish Rule	47
Buccaneers and Pirates	48
Creole Society	48
A Controversial Territory	49
Independence and Democracy	51
Towards the Year 2000	52
Economy	52
Modern Society	54

Pre-Independence History

> *Land as slim as a whip,*
> *Hot as torture,*
> *Your step in Honduras, your blood*
> *In Santo Domingo, at night,*
> *Your eyes in Nicaragua...*
>
> Pablo Neruda, *Centro América*

Flying across Central America, the view is astonishing. Far below, you see the Atlantic and Pacific oceans at the same time, only a narrow strip of land keeping them apart—a narrow strip which also separates (or connects) the great land masses of North and South America. Central America has somehow always been viewed like that: a ragged bridge connecting two huge continents, or worse still, simply a peninsular extension of North America, 'America's Back Yard'—after all, the Darién Gap is a dead end in terms of overland travel. The jungle there is so inaccessible and the land so swampy that no road or rail has yet succeeded in penetrating to the South American mainland. The only way to proceed is either on foot or to fly.

There is nothing homogeneous about this region that stretches from the Mexican-Guatemalan border all the way to the swampy jungles of the Panamanian border with Colombia. What looks like geographical unity is in fact a collection of seven very different countries. However, there are features which they all have in common, such as the Spanish language, certain tropical export crops, and a subtropical climate. But the human histories of the countries could hardly be more dissimilar. From prehistoric times quite distinct cultures have emerged, largely defined by the regional differences in geography and vegetation.

Prehistory

During the last Ice Age, such vast expanses of ocean were frozen that the earth's general sea level was lowered. One effect of this was that Asia and North America were at times connected by a land bridge, known as the Bering Passage, and it is believed that humans first came into the Americas via this route about 60,000 years ago. Radiocarbon emitted from polished bone tools suggest that the entire North and South American continents were populated by 11,000 BC.

The people who lived here in those times were hunter-gatherers, who lived a nomadic existence, following a seasonal cycle after a large variety of animals and easily gathered fruits, nuts and roots. Small family groups would have roamed the landscape, only occasionally coming together into larger camps in order to hunt the giant mammals of the age, such as mammoth, mastodon or bison. But there were many smaller animals they hunted too, such as rabbits, foxes, squirrels, turtles, lizards and quail.

Between 11,000 and 6000 BC the climate gradually became warmer and drier. Huge lakes dried up, grasslands became deserts, and the woodlands shrank, so that slowly the giants of prehistory became extinct. New kinds of food eventually had to be found by humans, and very, very slowly, people evolved new ways of life, where food came from a greater variety of sources.

In the time from 7000 to 1500 BC domesticated plants played an increasingly important role, and larger camps of people developed in response to the greater numbers needed for effective food gathering and hunting. In particular near rivers, lakes and oceans, sedentary groups emerged, who supplemented their fishing culture with gathering a great variety of other food, such as wild cereal plants, fruit, nuts, avocados, squashes, chilli peppers and prickly pears.

The Origin of Agriculture

The evidence for how and when humans first developed agriculture in the Americas is hotly debated. By its nature, plant evidence is hard to come by, and archaeologists have had to make do for their clues with a few cave sites in dry areas, such as in Oaxaca in central Mexico or the Ayacucho basin in the Peruvian Andes. It is at those sites that they have analysed the ground layers relating to different ages, as well as studying coprolites (fossilized faeces) and human bones. From these combined studies scientists have established that a major change took place in human diet after 4500 BC, and that agriculture was important from this time on.

To look for an exact point at which hunting and gathering stopped and agriculture began is fruitless. Development is the key word, and the transition from a nomadic hunting way of life to a sedentary agricultural life was gradual. The cultivation of certain plants may not have resulted from the extinction of the larger animals, nor because of the changing climate or population pressure, but for simple practical reasons. For example, one of the earliest domesticates was the bottle gourd for carrying water, and other plants were cultivated for dyes. Some plants, such as the tomato, are believed to have been domesticated incidentally, when genetic changes in the plant, such as increased size, made it a more important and easily gathered food source.

This must particularly apply to the all-important food plant, maize. Whatever the plant ancestor of maize, its cob would have been no larger than a thumbnail, and its use as a food source cannot have been obvious to early man. Instead, the combined effect of incidental domestication and genetic changes in the plant very gradually made it more and more useful, and eventually people began planting and gathering it specifically for food. These changes must have been slow; by 1500 BC maize was still only one-fifth of its present size. What is certain, however, is that human beings' changed relationship with the environment eventually allowed the first settled cultures to develop.

Early Societies

The earliest evidence for settled communities comes from household objects, such as simple pottery, and cotton fibre cloth which was probably also used. From 3000 BC onwards, and certainly from 1500 BC, settled communities of between twelve and several hundred people gradually developed a new culture that included ritual and religious belief. Small figurines, believed to relate to ancestor worship or fertility rites have been found from this time. Homes were probably windowless houses made of pole and wattle, with palm-thatched roofs. In the highlands, houses would have been made of mud bricks (adobe), and thatched with straw or coarse grasses. Both types of housing can still be seen in Indian villages today.

Elite centres appeared by around 1000 BC; flat temple platforms from this date indicate ceremonial sites, and unequal burials testify to a rigidly stratified society. Some were simply wrapped in a sleeping mat and buried under the family house, while others were buried with immense finery and even human retainers to accompany them in their graves.

One of the earliest Mesoamerican civilizations were the Olmec, who existed between 1200 and 100 BC: with their heyday from 900 to 600 BC. However, their territory was almost entirely restricted to the Gulf Coast and the Tuxla Mountains of modern Mexico. The only significant satellite further south was at Izapa, on the Mexican Pacific coast near modern Tapachula. Another Mesoamerican people were the Toltecs, whose capital was the Yucatán ceremonial centre of Tula, and yet another were the Mixtecs, who ruled the area around modern Mexico City after the demise of the nearby city of Teotihuacan. The only Mesoamerican civilization to develop further south was that of the Maya, whose earliest beginnings go back as far as 2000 BC. They are generally divided into three regional groups: the Highland Maya of the Guatemalan highlands, the Lowland Maya of the Guatemalan Petén and adjacent Maya Mountains, and the Northern Lowland Maya of the Mexican Yucatán.

The Maya

The history of Maya civilization is divided into three periods: the Pre-Classic (2000 BC to AD 250), the Classic (AD 250 to 900), and the Post-Classic (AD 900 to 1530). They are generally held to represent the development, maturity and decadence of the civilization.

Pre-Classic Maya: 2000 BC to AD 250

From 2000 BC to around AD 150, Maya ancestors lived in the small communities already described. In particular along the Pacific plain of Guatemala, villages were established to harvest both the land and the sea. Their inhabitants lived off shellfish, crab, fish, turtles and iguanas, as well as maize from cultivated fields. The earliest village culture in this region is known as Ocos, and flourished from 1500 BC onwards. Later came the Cuadros village culture, which lasted until around 850 BC. Both evolved fine pottery skills, making a variety of bowls, pots and figurines. A common artefact of the period was the tripod bowl or jar, often decorated with crisscross and zigzag designs and patterns made by pressing rope or twine into the wet clay, only found in Central America.

Another important centre of early civilization Kaminaljuyú, lies in the central valley of Guatemala, close to the modern capital. A significant ceremonial centre from earliest Pre-Classic times, it eventually developed into a huge site of at least one hundred buildings, with political and trading links reaching all the way to Mexican Teotihuacán. Even the inhospitable Petén lowlands show evidence of early cultures, and sites such as Altar de Sacrificios, Ceibal, Tikal and Uaxactún were certainly inhabited by 400 BC.

Eventually, some time between 250 BC and AD 300, these simple village cultures scattered across the Maya territory developed the traits of a great civilization. Monumental architecture, sophisticated art forms, timekeeping and elaborate calendars, writing, and the science of astrology were all components of that development. Society became structured by an official religion and a rigid, hereditary class system where even slaves were a hereditary group.

Kaminaljuyú developed into a vast and prestigious city. Temple platforms were raised from the ground, reaching up to 18 metres, and on these stood the simple temples of pole and thatch that so disappointed the Spanish in their search for riches. For those were not to be found in the temples, but in the burial chambers underneath them and around the pyramid platforms.

Classic Maya: AD 250 to 900

The Classic Age was a Golden Age for the Maya civilization, and their sophistication in architecture, art and science can easily match that of the ancient Egyptians or Greeks. Their astronomers could accurately predict lunar and solar eclipses and had recognized many planets, while the Maya calendar reached far beyond the Christian calendar, and the complexity of their writing system has yet to be fully understood (see p.00).

It is during this age that Maya lords built the imposing pyramids of Tikal and Caracol, and sculptural art reached its peak at sites like Copán and Quiriguá. Often these sites are referred to as cities, since as many as 50,000 people once lived in and around them. But that is a misleading term, imposing modern conceptions on the past. It is now generally accepted that it is better to speak of ceremonial centres, since Maya civilization was fundamentally ruled by religious faith and ritual, and all aspects of life, whether the planting season, dates for war, or people's names, were decided by the Maya astronomers and diviners. They were at the heart of all decisions, and the position of every person in society was dominated by their interpretation of the celestial and divine cycle.

Only a very small group of nobles and priests lived at the core of what we see today: the great plazas and pyramids. Nearby there were quarters of artisans, craftsmen and slaves, and spreading out over a much larger area were the dwellings and clustered communities of the peasant majority, who were involved exclusively in food procurement and processing for the central elite, who then redistributed it among the population.

Post-Classic Maya: ad 900 to 1530

Between AD 790 and 889 the Classic Maya civilization abruptly disintegrated. Within a hundred years, the Lowland Maya populations seem to have left, state architecture and monumental building stopped, and even the Maya hieroglyphics appear to have degenerated into simpler forms of pictographic symbolism. Many explanations have been put forward for this collapse: earthquakes or hurricanes, epidemics, ecological disasters, social revolt, foreign invasion or economic decline. Certainly, the warlike Toltecs seem to have moved in from the north around 900, but the evidence from some sources suggests that the decline began before then. Until the Maya script is fully understood, we shall never know more than a fraction of the story.

All we can say for certain is that the Classic Maya civilization did collapse, and from the 10th century onwards, the glorious temples and plazas of most lowland ceremonial centres were left to itinerant squatters, who camped among the abandoned buildings, periodically looting the royal burial chambers or using masonry for their own building needs. Soon the great buildings were reclaimed by surrounding jungle, and by the time the Spanish arrived, the temples and pyramids of the Maya had been derelict for over 500 years, remnants of a 'lost civilization'. The surviving Maya Indians could not shed much light on the magnificent art and architecture of their ancestors, nor adequately explain their culture's historic knowledge of astronomy, science and writing.

But while southern lowland centres of power, such as Tikal, declined, northern lowland centres, such as Chichen Itzá in modern Mexico, expanded. They developed a new style of art and culture, and traded goods along the coast in canoes. Much of this phase of Central American history remains obscure, though Post-Classic culture may have been a fusion of Maya and Toltec. By the time the Spanish arrived, however, Chichen Itzá was also in ruins. In the Western Highlands of Guatemala, though, the Quiché Maya had their powerful kingdom with its capital at Utatlán, the Mam Maya ruled their domains from Zaculeu, and the Cakchiquel Maya governed theirs from Iximché. All these peoples preserved many aspects of Classic Maya culture, and continued to do so after the Conquest. CHK

European Discovery and the Colonial Era

Europeans first came to Central America on Columbus' fourth and final voyage in 1502. His ship dropped anchor at Guanaja, one of the Honduran Bay Islands and, much to the excitement of his teenage son, his forces captured a Maya trading canoe, filled with exotic goods such as quetzal plumes, cacao beans, shells and fine pottery. Soon Columbus set sail once more, heading east around the Mosquito Coast, and discovered the Veragua region, which yielded enough gold finds to encourage a steady stream of expeditions to beach on today's Nicaraguan and Panamanian Atlantic coasts.

In 1513, the conquistador Balboa discovered the Pacific Ocean while travelling inland near the Darién forest, and soon Panamá City (1519), León and Granada (1524) were founded. They were some of the earliest colonial settlements in Central America, and flourished as bases from which to explore, as well as exploit local minerals and the Indians. Slavery was good business, and many thousands of Indians were shipped off to South American silver and gold mines. Most died of European diseases and malnutrition before they reached their destination, and those that did arrive proved unsuitable for heavy mine work. It was then that the Spanish began importing the stronger African slaves, thus introducing a significant black society to Central America.

Spanish forces were also penetrating south from Mexico City, soon to discover and conquer the Highland Maya of Guatemala and establish the brutal reign of Pedro de Alvarado. It was he who founded the most glamorous colonial city of Central America: Antigua, Guatemala, situated in a beautiful highland valley embraced by three volcanos. Meanwhile Spanish forces also traced the Atlantic coast southwards from the Yucatán, establishing strategic forts near the Honduran ports of Puerto Cortés and Trujillo, as well as inland at San Pedro Sula. These were important in repelling Portuguese and English expeditions, and also as bases from which to exploit the fertile interior for cacao.

After the Conquest, population centres followed the ancient patterns so that the main centre of Spanish rule grew up in the Guatemalan highlands. From there it spread thinly south, neglecting the traditionally 'empty' regions, such as the swampy jungles of the Atlantic littoral, as well as many inland areas, such as the inaccessible Honduran highlands. Much of the interior was left to its own devices by the colonial authorities, with the exception of vital ports along the Pacific, such as Colón in Panamá, and fortifications along the Atlantic, such as Omoa and Trujillo in Honduras.

The Spanish were too preoccupied with extracting the riches of Mexican silver and Peruvian gold to bother much with Central America; its mineral resources were limited, and its largest asset was an enslaved Indian population which did little to increase the wealth of Spain itself. Since the conquistadors had little interest in farming, the region was not farmed intensively until after Independence, although indigo and cacao were relatively lucrative exports from El Salvador and Guatemala. Soon the region became a colonial backwater. Panamá was lumped in under the jurisdiction of New Granada, ruled by the Viceroy of Peru, while the rest became the Captaincy-General of Guatemala in 1543, beholden to the Viceroy of New Spain, the forerunner of modern Mexico. This political division still influences Central American politics today and Panamá retains a unique position, not least because of the US-controlled Panamá Canal.

Unlike the Europeans in North America, the Spanish came as soldiers, not settlers. They did not bring their families, but married and had children by Indian women. The mestizos who resulted from this union soon formed the majority of colonial society. The Spanish crown, however, reserved the positions of highest authority for peninsulares—those born in Spain, who brought their families with them—a division that was eventually to spark off the independence movement. Along the Atlantic coast, the presence of African slaves led to a significant society of blacks and mulattos. Added to these peoples were small, tight-knit groups of Chinese, East Indians and white settlers, usually of religious groups, such as the Mennonites, as well as non-Maya indigenous groups, like the Miskitos or Darién Indians, who survived by nature of their inaccessibility. The Maya themselves succeeded better than any other indigenous people of the Americas in retaining their racial and cultural heritage, and to this day they make up over half the population of modern Guatemala, and a significant proportion of Belize.

Neglect by the Spanish authorities allowed others to make inroads into the territory. English, Dutch and French pirates made their homes along the Bay of Honduras and, by the 17th century, English pirates had even helped their country establish claims to what became known as the Crown Colony of British Honduras. Their legacy still exists in Belize, which has only been independent from Britain since 1981, and the English-speaking inhabitants of the Honduran Bay Islands.

Independence from Spanish Rule

Central America gained independence on the coat-tails of Mexico in 1821. There was no battle for independence in the region, and there were plenty among the economic élite who remained loyal to Spanish authority. They were virtually let go against their will; once the rest of Latin America had gone, the Spanish colonial authorities had no further interest in a region that had always been one of the least profitable possessions.

It was a confusing time, when such disparate groups as the mine owners from Honduras, cacao planters of El Salvador and cattle ranchers of Panamá found themselves in a territory with no political authority and little common ground. As a result the various regions turned inwards, trying to consolidate their own interests, while sporadic battles raged between forces loyal to Spain and those with ambitions for wider political control of the region. A limited consensus was reached in 1823, when all but Chiapas decided not to become part of Mexico, and instead founded the United Provinces of Central America, whose capital was to be Guatemala City. This union was made up of five newly founded provinces: Guatemala, El Salvador, Honduras, Nicaragua and Costa Rica, whose borders were more or less the same as those of the countries of today. Belize (then British Honduras) remained outside the union, while Panamá became a part of Colombia. It was a recipe for political fragmentation, and the union was soon rent asunder by conflicting economic and political interests, falling apart completely in 1839.

Ever since, Central American unity has been a lost cause. Honduras and Guatemala soon emerged as the original 'banana republics', their economic and political destiny closely supervised by US interests such as the United Fruit Company. Panamá declared its independence from Colombia in 1904, supported by the US to facilitate the building of the canal. Central America's role as the 'back yard' of the US has been a constant theme of its history since Independence, and on several occasions economic and political influence has spilled over into direct military intervention: the US occupation of Nicaragua from 1909 to 1933, the CIA-backed coup in Guatemala in 1954, or the invasion of Panamá in 1989. Admittedly this has produced a level of economic investment which the local governments could never have generated. But the price has been high, and remains the foremost cause of political instability in the region.

Buccaneers and Pirates

The history of Belize is unique among the Central American countries. It was ignored by Spanish conquistadors, who only passed by on their way from Mexico to Panama, and the coast was left to be settled by British seafarers, the first of whom were shipwrecked on the treacherous Barrier Reef in 1638.

In the early days, the region was known as the Honduran Bay Settlement, and only consisted of a tiny patch around Belize City and St George's Caye, which was an ideal base for maritime bandits. The Barrier Reef provided protection from heavy Spanish galleons, who were unable to pass through the shallow waters, yet the pirates could still swoop on the seasonal migration of colonial ships weighed down by gold and other treasures.

The British government, eager to crack the Spanish monopoly on trade in the Americas and West Indies, actively encouraged piracy at that time. Some were even commissioned by the British government, such as the buccaneers and privateers. Buccaneers were a motley crew of sharpshooters and runaways of all nationalities; those who were seeking out adventure. One of the most famous was Sir Henry Morgan, whose most spectacular feat was capturing Panama in 1670, and holding it to ransom for 750,000 pieces of eight, double-crossing many of his buccaneers. His reward was to be named Lieutenant Governor of Jamaica.

Privateers were simply hired to rob trading vessels of competing nations such as Spain, and their reward was to keep whatever bounty they found. Finally, at the bottom of the criminal scale were the pirates, who served no one but themselves and robbed any boat they could.

Among the many legendary figures is Edward 'Blackbeard' Thatch, who apparently was so fearsome and formidable that Spanish ships would give up their cargo without so much as a fight. His outrageous dress and intimidating appearance helped build his notoriety.

Creole Society

From the early pirate camps developed a society that was not characterized by a blending of Spanish and Indian blood, but of mainly British and African, with a limited amount of Indian. It was a society that eventually developed its own governmental institutions, far removed from the 'strongman politics' that grew up elsewhere in Central America. No plantation elite developed here, with a country enslaved to bananas, coffee or sugar, rather a society that lived from logging and the sea. The Baymen, as they were called, constructed an early form of democratic rule, where they elected governing magistrates at public meetings. For over 200 years the Honduran Bay Settlement survived even though it was entirely surrounded by hostile Spanish forces, and did not become a British Colony until 1862. Not only does the racial and political heritage differ from that in the rest of Central America–the social and economic history does too.

Slavery was officially abolished in 1838, and multiculturalism flourished throughout the 19th century, though certainly not without tension. Not all blacks who came to the Honduran Bay Settlement were slaves in the first place. In 1817 500 black members of the 5th West India Regiment arrived, after their regiment was disbanded and they were given the option of land grants here. Most became free woodcutters in the emergent logwood and mahogany trade. Other blacks arrived as free survivors from shipwrecked slaving vessels or were simply given their freedom by captains who had fallen out with their contractors.

The racial melting pot was not just one of white and black, however. At least 8000 mestizo and Indian refugees remained after the end of the War of the Races in the Yucatán, in 1874, while almost twenty years earlier, 1000 East Indian Sepoys arrived after being deported by the British. The Sepoys had been responsible for a bloody uprising against British rule in India, killing many colonials in New Delhi and elsewhere. Once the British had granted the territory Colony status, they also began an immigration incentive programme for Chinese farm workers. By that time the logging trade was already going into decline, and new labour was needed to develop agriculture. Unfortunately, less than half of the 474 Chinese arrivals in

1865 remained three years later; they had either died from tropical diseases or returned to their own country. A small number of Lebanese mercantile families also settled in British Honduras, as did German-speaking Protestant Mennonites, emigrating from Canada and Mexico.

A Controversial Territory

At first Belize consisted solely of Belize City and St George's Caye, but soon the settlement spread. One reason for the expansion was that the logging trade required large tracts of forest to search for mahogany. The Spanish were always keen to assert that the British settlers had no territorial rights, and could not found permanent towns and villages. However, the 1783 Treaty of Versailles established the first outline for the Baymen's territory.

According to that agreement, the northern border was the River Hondo, the southern one the Belize River, and the western border Petén Itzá. But only three years later Belizean loggers were operating as far south as the Sibun River, and the country's present-day outline was established from this time onwards, even if the Spanish and British authorities both tried to deny it.

The 1783 Treaty had been signed by the Spanish on condition that the British government did not establish a colonial government in the region, and also gave up its claim to the Mosquito Coast. But the Baymen, with their tradition of self-rule, were never easily persuaded to curtail their operations according to British foreign policy, and thus this early territorial agreement was soon ignored. It was a thorn in the Spanish colonial side, and forces from the Mexican Yucatán repeatedly threatened the Baymen.

Finally, in 1798, a huge Spanish fleet of 32 ships, 500 seamen and 2000 soldiers set sail to rout Belize City once and for all. But as luck would have it, three ships of the West India Regiment came to the aid of the ragged flotilla of Baymen boats, in addition to 171 slaves who agreed to fight in return for their freedom, and their combined forces actually succeeded in repelling the enemy fleet. It was the last time the Spanish tried to remove the settlers by force, and the Battle of St George's Caye is still celebrated as a national holiday in modern Belize.

Once Mexico and the Central American region had gained independence from Spain, in 1821, the United Provinces of Central America were founded, from which British Honduras remained apart. However, in 1839, when the union disintegrated, Guatemala claimed it had inherited sovereign rights over Belize from Spain, thus initiating a conflict that is still simmering at present. The British, in turn, declared the territory to be under the law of England and instituted a governor general to rule the country. As far as the Baymen were concerned, it was a necessary evil, but British rule always sat uneasily with a society that was founded on personal freedom and home rule.

The conflict between Britain and Guatemala continued until the Treaty of 1859, when Guatemala officially recognized British sovereignty over British Honduras–now known as Belize. The agreement was signed on condition that the British would build a road connecting the Petén with the Caribbean coast of Belize, but this part of the bargain was never kept, and thus successive Guatemalan governments have declared the 1859 and later 1863 Treaties invalid, and laid claim to the entire territory of Belize

This is the principal reason why the British armed forces remained in independent Belize, and why the country did not gain full independence until 1981. A new treaty of recognition was signed in 1991, but it may not hold since many Guatemalans oppose it and the next president could easily revoke it. In the meantime, though, the British presence has been scaled down considerably since 1993, and most of their army bases have been handed over to Belizean control. Officially this was because of the 'democratisation' of Guatemala, but the real reason has more to do with budget cuts in the U.K.

Independence and Democracy

British Honduras officially became known as Belize in June 1973, and instituted its own Belizean dollar in 1974, but did not become a fully independent member of the Commonwealth of Nations until 21 September 1981, with George Cadle Price elected as the first prime minister. He is the leader of the People's United Party (PUP), founded in 1950, and has been the country's premier on many occasions, most recently elected in 1989, when his party narrowly won the elections with a majority of just two seats. Elections must be held at least every five years, and there is universal suffrage for all over the age of 18.

The system of government in Belize is a parliamentary democracy based on the British model, and the prime minister rules the country with an elected cabinet of ministers and ministers of state. The Queen is still the titular head of state, but she is represented by a governor general who is always a Belizean and takes his cue for appointing members to the cabinet from the Belizean prime minister.

The 1993 elections gave a surprise win to the nationalist United Democratic Party (UDP), led by Manuel Esquivel largely due to the popular sentiment stirred up by the coup in Guatemala that same year, combined with the withdrawal of British Troops, which many felt made the country extremely vulnerable. Price's ruling PUP was blamed for allowing the British withdrawal to go ahead and thus the UDP won—albeit with only 49% of the popular vote—to form a coalition government.

Towards the Year 2000

Economy

Like many developing countries, Belize is economically vulnerable because of its small size and over-dependence on imports. It imports almost a quarter of its food requirements, which seems extraordinary for a country so rich in fertile land and seafood. But the problem is that the agricultural and fishing industry is dedicated to earning foreign exchange, rather than catering to internal needs. Most farming land is therefore used to produce sugar— still the country's number one export and foreign exchange earner—as well as bananas and citrus fruits. As a result, local markets are characterized by a very limited range of home produced food and a great many expensive tinned items from abroad, including tinned meat, fish and butter. A kind of inverted snobbery exists that means people would rather have expensive tinned sardines than local fresh fish. The exception to this rule are the markets close to Mennonite settlements, which are successfully producing and selling dairy products, as well as the finest handmade furniture. Crop diversification has taken place, though, and the country is now self-sufficient in bean and corn production, and also produces rice and cacao. Meat production has also expanded a great deal in recent decades, and Belize produces all its own beef, and a good deal of its pork and chicken needs.

Falling international sugar prices, high fuel prices and production costs have resulted in up to 30% of sugar cane fields being abandoned, increasing the country's dependency on imports and the fluctuations of the world market. Industry, meanwhile, only accounts for 20% of the national income and is threatened by cheap imports from neighbouring countries. Here the problem is not so much local as imposed by the International Monetary Fund (IMF), which has dictated a policy of free market economics in effect making imports cheaper than locally produced products. This and the North American Free Trade Agreement threaten the development of the Belizean economy meaning its favoured trading status for sugar and banana exports is likely to end by the turn of the century. By then it will no longer be able to sell up to one fifth of its sugar at double the world market price under the US sugar import quota programme, which could trigger a collapse of the Belizean sugar industry. Similarly, preferential trading of Belizean bananas to Europe under the Lomé Convention could also end after the year 2000, threatening the collapse of the country's second most important export. Meanwhile, the citrus concentrate production industry is threatened by a possible opening up of the Caribbean market, which has so far been party to a protected trading block (CARICOM) in which Belize is the largest producer and seller of citrus concentrate.

The economic future of Belize therefore faces several external threats that it will be hard pushed to overcome entirely. Internally there are also serious problems, mostly to do with a lack of infrastructure, local capital, education and training, and a sufficiently large population. The debate over whether Private Sector or Public Sector investment should be responsible for developing the country's infrastructures remains unresolved and, as yet, any work in these areas has tended to concentrate on regions of special interest to tourism or agricultural development, rather than deprived areas. Thus, although the road network and paved highways have been greatly improved, it has not extended to the remote southern districts, where up to 40% of the country's poor live. The same can be said for telecommunications, water and sewerage provision, and electricity provision.

Health and education, and how they should be provided, are also contentious issues. Although Belizeans generally enjoy far better living conditions than neighbouring countries, there is still a strong disparity between Belize City and the rest of the country, which have to rely on mobile health clinics that can only attend to basic needs. Although 75% of the population has access to medical facilities, half the rural population is forced to travel long distances for surgical care, which is almost exclusively available in Belize City.

No wonder, then, that the booming tourism industry has been targeted as an important part of the country's solution to dependency and debt. It is now the second most important source of foreign currency, after sugar, and has been increasing dramatically with every decade. As recently as the 1960s there were an average of 11,000 visitors annually to Belize. During the first half of the 1990s that figure had risen to 225,000. Unfortunately, the tourism industry suffers from a number of flaws, which lessen its economic contribution to Belize. For example, most of the coastal tourist resort hotels and top jungle lodges are controlled by foreign (mostly American) investors, raising doubts as to how much profits actually remain in the country. Furthermore, expensive imports are needed to provide tourist facilities of international standards, diminishing economic benefits. Other problems are associated with an over-dependence on a single market, namely the North American one, which is set to continue as long as there are no direct flights from Europe to Belize.

On the other hand, tourism has provided an important boost to many employment sectors, notably in hotel and catering, construction, transport provision, guiding, sport and leisure, travel and touring agencies, and environmental protection work. As much as 10% of the working population is now thought to be employed in the tourism industry. The government's objectives for tourism are therefore not only to increase foreign exchange earnings and job creation, but also development of environmentally sustainable tourism, improved links with other sectors, such as agriculture and craftwork, and to target high-spending, luxury tourism over mass tourism. Training and government-led investment incentives promoting Belizean participation as well as foreign development is also planned.

Modern Society

The most notable feature of Belizean society in the second half of the Twentieth Century is the changing balance between ethnic groups, which has inevitably become a hot political issue. What was once a society dominated by Afro-Belizeans and Creole culture is rapidly becoming more Hispanic, so that half of all Belizeans now have Spanish rather than English as their mother tongue. The change has been most dramatic since the early 1980's, when up to 40,000 Central American refugees and displaced persons arrived in Belize. Considering the total population is only around 205,000, this represents a huge influx of people. Hence there has been a significant amount of ethnic tension between Creoles and recent Mestizo arrivals, not least because of the difficult economic times and limited job opportunities. Resentment has also been aimed at others, though, such as the several thousand Hong Kong Chinese, who bought Belizean passports under a government scheme to increase foreign exchange revenue.

Yet this cultural and linguistic change is not just due to immigration. Emigration has played a very important role as well, with up to 60,000 Belizeans (mostly creole and garifuna) believed to be living in the United States. Some left after World War II, when they were invited to boost a labour shortage in the American agricultural sector, but many more left after Hurrican Hattie, in 1961, attracted by better educational and work opportunities. A steady flow has been established ever since, made easy by an ability to assimilate into American culture without any language problems. But while some locally may view this population shift as negative, it has had definite positive results as well. For example, ex-patriate Belizeans contribute over 10% to the country's GDP in money sent 'home', accounting for millions of US dollars.

Wildlife	56
Birds	57
Mammals, Reptiles and Insects	59
Flora	61
Life on the Reef	62
A Short Note on Reef Hazards	64
Ecotourism in Practice	65

Natural Belize

Wildlife

Considering Belize is barely larger than Wales or the US state of Vermont, the size of its animal and plant population is impressive. The country's geographical features not only include mountains and rainforest, but also flat savannah and coastal plains, marshy lagoons and wind-swept pine forests, pristine rivers and islands hugged by mangroves. Add to these a sub-tropical climate and you find a biodiversity that is unmatched in Central America, except perhaps by Costa Rica.

Most important of all, the relatively large amount of protected land in Belize means that many endangered species of birds and mammals still survive here. Both the American crocodile and manatee thrive, as do jaguars and Baird's tapir. *See* p. 127. The giant jabiru stork and the rare red-footed booby are just a couple of the 520 species of birds recorded in Belize, while 250 different types of orchids make up some of the more glamorous of 4,000 species of flowering plants.

Though the country is a naturalist's heaven, the casual visitor should note that not only patience and a good guide is required to find the most exotic stars, but also luck and correct timing. The best time of year is the dry season, from February to May, when forest roads and trails are easily accessible, the country's bird population is high and very visible, and the seas are calm, allowing for good diving and snorkelling. The time of day is also vital, and you will find dawn and dusk the most rewarding times to be out looking for wildlife. Some of the most beautiful and enchanting animals are nocturnal including the country's famous five: the jaguar, jaguarundi, margay, ocelot and puma, although you are unlikely to catch a glimpse of them in their natural habitat. You do have an excellent opportunity to see many of the country's smaller species, however, especially its birds, reptiles and insects, flowers and other tropical plants, not to mention the marvellous array of life in the Caribbean Sea. In all cases, the best places to find any wildlife are the reserves and national parks, most of which are administered by the **Belize Audubon Society** (12 Fort Street, Belize City, ✆ 02 34987, ℻ 02 78562. *(open Mon–Fri, 8–noon and 1–5)*. See p. 78. Some are also in private hands, such as the Rio Bravo Conservation Area, which is run by **Programme for Belize** (2 South Park Street, Belize City, ✆ 02 75616, ℻ 02 75635. *(open Mon–Fri, 8–5)*. Contact either of the above for the latest practical information, as well as their informative leaflets covering each reserve.

Birds

Of the many hundreds of bird species found in Belize, approximately 370 are permanent residents, which makes Belize a twitcher's paradise. The largest bird, the five-foot jabiru stork, which has an impressive nine-foot wingspan, is easy to spot, especially at the Crooked Tree Wildlife Sanctuary where couples arrive in November to build huge nests for the young that will hatch in April and May. Others in the big league include the harpy eagle, whose females stand a proud three feet tall, with a wingspan of over six feet. A fast and agile killer, this black and white bird hunts in the country's forests, swooping on unsuspecting monkeys and parrots with terrifying speed. In contrast, the red-footed booby is so docile that sailors used to smack it off its perch for supper for generations before it was officially saved. Only one colony remains, though, and you have to travel all the way to Half Moon Caye Natural Monument to see them. Go between February and April, and the viewing platform will reveal branches heaving with noisy chicks, one fluffy white bundle for every nest. The boobies are not the only residents either, there are also thousands of huge black frigate birds, and visiting pelicans too, though you can see both of these in virtually any coastal area of Belize.

Some of the most entertaining birds are the parrots and hummingbirds, and Belize boasts seven kinds of the former and twenty-two species of the latter. Sit quietly in any garden, and you are bound to hear the buzz of a hummingbird's wings. Look in the direction of the noise and soon you will focus on a tiny body of fabulous colours and delicate bill, hovering just long enough to lick nectar from a flowering bush. The parrots, meanwhile, are likely to wake you early in the morning, squawking manically as they chase among the tree tops.

The finest of them all is the scarlet macaw, whose striking red body is usually framed by bright yellow and blue wing feathers. A smaller cousin is the yellow-headed Amazon parrot, popular locally because of his mimicking talents.

Travel along any river and you are likely to see kingfishers, herons, white ibis, egrets and snail kites amongst others. Walk in the rainforest, and you might encounter keel-billed toucans perched high above, and elegant curassow stalking the ground for seeds and fallen fruit. Curassow are distinctively long-legged with a curled crest on top of their heads. Spend time sitting quietly in any of the country's gardens and reserves, and you are likely to spot all manner of tropical finches, jays and orioles, including the blue-crowned motmot.

When it comes to the best locations for bird-watching, preferences are defined by time and money, the level of comfort and convenience you require, and what type of birds you most wish to see. An excellent region for birds is the remote Shipstern Reserve in northern Belize, where you will not only find a Butterfly Breeding Centre, but also an impressive area of land that encompasses lagoons, rivers, swamp and forest.

A more comfortable and up-market option would be a visit to Chan Chich Lodge, which is a luxury resort hotel tucked among ruined temples in the rainforest of western Belize. A compromise between these two, both in terms of comfort and cost, is the Crooked Tree Wildlife Sanctuary. *See* p. 175. Easy to reach from Belize City, it has a variety of places to stay and a selection of self-guided trails or booked tours to explore its lagoons and marshland.

Finally, a few nights spent at any of the jungle lodges surrounding San Ignacio would also result in an excellent crop of bird sightings, as would any hike in the

Mountain Pine Ridge Forest Reserve. A good specialist guide on the subject is *A Guide to the Birds of Mexico and Northern Central America*, by S. Howell and S. Webb.

Mammals, Reptiles and Insects

Some of Belize's most endearing and easily encountered mammals are its monkeys, and a visit to the Community Baboon Sanctuary will almost certainly guarantee a close encounter. Expect to find not a baboon, but at least one family of howler monkeys. How these monkeys came to be called baboons in Belize is unknown, but their name is apt. The fearsome bark of one is enough to stop anyone in their tracks. Find yourself surrounded by a whole troop at nightfall, and you could be forgiven for thinking that your last hour had finally struck. In fact, the howler monkey is quite harmless, and the ones living in the sanctuary are so used to people, they will let you get very close before haring off and disappearing into the tree tops. A much rarer creature also found at the Baboon Sanctuary is the spider monkey, an agile creature which moves at terrific speed. Using its tail as an extra limb, sometimes picking up objects with it, it will hang upside down, with all four limbs plus its tail grasping a tree branch, resembling a spider in this position. They live in troops of 2 to 100, spending most of their time feasting on fruit and nuts high in the trees. Different species have black, brown, golden, reddish, or tan fur and one of their other distinguishing marks is their four fingers and no thumb, unlike other monkeys.

A few days at the Rio Bravo Research Station or camping in the Cockscomb Basin Wildlife Sanctuary provides the opportunity to explore the country's inland rainforest, which is where a great many animals reside. Some of the most prevalent species are the insects and although you will want to avoid the biting and stinging ones, there are plenty you will enjoy, not least the many butterflies. One of the most beautiful is the blue morpho, whose large wings glow an iridescent blue. (If you want to be sure of seeing one, make sure you visit the Butterfly Breeding Centre at Chaa Creek (*see* pp. 00), which is entirely devoted to them).

Try not to be disappointed if few animals dutifully present themselves to you. Most are nocturnal and rarely wait around for humans. But tread carefully and quietly with a guide, and your senses will gradually become accustomed to the forest's sounds. Look up into the canopy and scan the forest floor, stand still and listen, and you might catch a coati rummaging for bugs. Its distinctive ringed tail and pointy nose are reminiscent of a raccoon. Perhaps a shy white-tailed deer will flit across the path ahead or a long-legged agouti will dash off, forgetting the seed it was just cracking. Sit by the river bank and watch iguanas sunning themselves on overhanging branches, while underneath, little hickatee river turtles sit immobile on a log. If you're really lucky, the country's largest animal might stumble from the forest for a drink: the Baird's tapir, Belize's national animal, is easily recognized by its flexible long snout, which it uses for rummaging, and of course its sheer bulk, which can weigh up to 650 pounds. *See* p. 127.

After rainfall, forest paths are favourite sleeping spots for snakes, so tread extra carefully. Very few are actually poisonous, and none will attack humans unless trodden on or provoked. (Its therefore a good idea to stamp your feet, giving snakes a chance to move before you reach them). However, the deadly fer-de-lance is easily provoked and found not only in the forest but also in the countryside and around villages. It has velvety scales, a yellowish throat and marks of rich brown and grey. Feeding on small birds and animals, there may be over 60 young snakes in a brood, all carrying fully formed fangs at birth which can deliver a poisonous bite. The fer-de-lance can grow to 2.5 metres long. The impressive boa constrictor is also common in Belize, and despite the mythology, is hardly dangerous to humans, although its bulk and length (approx. six feet) make it seem intimidating.

Even though you are unlikely to see any wild felines, you might just hear the odd grunt at night, which your imagination will immediately identify as a jaguar, but which could just as well be coming from a peccary (similar to wild pigs, very bristly and smelly). But the cats are roaming the forest, patrolling their territories and searching for prey. Largest of them all is the jaguar, which can weigh up to a hefty 150 pounds in this region. The puma only weighs around 70 pounds and is more likely to range in the highland pine forests of the Mountain Pine Ridge than rainforest areas, though both will do.

The delicate and rare ocelot is about half the size of a full-grown puma and hunts much smaller animals, such as gibnut (a type of rodent which is also a popular food with humans). The reddish or brown jaguarundi, on the other hand, is the most common wild cat in Belize, and favours small birds, rodents and lizards for its supper. No larger than a house cat, but with a lean, short-haired body, the loveliest feline of them all is the tiny margay. Very shy and strictly nocturnal, its large eyes blink from a finely drawn face, brilliantly adapted to hunting in the night time canopy, where sleeping birds and creeping insects move at their peril.

Head for the coastal areas and you will not only have the opportunity to discover fish and coral, but also the continent's healthiest populations of manatee and American crocodile. Both can actually be found in many habitats, including inland rivers and among salt-washed mangroves. But the manatee has very specific areas it likes to congregate in, and is therefore quite easy to find. Manatee spotting tours leave from San Pedro daily, though a more tranquil option is to head for the sleepy village of Gales Point, where local boatmen will take you to a warm water spring adored by these huge creatures. Their shape and 400–1,300 lbs blubbery bodies most closely resemble a walrus, although their nearest relative is, in fact, the elephant. Like the elephant, the 'sea cow' is strictly herbivore and does an excellent job of keeping the waterways clear of choking weeds, such as the water hyacinth.

If you want more background information, track down *Neotropical Rainforest Mammals*, by L. Emmons which offers detailed accounts of Belizean wildlife.

Flora

As with its animal life, the most exciting aspect of Belizean flora is its astonishing variety. The climate and different natural environments mean you can just as easily encounter rainforest or pine forest, marshes and mangrove swamps, beds of floating water lilies or sandy palm groves and flowering heath. In fact, there are no less than twelve different vegetation types in Belize, all of which can be found in the Rio Bravo Conservation Area, which makes it an excellent destination not only for animal lovers, but also for plant enthusiasts. Special interest trails have been cut in the surrounding forest, one of which is the Orchid Trail, where you might just spot the Black Orchid (*Encyclia cochleata*), the country's national flower, which is not black at all, but mostly yellow.

Hike in the Mountain Pine Ridge, and you will also have a good chance of finding orchids, especially the *Maxillaria* species which favour the damp environs of streams. (But please remember that picking orchids is illegal). The reason why this region is particularly good for orchids lies in the abundance of fire-resistant trees, such as craboo and oak, whose mighty boughs can support huge colonies of all kinds of epiphytes. In the rainforests of the south-western region of the Mountain Pine Ridge, meanwhile, you can expect to find *Cattleya bowringiana* and *Encyclia belizenis*, and even the rare *Encyclia alata*. Outside these areas, forest clearance for agriculture has caused a significant loss of habitats: for example, certain orchid species thrive on grapefruit trees and rarely grow anywhere else.

One of the most fascinating and mysterious aspects of tropical forests is the vast number of medicinal plants that they conceal, most of which we have yet to discover. An excellent introduction to some of those we do know about is the Medicine Trail at the Ixchel Farm, outside San Ignacio. Here you will learn that poisonous plants usually grow close to their natural antidote, and that many of our most serious diseases can be cured naturally. Dysentery can be stopped by drinking an infusion made of bark from the negrito tree, while the humble yam not only has contraceptive properties, but is also used to derive steroids and several other crucial drugs used daily in the West.

Life on the Reef—Underwater Flora and Fauna

Divers and snorkellers visiting the underwater wilderness of Belize could easily spend their entire vacation just looking at fish. More than 500 species inhabit the Belize Barrier Reef, among them all five species of the graceful Butterfly Fish. The easiest to recognise is the six-inch Foureye Butterflyfish, which has a distinctive false eye at the tail end, part of its defense mechanism to confuse predators. Commonly found in pairs in shallow waters, you will see them fluttering over the coral in search of food. The Trumpet Fish, meanwhile, is more likely to be seen hanging vertically among Purple Sea Reds, perfectly camouflaged. Schools of Blue Tang are a favourite sight, and so is the rarely glimpsed Spotted Drum, which spends most of its time hiding in the crevisses and tunnels of the reef.

Sighting an unusual fish is always a treat. A snorkel through Twin Cayes— a mangrove island a short distance from South Water Caye — often turns up a Short-nose Batfish, for example, which looks like a cross between a very ugly toad and a unicorn. Diving near Long Caye, on Glover's Reef, you can find a colony of Brown Garden Eels in the open sand patches. A shy fish, they peek out from burrows, waving back and forth to catch plankton, but dart away instantly into their holes when disturbed.

The deeper the waters the larger the fish, such as Jewfish (a type of Sea Bass), which can grow up to a mighty 8 ft long. But while encounters with the larger varieties are incredibly exciting, the sight of thousands of smaller fish swimming along is just as enchanting. A curious sight is the common activity of fish cleaning, whereby small species of fish feed on the parasite and debris encrusted on larger ones. This usually takes place at specific locations on the reef, where small fish such as Spanish hogfish and other young Wrasse await the arrival of larger species, such as Grouper, who will gently flounder on the sea bed, while they get the once over from their 'cleaners'.

If you enjoy the thrill of spotting sharks, Nurse sharks are probably the most often encountered, usually found under ledges and overhangs during the day. They tend to lie motionless unless provoked. The lucky diver may even find the world's largest fish diving here: the Whale Shark, which can reach a length of up to 55 feet.

It is normally considered an open water oceanic specimen, but it does occasionally cruise along the Barrier Reef and its walls to feed on plankton, especially in the spring months.

Many species of reptiles and mammals inhabit the waters of Belize. One of the most graceful is the Hawksbill turtle, which is rarely seen by divers because it is endangered due to over harvesting and loss of nesting habitats. Formally valued for its beautiful brown and yellow shell, a Hawksbill can reach three feet in length and weigh up to 150 pounds. Two species of crocodiles also live in Belize, one of which is the Saltwater crocodile and the other is the American crocodile. The latter has become an endangered species because it has been overhunted. Most sightings occur in coastal swamps and rivers, though some of these giant reptiles are regularly seen around mangroves on the Cayes.

Aquatic mammals include whales, dolphins and manatees. Bottlenosed dolphins are the most abundant dolphin species here, and can usually be found jumping in and out of the wakes of boats and ships. They may swim near reefs, especially in lagoon areas, while feeding. The Southern Lagoon, near Gales Point, is a popular site for spotting manatees, although occasionally they are also to be found gliding through the crystal waters near the reef. Whales are infrequent visitors to Belizean waters, preferring colder oceanic waters. Certain species do sometimes migrate through warm Caribbean waters, though, as was the case in 1992, when a pod of Orcas was sighted by divers on the Aggressor dive boat.

As entertaining as these vertebrates may be, they only make up between four and five percent of all the multicellular animals in the world. The majority, about 88%, are invertebrates. The sea is host to many well-known groups of these, including sponges, jelly fish, coral, shrimp, crabs, snails, octopus, sea stars and sea urchins. The fact that sponges are animals often goes unnoticed, though their size and beauty ensures that that they are rarely overlooked by visitors. Colours range from browns and greys to vibrant shades of red, orange and purple. Giant Barrel Sponges may be over six feet in diametre, indicating an animal over one hundred years old.

Jellyfish are common on the reef and best known for their stings, but most have no harmful effect on divers or snorkellers, if left undisturbed. *See* A Short Note on Reef Hazards p. 64 for both the common and toxic varieties to be avoided.

The Caribbean Spiny Lobster, a commercially fished species, is commonly harvested in Belize. It inhabits the reef, hiding in recesses and crannies during the day. Another over-harvested animal of the reef is the Queen Conch, found within the grass beds. Sadly many cayes are piled high with their shells. Focusing on the plants and algae, the producers of this system, only two genuine plants are found in the sea of Belize: Turtle Grass and Manatee Grass. The diversity of algae, however, is vital, because after their death many of them contribute to the formation of sand on the Cayes.

Corals are also often mistaken for plants, and were actually classified as such until the 1700s. We now know they are intricately formed animals. Not only do reef formations vary in size, shape and location, but individual coral species vary. The variety found in Belize is typical of the Caribbean including chalice, but what sets it apart is its pristine condition. **(co-written with Jennifer Hall)**

A Short Note on Reef Hazards

Remember that the worst accidents are caused by human beings rather than anything you'll find in the sea. Moving propellers cause horrific injuries to anyone who comes across them, and it is the responsibility of both captains and swimmers to take great care. It may be stating the obvious but alcohol and water-sports don't mix though of course this is often ignored with disastrous consequences.

Making sure all your diving equipment is in good working order is essential and, if you have any doubts about the safety of your diving outfit, go with someone else. (Better still, make sure it works!) Bearing in mind that the most common injury of all is sunburn, which mostly affects snorkellers, wear a T-shirt and put on plenty of waterproof sunblock.

There are dangerous fish in Belizean waters, but none of them are the human-devouring sharks you've seen in the movies. Funnily enough, very few sharks are actually interested in humans for supper. The Bull Shark, Great Hammerhead, Nurse Shark, Lemon Shark, Black Tip Shark, and White Tip Shark are all found in Belizean waters. They are all exciting big fish you might be lucky enough to spot who are certain to leave you unscathed if you remain calm and neither provoke by sudden movements nor attack. No matter how impatient you are to spot a shark, don't be tempted to wave around fish on a spear gun that might act as a bait.

Sometimes it is the smaller fish in the sea which should inspire fear. One of the more dangerous in Belizean waters is probably the Spotted Scorpionfish, which is a mottled red colour (commonly around 10 inches long) and well-camouflaged as it sits motionless on eroded roof tops, in coral rubble or near jetties. If disturbed, it will flick up its dorsal fin and inject poison from every spine you come into contact with, which causes horrible pain. The wounds are liable to become infected so a doctor should be consulted but it is not life-threatening. Moray eels are common on the Belizean reef and although they will not attack without reason, they have teeth large enough to inflict a nasty bite wound.

Stingrays have venomous serrated spines on their tails, which they are capable of arching over their backs to stab an oncoming threat or a careless foot stepping on them. Snorkellers are most at risk as stingrays stalk their prey by burying themselves just below the surface of the sand. If you are vigilant, though, you can just about spy their outline in the sand. Again acute pain and infection are likely so see a doctor.

Jellyfish have pendant tentacles which they use to stun their prey so a brush on human skin results in burning pain, which is very uncomfortable but not serious. A splash of alcohol on the affected area is a recommended remedy, or a little antihistamine cream, but the area must not be rubbed as this will only increase the inflammation. The most common jellyfish found here are the Moon Jellyfish, which have a disc shape about one foot across, fringed with white tentacles, and the Stinging Jellyfish, which has a slightly smaller disc shape and longer tentacles. The Portuguese Man of War is the only jellyfish which is genuinely harmful and should definitely be avoided. Easily recognizable by its bright blue floating body and tentacles up to 40 feet long, its sting can cause respiratory paralysis, which can result in drowning for the diver or swimmer.

Stinging Corals are a hazard that should encourage people to leave all corals well alone. Among those that might harm is the Fire Coral, identified by its smooth yellowish 'leaves' that can grow up to one foot high; the Square Coral, which has a box-like shape; the Leafy Coral, which grows in a fan shape; and the Encrusting Coral, which forms branching colonies that tend to cling to the sides of ancient boats. All of these will cause stings of varying degrees that are best treated with a mild antiseptic. Finally, an occasional problem in Belizean waters is presented by Sea Urchins whose sharp and very brittle spines can become embedded in carelessly placed feet. Virtually impossible to remove, the spines will cause intense pain and infection, which can take several weeks to heal. Be thankful that they are relatively rare.

Ecotourism in Practice

No one in Belize is unaware of their country's magnificent natural heritage, and no visitor can fail to notice it. Even the most inobservant tourist will be awestruck by the fantastic variety of wildlife that survives here—whether on land, airborne or underwater—and will most certainly find it memorable. No wonder that the government's '1990-94 Development Plan' stated that it aspires to 'sustainable economic growth, consistent with the maintenance of ecological balance...'

Ecotourism has become a popular term to describe that effort and as a buzz word is generously bandied around. In fact, Belize has succeeded in promoting itself as one of the foremost ecotourism destinations in the world, hosting major conferences on the subject. But what does 'ecotourism' really mean? In many cases it just seems a politically correct phrase that is conveniently tagged on to tourism businesses, which have no real commitment other than to increase their profit on the back of an honourable concept. Think of the 'eco-lodge' that nevertheless empties all its sewage straight into the sea or river, or the 'eco-tour' that disturbs fragile animal habitats, just so that tourists can tick as many sights off their list as possible. The catalogue of possible scenarios is endless and a certain responsibility lies with the visitor, who should endeavour not to support tourism ventures that exploit the environment, ravaging its precious resources.

On paper almost 40% of the country's 22,960 square kilometres are protected. Belize has an outstanding variety of officially protected entities: there are forest reserves, nature reserves, wildlife sanctuaries, national parks, private reserves, natural monuments, marine reserves, archaeological reserves, and conservation management areas. Some might argue that this plethora of names is unnecessarily confusing, but the important thing is that protected areas exist and are not only officially recognised, but are also supported by legislation.

There are also several organisations in Belize promoting educational programmes highlighting the importance of nature conservation and sustainable management of the country's flora and fauna. Foremost among them is the Belize Zoo, (*see* p. 85) which promotes environmental awareness with a variety of programmes for school children. The Belize Audubon Society does invaluable work (*see* p. 78), administering most of the country's protected areas and publishing several information pamphlets for visitors. The Belize Centre for Environmental Studies and the Coral Caye Conservation Association conducts important scientific research and monitoring, while Programme for Belize is making a vital contribution to practical solutions for sustainable forest management.

The human factor is also being addressed in projects such as the Community Baboon Sanctuary, north of Belize City, and the Village Guest House Programme in the remote southern district of Toledo, which are trying to ensure that the local population benefits economically from ecotourism, giving them a genuine incentive to support it. *See* p. 65. In addition to these official bodies, a large number of Belizean and ex-patriate tourism businesses promote ecological awareness among their customers, and try to set an example to others in their day-to-day practices. Many have joined the Belize Eco-Tourism Association (BETA) which monitors things regularly.

However, in reality the enforcement of protective legislation is simply not happening, and unless the political will is found to change, Belize is in serious danger of losing its splendid natural riches. Considering that tourism receipts are rapidly overtaking other exports for foreign currency earnings and an estimated 10% of the working population are employed in the tourism industry, the need for action is urgent. Furthermore, if Belize wishes to set an example of good ecotourism practice it must be able to bear close scrutiny which, currently, it cannot.

In many cases the problem arises because of the country's limited infrastructures and funding sources, which means large parts of Belize, including its protected areas, lack effective policing, leaving them vulnerable to illegal hunters, poachers loggers and looters of archaeological sites. The funding available from PACT (Protected Areas Conservation Trust) will hopefully contribute towards solutions. Yet even when someone is caught red-handed they often escape prosecution, which betrays an official lack of commitment to environmental protection in practice. One Belizean's comment is revealing, 'these days it makes me sad when I hear a jaguar's call in the forest. If I can hear him so can the poachers, and it won't be long before he is dead.'

Unfortunately examples of actions destructive of sustainable tourism and ecotourism are easy to find. One of the most glaring is the almost daily damage done to a 30-mile stretch of the New River caused by obscenely fast motor boats travelling to and from the Maya ruins of Lamanai. Another is the destruction of coastal mangrove forests as more and more hotels and holiday homes are built on the most popular cayes, and the seabed is dredged to create artificial beaches. In theory these things should not be possible, but in practice they happen anyway, though popular opposition does sometimes result in the closure of certain ventures. Recently the logging concession granted by the government in the Columbia River Forest Reserve, was later withdrawn after successful and prolonged lobbying by various non-governmental agencies and Maya community leaders.

An important factor limiting successful development of sustainable tourism is the lack of trained human resources. This applies especially to community tourism projects, many of which are rendered unviable by personal disputes and lack of organizational and financial support from local and national government. Around Punta Gorda and Five Blues Lake, sadly local villages have failed to benefit economically from tourism, thus making destructive activities, such as illegal hunting, far more likely.

To be fair, the issue is complicated by economic, social and political considerations. However, as long as ecotourism is little more than a lucrative catch phrase, the onus is on the visitor to ask questions and not be seduced by slick marketing. The tourist's spending power is a potent and valuable incentive, so it is up to the visitor to spend it with those who are genuinely committed to a sustainable natural and human environment.

The opportunity to preserve Belize for future generations is not yet lost. (For up-to-date information on the latest issues relevant to eco-tourism in Belize, pick up a copy of the *Journal of Environmental Information* (ECO), published by the Environmental Conservation Organisation. It costs around BZ$7.50 and is most likely to be found in the bookshops and tourist shops of Belize City.)

Whether you choose to join an ecotour or not, and notwithstanding the lack of enforcement, note the specific Belizean laws enacted to protect its natural resources. The following are the most important to support.

In particular, do not order seafood in restaurants during their closed season.

- do not remove or export black coral without a licence.
- do not take, buy or sell any other type of coral
- the closed season for shrimp is 15 April–14 August
- the closed season for conch is 1 July–30 September
- the closed season for lobster is 15 February–14 June
- the closed season for hickatee turtle is 1 May–31 May
- the closed season for marine turtles (Green, Loggerhead and Hawksbill) is 1 April–31 October
- do not hunt without a licence
- do not pick orchids in forest reserves
- do not spear-fish without a licence

Belize City

History	72
Getting There	72
Getting Around	73
Belize City Directory	74
Around Belize City	78
Where to Stay	80
Eating Out	82
Entertainment and Nightlife	83
Trips From Belize City	84
Nearby Cayes	86

Belize City is no longer the dangerous place travellers warn each other about, though wandering alone at night is still not a good idea. (Take a taxi, especially to and from the bus stations). In fact, the city's dilapidated wooden buildings and putrid canals have something magnetic about them, and a handful of colonial buildings add a dash of faded glamour.

Built on reclaimed swamp, many of the houses stand raised off the ground on short wooden posts, allowing just enough space for chickens to scratch the dirt. Their back doors look onto the canals that are more like ditches. The main streets are lined by modern concrete architecture, billboards and neon signs jostling for attention over unhurried pedestrians.

There is just one large waterway, Haulover Creek, with a humpy swing bridge, with people and traffic at its hub, which soon becomes a familiar marker for all visitors. Most boat traffic to and from the sea passes by this bridge, and local captains are always tempting passers-by to hop on and visit the coastal cayes, just a short distance from the city.

It takes no more than half an hour to walk from end to end of the city centre yet its cracked pavements and dirt roads, its ancient beggars and wanna-be studs—seedy details in themselves—do not seem so sleazy. The city is too small to be intimidating, and street crime is not a major problem, though unlit side streets should be avoided at night. The city is relaxed (by Central America's standards), but women should take precautions such as not wearing expensive jewellery, walking briskly and avoiding eye contact.

The atmosphere is more reminiscent of a Caribbean town than a major city. Uniquely in Central America too, the voices around you speak the languid English of creoles, and the hustlers somehow seem less frightening because of it, though don't let that lull you into a false sense of security: changing money on the street, for example, is risky. Drugs are frequently offered to tourists on the streets, and crack is a serious problem, but if you ignore the pushers you will not generally be pursued.

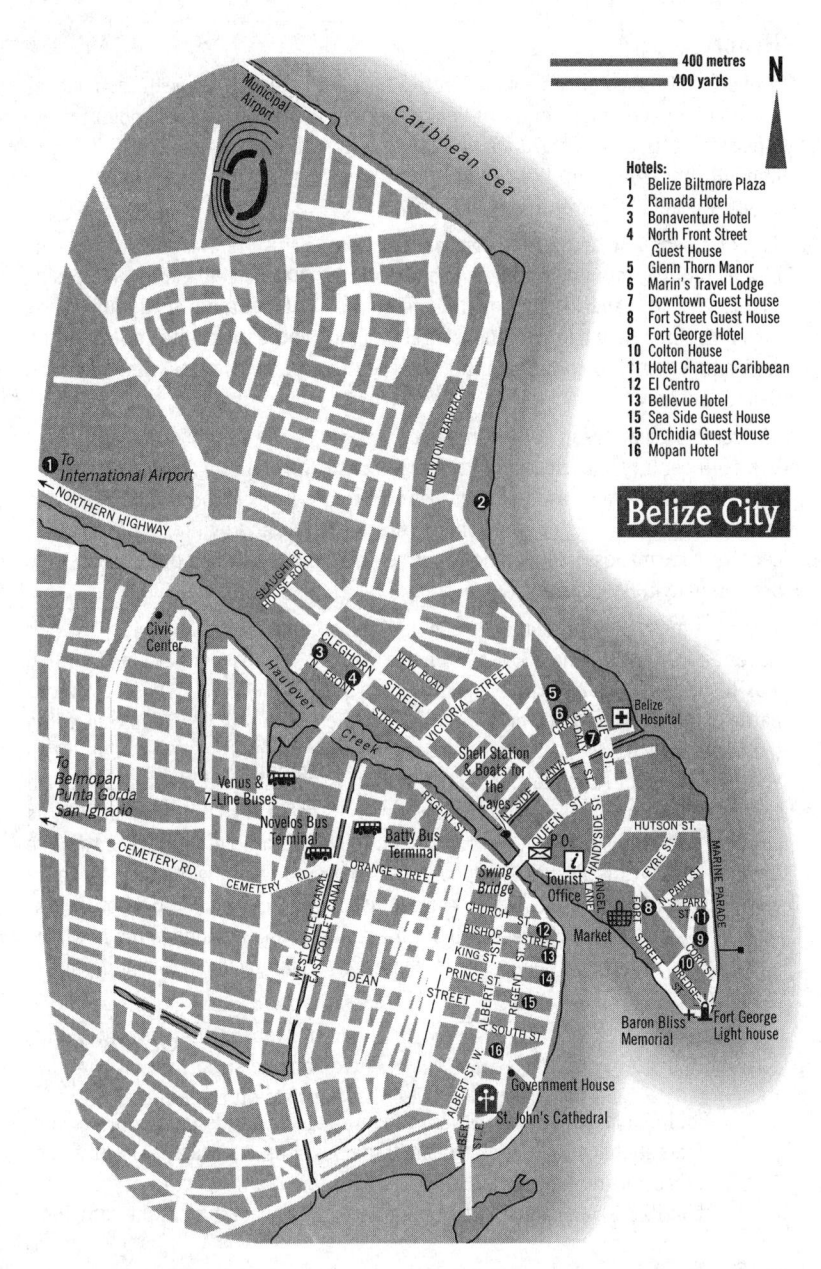

Hotels:
1. Belize Biltmore Plaza
2. Ramada Hotel
3. Bonaventure Hotel
4. North Front Street Guest House
5. Glenn Thorn Manor
6. Marin's Travel Lodge
7. Downtown Guest House
8. Fort Street Guest House
9. Fort George Hotel
10. Colton House
11. Hotel Chateau Caribbean
12. El Centro
13. Bellevue Hotel
15 Sea Side Guest House
15 Orchidia Guest House
16 Mopan Hotel

Belize City

History

A quarter of the country's population live here, and the city has been the political, cultural and economic centre of Belize for over three centuries. Though it is no longer the capital, this has done nothing to lessen its leading role, which is underlined by the reluctance of foreign embassies to move out to Belmopan, the country's capital for over thirty years now.

The first people to settle here permanently were British pirates and loggers: the pirates hiding amongst the many islands of the Barrier Reef, the loggers basing themselves at Belize Point, on the mainland. The loggers called themselves Baymen, since they had operations stretching along the whole Bay of Honduras, searching out mahogany trees for Europe's gentry, and it was from their camps that Belize City grew.

The settlers used broken bottles and wood chips to fill the swampy land, and by the late 18th century, the city was a thriving frontier town: a rough place, where the families of the Baymen awaited their periodic return from the bush. The tough and dangerous work of logging was done by African slaves, and by the end of the 18th century, they made up 75% of the country's population, it is their descendants who predominate in Belize today.

The city's most glorious moment came in 1798, when the Baymen, helped by their slaves and the British navy, resoundingly defeated the Spanish naval assault that was to have established the Spanish Crown's claim to the region. The famous Battle of St George's Caye was fought in the waters off Belize City, and centred on the island which has given the battle its name. In spite of this, it took the British another 73 years to make their territorial claim official, and create the Crown Colony of British Honduras with Belize City as its capital in 1871. The city lost its political status in 1961 after Hurricane Hattie pushed a huge tidal wave through the city, destroying most of its wooden buildings and claiming many lives, and it was decided to move the capital 50 miles inland. The new capital, Belmopan, was carved out of the bush. However, all but the civil servants working in the new government offices have chosen to stay in Belize City so in practice it is still the capital of the country.

Getting There

by air

Philip Goldson Airport, 16 km outside Belize City, is the country's only international airport. Unfortunately the bus shuttle service to the city from the airport no longer exists. But if you hire a taxi, expect to pay no more than BZ$30, and always agree on a price before departure as the cabs don't use meters.

There are daily flights from the following Central American cities: San Pedro Sula, Tegucigalpa, San Salvador, San José and Panamá, Flores.

The Municipal Airport lies a few kilometres north of the city centre. Taxis should cost about BZ$5. Domestic flights from here include Corozal, Placencia, Punta Gorda, San Pedro, Caye Chapel and Dangriga.

If you don't wish to go to the main representatives of the airlines, you can always buy tickets via any of the travel agents situated along Regent or Albert Street.

by boat

There are regular connections between Ambergris Caye and Caye Caulker, as well as many smaller islands near the city. Things are much easier thanks to the completion of the **Water Taxi Terminal** ✆ 02 31969, on North Front Street, across from the post office. Times and prices are clearly advertised and maintained and all tickets can be bought from the central booth. (Belize City to Caye Caulker: BZ$15 one-way; daily 9am, 10am, 1, 3 & 5.30pm. Return from Caye Caulker daily at 9am. Belize City to San Pedro: BZ$30 one-way; daily 6.45am, 8am, 10am, 3pm. Children under five years go free).

A café, toilets, payphone and gift shops surround the seated waiting area, so it is now safe and convenient to kill some time here while waiting for transport. There is also a baggage lock-up—ask at the ticket booth. This is also the place to arrange water taxis to any of the islands not regularly connected, such as St George's Caye, Caye Chapel and the picnic and snorkel spots on Sargeant's Caye, Goff's Caye and English Caye.

If it is raining or the sea is rough, you may prefer to travel by covered boat, however. In which case you need to head for the **Courthouse Wharf**, the other side of the river, where the 'Triple-J' leaves daily for Caye Caulker at 9am, and for San Pedro (& Caye Caulker by request) at 3pm. The 'Yara Andrea' departs Mon–Sat at 3pm, calling at Caye Caulker and then San Pedro. Returns from San Pedro at 7am. Prices are the same as the Water Taxi Association boats. Note that these covered boats take at least half an hour longer to reach their destinations because they also carry cargo. (Please *see* pp. 5–6 under the 'Travel' section.)

by bus

There are four main bus companies connecting Belize City with the rest of the country and several smaller ones operating minor routes, such as to the Baboon Sanctuary. They all have their main terminals here.

Batty Bus Line covers western and northern Belize, and has its terminal at 15 Mosul Street, ✆ 02 72025. For Belize City to Chetumal, stopping in Orange Walk and Corozal on the way, buses leave on the hour between 4 and 11 am.

The Northern Highway is the country's best road, and the journey only takes 4 hrs to Mexico, 3.5 hrs to Corozal. Services to San Ignacio, via the capital, Belmopan, leave Mon-Sat at 5, 6, 6.30 (express), 6.45, 7, 9, 10 and 10.15 am.

On Sundays buses leave at 5, 5.45. 6.30, 6.45, 7.30, 8.30, 9.30 and 10.30am. Venus Bus Line also runs a service to the north, and its terminal is on Magazine Road, ✆ 73354/77390. Buses to the Mexican border and all towns along the way leave daily at 11.45 am, 12.30 (for Sarteneja) 1, 2, 3, 4, 4.30, 5, 5.30, 6, 6.30 and 7 pm. The one-way fare to or from the Mexican Chetumal is BZ$12.

Novelo Bus Service goes to the Guatemalan border, passing Belmopan and San Ignacio. The terminal is at 19 West Collet Canal, ✆ 02 77372. Buses leave on the hour between 11 am and 9 pm Mon–Fri, and also at 3.30, 4.30, 5.30 and 6.30 pm. Saturdays buses run until 7 pm, Sundays until 6 pm. The fare to or from the Guatemalan border town of Benque Viejo is BZ$5.50.

Z-Line Buses run to southern Belize, calling at Belmopan, Dangriga, Big Creek and Punta Gorda. Their buses leave from the same terminal as Venus buses. Buses for Dangriga leave at 9 am, noon and 2 pm, Mon-Sat (9 am and noon, 2 and 3.30 pm on Sundays). Buses for Punta Gorda leave 8 and 10 am, and at 3 pm (Sundays 10 am and 3 pm).The journey to Punta Gorda takes up to ten hours due to the unpaved road south of Dangriga, so breaking the journey in Dangriga is recommended.

Jex Bus Service leaves Belize City for Crooked Tree Mon-Sat, 10.55 am and 5.15 pm (returning 5.30 and 7 am, and 2.15 pm). Their white buses are easily recognizable, parked alongside the canal. Ask someone for help if you can't find them.

For Bermudian Landing and the Baboon Sanctuary, you need the unnamed yellow schoolbus, which also leaves from the canal (usually near the corner of Orange Street) daily at 12.30 pm (returning at 5.30 and 6.30 am).

Remember there is no **railway** system in Belize.

Getting Around

You can easily walk around the centre and find everything you will want to see. You only need transport to and from the international and municipal airports, and the bus terminals. Taxis are plentiful on the main streets. Official taxis have green numberplates, and a journey within the city should cost no more than BZ$5. Remember that there are no meters, so always agree on a price before departure.

Car and **motorcycle hire** are easily available: Avis, 50 Vernon Street, ✆ 02 70730, ✉ 02 70728; Bike Belize Motorcycle Rentals, 74 Cleghorn Street, ✆ 02 33855; Budget, 771 Bella Vista Northern Highway, ✆ 02 324335, ✉ 02 30237; National Car Rental, 12 North Front Street, ✆ 02 31587, ✉ 02 31586; Safari Car Rental, 11a Cork Street, ✆ 02 35395; Smith's Auto Rental, 12a Banak Street, ✆ 02 73779, ✉ 02 75199.

Tourist Information

The Belize Tourist Board is at 83 North Front Street, ✆ 02 77213/73255, ✉ 02 77490 *(open Mon–Fri, 8.30–4, Sat 8.30–noon)*. The Office is on the first floor. The staff are helpful and there are a great variety of free brochures on everything from car rentals, boat schedules, to tours. A few interesting books and some maps are also available.

Available free in most hotels, try to get hold of the latest edition of Destination Belize, published by the private sector association, The BelizeTourism Industry Association, and full of useful information, shopping advice and travel articles. If you can't find it anywhere, try their offices at 99 Albert Street, ✆ 02 71144.

Bellize City is such a small place that the main thoroughfares are never far away, and even if you lose your bearings, the noise from the commmercial streets or sight of the sea will guide you back on course.

Around Belize City

As you walk along the seafront, with the waves lapping at the crumbling sidewalk, you sense how easily houses can be washed away–something that has happened on a number of occasions, most notably during Hurricane Hattie. As a result the central city is a mix of old and new, with wooden colonial houses, raised slightly off the ground, breaking up the streetlines of modern concrete homes. There are no grand palm-fringed boulevards here. Instead you have a handful of main streets that cut through a tangle of quiet back streets, and after a day of wandering around, the city quickly becomes familiar.

Belize City Directory

airline offices

The following are the most important airlines you may wish to use to or from Belize City.

Aerovías, Mopan Hotel, 55 Regent Street, ✆ 75445, @ 75383.
American Airlines, Queen Street, ✆ 32522, @ 31730 (New Road office).
Caribee, municipal airport, ✆ 44253, @ 31031 (for private charters).
Continental, 32 Albert Street, ✆ 78309, @ 78114.
BWIA, 41 Albert Street, ✆ 77185, @ 75213 (for flights to the West Indies).
Eastern, 26 Queen Street, ✆ 78646.
Island Air, municipal airport, ✆ 31140, @ 44502.
Javier's Flying Service, municipal airport, ✆ 45332, @ 31731 (for private charters).
Maya Airways, municipal airport, ✆ 35794, @ 30031.
Taca, 41 Albert Street, ✆ 77185, @ 75213.
Tan-Sahsa, Valencia Building, on the corner of Queen Street and New Road, ✆ 77080.
Tropic Air, municipal airport, ✆ 45671, @ 32794.

books and newspapers

The largest **bookshop** is the Belize Bookshop, opposite the Mopan Hotel, and there's also a newsagent that sells foreign papers on North Front Street, by the Swing Bridge. The major hotels should also sell Time and Newsweek. *The Belize Review* no longer exists. Instead try *The Belize Sun*, the 'national tourism paper', which is only available in San Pedro.

emergencies

The main **police** station is on Queen Street, near the Swing Bridge, ✆ 72210. In a **medical emergency**, contact the Belize City Hospital, Eve Street, ✆ 77251. Also check with your embassy or consulate for recommended doctors. You can also contact the private Belize Medical Association, St Thomas Street, ✆ 30303.

immigration

The **immigration office** is on Mahogany Street, ✆ 22046 (*open Mon–Fri, 8–noon and 1–5*).

laundry

The best is **Stan's Laundry**, 22 Dean Street (*open daily 8–noon*). One wash and dry will cost around BZ $10.

Photographic Development can now be done reliably by **Pooner's Hour Minilab**, 89 North Front Street, ✆ 31043, ✉ 31058.

dive boats operating out of Belize City

All three boats listed are American-run, but operating in Belizean waters. All will take you to many of the best diving spots, usually over a period of two to six days, and offer the most comfortable live-aboard diving to be found in Belize. Expect a week's diving to cost between US$1500 and US$1800 per person, which includes all meals and many small luxuries, such as fresh towels when you emerge from a dive. If you don't need quite this level of luxury, much cheaper live-aboard diving is available out of San Pedro, on Ambergris Caye, and groups are also much smaller. (*see* p.99).

Wave Dancer is a 120ft luxury motoryacht, complete with air-conditioned cabins and film processing facilities, which will take you out to all the best diving spots for up to a week. (Takes a maximum of twenty people). Either book in advance via 6851 Yumuri Street, Suite 10, Coral Gables, FL 33146, ✆ 305 669 9391, ✉ (305) 669 9475, or e-mail: dancer@winnet.net or via the Radisson Fort George Hotel in Belize City.

The *Rembrandt* is a stunningly beautiful herring lugger from Holland, originally built in the early 1900s, but now totally modernised to include air-conditioning and private baths for every cabin. 184 feet long, its wooden sundeck provides plenty of room for the maximum of 32 passengers.

Reservations via Oceanwide Expeditions in the US, ✆ (1 800) 453 7245 or ✆ (713) 591 1616, ✉ (713) 591 1082.

The *Aggressor* is a 110-foot motoryacht offering very similar services to *Wave Dancer*. Reservations in the US, ✆ (1 800) 348 2628 or 504 385 2416, ✉ (504) 384 0817, or via the Ramada Hotel in Belize City. Mayaland Tours, ✆ 02 32810, ✉ 32242 also acts as agent for the *Aggressor*.

Belize City Directory

money

The most efficient place for exchanging money is Belize Bank, on the small park south of the Swing Bridge. Barclays Bank and Bank of Novia Scotia are both on Albert Street. It is possible to change up to US$100 traveller's cheques directly into US dollars, but you must prove that you are about to leave the country with an airline ticket. The major banks will also change money. Street vendors are not recommended since dubious practices are very common—you certainly do not get a better deal than those the banks offer.

The American Express office is at Belize Global Travel, 41 Albert Street, ✆ 77363 (*open Mon–Fri, 8–noon and 1–4.30; Sat, 8–noon*).

national parks

The **Belize Audubon Society** is at 12 Fort Street, ✆ 34987, 🖷 78562. It manages the country's national parks and has information on access, opening times and self-catering accommodation facilites, wherever available.

Programme for Belize, 2 South Park Street, ✆ 75616, 🖷 75635, is a non-governmental organisation which administers the huge Rio Bravo Conservation Area in northwestern Belize, which you can visit on a variety of tours.

post office

The main post office (*open Mon–Thurs 8–5, Fri 8–4.30*) is on the corner of Queen Street, just north of the Swing Bridge. The poste restante is on the ground floor. The parcel office is next door to the main post office, just along North Front Street.

The heart of the city is divided into a northside and a southside by Haulover Creek, with the Swing Bridge the main crossing point. The southern part of town is the oldest sector, with just two main streets: Regent Street and Albert Street. Both streets are lined by shops and offices and, before you know it, you find yourself at the far end, where Government House and St John's Cathedral mark the beginning of a grand residential quarter, where many gardens are met directly by the sea.

Government House (*open Mon–Fri 8.30–4.30, BZ$5*) is a fine colonial wooden building, painted white and set in an attractive tropical garden, both now open to the public. It is worth a visit, if only to see an example of the sumptuous housing that the British colonial authorities used to enjoy. Most of the original furnishings have been removed, but you still get a good feel for the place, and the historically minded can cruise a large portrait gallery of every governor of Belize (then British

The cathedral's unassuming dimensions do not readily conjure up scenes of pomp and circumstance, and yet this has been the venue for many historic celebrations, not least of which was the thanksgiving held for the emancipation of slaves, on 1 August, 1838. Most glorious of all, however, were the coronations of the Mosquito Indian kings, which took place in 1815, 1825 and 1845. Keen to avoid Spanish colonial rule, the Mosquito Indians formed an alliance with the British between 1815 and 1845, thus ensuring protection for their 'kingdom', which stretched along the Caribbean coast, from Honduras to Nicaragua. Thus their 'kingdom' was under British protection and the Spanish risked the ire of the British Navy if they tried to encroach.

Near the Swing Bridge are the main BTL office, as well as the **Bliss Institute** (*open Mon-Fri, 8.30–noon and 2–8, Sat 8.30–noon*) , on the Southern Foreshore, which is the city's main cultural centre and library. Bliss was an eccentric Englishman, with a Portuguese title who loved the deep-sea fishing here so much that he bequeathed his fortune to the local authorities. He died on 9 March 1926, so that day is now a public holiday, celebrated as Baron Bliss Day to honour the extraordinary generosity of a man who never actually set foot in Belize, (he died before coming ashore), yet whose bequest has financed several of the country's major recreational and cultural facilities. Occasionally there are exhibitions of local art or national features at the Bliss Institute, such as the flora and fauna or the latest Maya finds, and it is always worth a look, even though the place usually seems rather quiet and neglected.

On the north side of town, Queen Street makes up the main thoroughfare, also lined by shops and bars, with the main post office at the intersection with North Front Street and the Swing Bridge. You will find yourself passing this way on many occasions, not least when you catch a boat from the new **Marine Terminal & Museum**, all sparkling white along the waterfront.

If you have time, do visit the Marine Museum (*open Tues–Sun, 8–5, BZ$4*), which offers an excellent introduction to the structure and life of the reef. Informative displays guide you from its physical nature and the fauna and flora you might encounter, through to interesting exhibits on the people who make their living from the reef. Photographs show fishermen's camps and captions offer home thoughts on some of the issues faced. One of the most pressing is over-fishing, which has resulted in a 60–70% decrease in fish populations in the Caribbean since the turn of the century.

Around the eastern tip are a number of beautiful colonial houses, as well as the market, where each morning traders sell the morning's catch. A fine example of colonial architecture is at no. 4, Fort Street, which is now a popular hotel and bar

telephones

Belize Telecommunications Ltd. (BTL) is on Church Street, open Mon–Sat, 8–6. It offers telephone and fax facilities. Another place for fax, e-mail and computer services, is **Angelus Press**, 10 Queen Street (*open Mon–Fri, 7.30–5.30; Sat 8–4*), which also sells books.

tour agencies

A full list of Belizean tour agencies (including diving), as well as ones operating from the US and Canada, is available from the Tourist Board. Very amiable and informed guides are used by **Discovery Expeditions**, 126 Freetown Road, ✆ 30748, ✉ 30750. There are many others as well, though, including: **Belize Tours**, 115 Albert Street, ✆ 75443, ✉ 77681. **Belize Travel Adventures**, 168 North Front Street, ✆ 33064, ✉ 33196; **Mayaland Tours**, 67 Eve Street, ✆ 30515, ✉ 32242; and **S&L Travel Services**, 91 North Front Street, ✆ 77593, ✉ 77594. **Native Guide Systems**, 1 Water Lane, Belize City ✆ 75819, ✉ 74007. For something a little different, why not check out the country's spectacular caves with **Caves Branch Adventure Company**, mile 41.5, Hummingbird Highway, ✆ & ✉ 08 22800.

Note: when comparing what's on offer always try to find out how large the groups are, what exactly you get to see and the general time frame, not forgetting the price.

Honduras). Rather incongruously, you will also find a small exhibition of the history of glass-making, with a variety of bottles, of which the round-ended 'torpedo bottles' are the most memorable. They were made for exclusive distribution in Belize—perhaps because they could be stacked better on people's boats.

Across the street, **St. John's Cathedral** is a small redbrick church, built in 1812, which looks rather provincial by comparison. Consecrated in 1826, it was the first Protestant episcopal church founded in Spanish America, and no doubt did not enjoy the kind of funding a Catholic counterpart might have enjoyed. Nevertheless, it was the country's first church and its simple but attractive interior displays many tablets bearing the names of some of the oldest families in Belize. Bowen, Quilter, Masson and Gentle are just a few of the names still well-known today.

and restaurant. Another attractive building houses the US embassy, on Hutson Street. If you follow Fort Street to the end, you come out onto the seashore, where the Fort George Lighthouse stands above the Baron Bliss tomb.

Shopping

Some of the best shops for handicrafts are located in the up-market hotels. For example, the shop inside the Fort George Hotel has a good range of books and publications, as well as clothes and trinkets. Equally, the shop at the Four Fort Street Guest House is well worth a visit.

The fish and vegetable market in Belize City is housed in the extension of North Front Street, past the post office. You will find all sorts of tropical food here and the vendors are always willing to explain their uses. On the other hand, you may be horrified by the writhing sea animals, and the stench can be quite overwhelming. Trading is finished by noon, so you need to get there early.

A smaller market operates in the new commercial building on the river front, across the street from the Belize Bank in Belize City.

The main shopping streets are Albert and Regent Streets, in the southside of the city. A popular spot is **Go-Tees** speciality T-shirt and gift shop at 23 Regent Street.

Cottage Industries, 26 Albert Street, and **Di Creole**, 7 Graboural Lane, both have a good selection of Belizean handicrafts. The best buy is probably wood carvings out of zericote wood. However it is always cheaper, to buy these from the street hawkers—best of all is to buy them direct from the woodcarver, if you can track one down. (If you go on any of the tours to Altun Ha make sure you get the driver to stop at the roadside stalls selling wood carvings, which are run by those who actually make the goods.) Duty Free Shopping is the latest service for tourists, available at the International Airport only.

Where to Stay

Belize City is not a cheap place to stay in comparison with other Central American cities. Most of the up-market hotels are in the northside of the city, while moderate and cheap hotels are located in the southside. All hotels are subject to a 7% government tax, and there may be a new 15% VAT tax by the time you read this, although small businesses are mounting a strong opposition campaign for fear of being squeezed out of the market.

Northside

luxury

The top-priced hotel in the centre is the **Radisson Fort George Hotel**, 2 Marine Parade, ✆ 33333, ✉ 73821, e-mail rdfgh@btl.net. All services, such as restaurant, valet service and swimming pool are provided. **The Belize Biltmore Plaza**, 3 miles out on the Northern Highway, ✆ 32302, ✉ 32301 boasts the country's largest convention centre, and is therefore mostly favoured by businessmen.

The newest up-market tourist hotel is the **Ramada Royal Reef Hotel**, on Newtown Barracks Road, ✆ 32670, ✉ 32660, which tempts customers not to leave by offering all services they could possibly require. But for those who want to be within walking distance of the city centre the Fort George is still really the only convenient option.

expensive

Hotel Chateau Caribbean, at 6 Marine Parade, ✆ 30800, ✉ 30900, is housed in a wooden colonial building, looking out to sea, and although the restaurant is excellent, the whole place is in urgent need of refurbishment. A beautiful family-run hotel set in a colonial building is **Colton House**, 9 Cork Street, ✆ 44666, ✉ 30451. And finally, the **Glenn Thorn Manor**, 27 Barrack Road, ✆ 44212, is an inviting and extraordinary place, squeezed into a colonial house, with every room a different colour ranging from pink to green. Fridge and kitchen are available to long-term guests and full cooked breakfasts are served to non-residents.

moderate

The attractive colonial mansion known as **Fort Street Guest House**, 4 Fort Street, ✆ 30116, ✉ 78808, has just six rooms, all with fans, and communal bathroom. Apart from the bar and restaurant, there is also a spacious lounge and a small library.

cheap

The best deal in town these days is offered by the **Downtown Guesthouse**, 5 Eve Street, ✆ 32057, clean and friendly in the heart of the city. Another friendly guest house—if you can find anyone to open the door—is the **North Front Street Guest House**, 124 North Front Street, ✆ 77595, which is conveniently located for catching boats to Caye Caulker. Close by, the **Bon Aventure Hotel**, 122 North Front Street, ✆ 44134 ✉ 31134 is friendly and basic. Cheapest of the lot, but still clean, safe, and nice, is **Marin's Travel Lodge**, 6 Craig Street, ✆ 45166.

Southside

expensive

Centrally located and extremely pleasant is the **Bellevue Hotel**, 5 Southern Foreshore, ✆ 77051/77052, ✉ 73253. All rooms have air-conditioning and TV, and there's also a popular bar/restaurant. The delightful hotel on St George's Caye, **Cottage Colony**, ✆ 12020 is now run independently of the Bellevue, although the hotel will still arrange reservations for you, if you wish. **Mopan Hotel**, ✆ 77351, ✉ 75383 is a little dingy, although it does offer the cheapest breakfast in town (also to non-residents), and the owner, Jean Shaw, is an excellent source of information on any aspect of Belize travel. The hotel bar is a good place to meet other travellers as well.

moderate

Good value is the **Sea Side Guest House**, 3 Prince Street, ✆ 78339 ✉ 71689. Just around the corner from the Bellevue Hotel, this place is close to the waterside and the hub of Regent Street.

Eating Out

The most widely available, cheap food, is usually Chinese, and there are plenty of places to choose from, especially around Queen Street. Of course there's the Creole beans and rice option as long as you've not sampled it one too many times already. Otherwise, you will find delicious food in some of the hotel restaurants, notably at the **Chateau Caribbean**, **Bellevue Hotel** and **Four Fort Street** (at the Fort Street Guest House). Note that many restaurants are closed on Sundays.

Northside

A good place for breakfast, and meeting other travellers, is **Glenn Thorn Manor**, at 27 Barrack Road. Pricey, but in beautiful surroundings of polished mahogany, the restaurant at **Four Fort Street** makes delicious fruit drinks and tropical cocktails, and their Sunday brunches are renowned. **The Nile** restaurant, at 49 Eve Street, is a simple place serving Middle Eastern food. Also on Eve Street, the **Paradise Sea Food & Steak House** (120 Eve Street) is an up-market restaurant popular with the local highbrow crowd. For an polished international menu head for **The Grill**, 164 Barracks Road, near the Ramada Hotel, where you can expect to pay around US$35 for a meal for two.

Southside

The best deal for breakfast is offered by the **Mopan Hotel**, on Regent Street, *see* p.83. On Regent Street, **La Cocinita** offers Belizean style breakfast and lunch, while the **Little Eatery Restaurant** is a decent Chinese place, with a pleasant shaded patio.

The Gourmet (*open Mon–Thurs, 9am–2pm only*), at 13 Prince Street, is an excellent place for pizza and pasta take-aways. Alongside the central square, by the Swing Bridge, the **Riverside Patio** offers decent creole food and breakfasts, and is a great place to watch life on the river. Nearby, **Big Daddy's Diner** is on the second floor of the Commercial Centre facing the Belize Bank, popular among travellers because of its cheap lunches.

The best creole meals are to be had at **Macy's**, 18 Bishop Street. Good, and even cheaper, is **Caribbean**, at 36 Regent Street. **G.G.'s Patio**, 2 King Street, has a pleasant little courtyard and makes the best stewed chicken in the country. Also on King Street, **Mexican Corner** has cheap, tasty Mexican fare whilst **Pizza House** offers filling meals for healthy appetites.

Entertainment and Nightlife

Belize City has the busiest nightlife in the country, which is not to say there is that much choice. Most places do not get going before 11 pm, and stay open till the early hours of the morning. You should note that drugs are a problem (crack, cocaine, grass), and you will most likely be offered them. Remember penalties are heavy and usually involve prison. (As always, take a taxi to any of the venues mentioned).

Of the hotel bars, the best are to be found at the **Fort Street Guest House**, the **Bellevue Hotel** and the **Mopan Hotel**.

The most popular nightclubs these days is **Club XS**, on Freetown Road, which plays anything from rock and reggae to soca and R&B, and **Pub Amnesia,** on Newtown Barracks Road, which is more disco than salsa.

Another drinking spot favoured by travellers and locals is the **Marlin Restaurant and Bar**, at 11 Regent Street. **Big Apple**, 67 North Front Street, is a dark and sweaty disco with a young crowd. **Legends**, 30 Queen Street, is best on Saturday nights. **Lindbergh's Landing,** 162a Newtown Barracks (near the Ramada Hotel), is where young professionals go for a romantic dinner and dance, from 8pm onwards, where the atmosphere is respectable and no one gets too loud.

There are two cinemas in the city, the **Majestic** on Queen Street and the **Palace** on Albert Street, usually showing imported American films.

Trips from Belize City

There are several places best visited from the city: the Belize Zoo, 48km along the Western Highway, and the Community Baboon Sanctuary, 40 km northwest of Belize City are both accessible by public transport, though the latter requires an overnight stay if travelling by bus.

Two important Maya sites, unfortunately not accessible by public transport, are Lamanai (on the New River Lagoon in Orange Walk District) and Altun Ha, 50 km north of the city. Tours go to both daily, so you can easily visit them from Belize City. If you would like a taster of what the cayes are like, there is a string of tiny islands, with St George's Caye in the north and English Caye in the south, easily visited from the city in a day.

Belize Zoo

The new **Belize Zoo** ✆ 0813004 (*open daily 9–4*; *BZ$10*) is a pioneering place that has endeavoured to show captive animals in as natural a way as possible. Large areas of bush, forest and riversides have been fenced in to house a great variety of indigenous species of the cat family, including jaguars, puma, ocelot and margay. Tropical birds, such as toucans, vultures, and parrots are to be found, as well as crocodiles, and forest animals such as tapirs. Nature trails take you around all the sights, giving you a good chance to spot wild animals in a controlled environment. You may not approve of zoos, but think again, this is one place where you are guaranteed to see some of the country's most reclusive animals. Across the road, a Tropical Education Centre opened in 1990 works in support of the country's natural environment, and is located on the former property of an American, Dora Weyer, who lived in Belize for thirty years. 140 acres of wilderness, with educational trails, a visitor's centre (including a dormitory) with a small library, and lecture rooms for slide shows, are all on offer here. Any bus heading for Belmopan passes the entrance to the zoo, but you must ask specifically to be dropped off here.

Community Baboon Sanctuary

The **Community Baboon Sanctuary** (*open daily 8–5; US$5*) is another pioneering place, since it is one of the first conservation projects in Belize that runs with the co-operation of the local population. The sanctuary covers an area of 18 square miles on the properties of over 60 different owners.

The local farmers living here have agreed to protect significant areas of forest on their land in order to sustain the troop of black howler monkeys (known locally as baboons) who live here. Your fee includes the service of a guide, who will not only find the monkeys for you, but also tell you all kinds of interesting snippets of information and lively anecdotes. Make sure you bring insect repellent to keep the mosquitoes at bay.

Administered by the **Belize Audubon Society**, you can find a useful booklet on the sanctuary at their offices (12 Fort Street, ✆ 02 34987). A system of trails leads visitors through the area, and there is also a visitor's centre and museum in Bermudian Landing.

To reach Bermudian Landing, follow the Northern Highway as far as the Burrel Boom turn-off, from where it is only a short drive. (You could catch any bus heading north as far as the turn-off, and then try to hitch, but there is little traffic passing this way.) Alternatively take the daily bus from Belize City to Bermudian Landing, leaving at around 12.30 pm, returning the next morning. (*See* 'Getting to Belize City' pp.72–74).

Where to Stay

For somewhere to stay try the new **Jungle Drift Lodge**, ✆ 014 9578, ✉ 02 78160 in the village of Bermudian Landing, where you get your own wood cabin and traditional meals of rice and beans for three times the price. To be fair, the level of comfort offered in the cabins is far higher than that you are likely to find in the local B&B's, which can sometimes be spartan. On the other hand, you won't find the human contact as readily. If you fancy a quiet day exploring by river in the company of a canoe, contact either the Jungle Drift Lodge or **Baboon River Canoe Rentals**, ✆ 02 82101, in Burrell Boom village.

Simple accommodation is available in the homes of local people; see the reserve manager, Fallet Young (✆ 02 12001), or contact the Audubon Society (at the above address). Room and board with a local family costs BZ$20 and is a great way of gaining an idea of how most Belizeans live.

Altun Ha

Altun Ha (*open 9–5; adm*), meaning 'Water of the Rock', is a small but attractive site that was only rediscovered in 1957, while work was being done on the Northern Highway. Close to the sea, it was an important trading post during the Classic Period (AD 250–900), and merchants came by sea and land from distant parts of the Maya empire.

Extensive archaeological excavations have produced some of the country's most exciting finds, such as the beautifully carved head of the Maya Sun God, Kinich Ahau, which was unearthed in 1967. This is one of the largest Maya jade carvings ever found, weighing almost ten pounds and standing nearly six inches high. Sadly, it is now kept in a bank vault in Belize City so you cannot see the original, but you can see a copy at Government House Museum in Belize City, *see* p.78.

A unique feature of Altun Ha is that the most important tombs here are those of priests, rather than war lords, which has led to the belief that Altun Ha was also an important ceremonial centre. Four of its temple structures are dedicated to natural forces—the sun, rain, wind and moon—all of which deeply affected Maya daily life, and most particularly their navigators at sea. Considering its strategic location near maritime and inland waterways, it appears that this site combined two roles of vital significance to the Classic Maya: commerce and religion.

To get there, the easiest option is to either go on a tour, or drive your own vehicle, which takes about 1 hour and 30 minutes each way. Many of the larger hotels organize tours, or you could enquire at the tourist board.

(You could also get any bus heading north, as far as Sand Hill, and then try to hitch. But be warned traffic is scarce so this is a very uncertain option). For a description of Lamanai ruins please *see* pp.180–182 in the Northern Belize Section.

Where to Stay

Accommodation nearby is either extremely simple, with locals in Maskall village, or mega-luxurious, at the sumptuous **Maruba Resort**, ✆ 03 22199, ✉ 02 34491, near Maskall village.

If your finances cannot quite stretch to luxury, but possibly to the expensive range, the latest jungle lodge to open around here is **Pretty See Jungle Ranch**, ✆ & ✉ 03 12005, which boasts 'moonlit jacuzzis' and 1360 acres of wilderness to explore.

Nearby Cayes

Only 14km northeast from the city, St George's Caye is the site of the famous battle and was the country's first official capital from 1650 to 1784. Even though virtually nothing remains to bear witness to the historic battle, it is a popular weekend picnic spot, and home to two resort hotels.

On St George's Caye, though other accommodation exists on the island, there is really only one place to stay, and that is the delightful **Cottage Colony**, ✆ 02 12020, ✉ 02 73253, (*expensive*). Fourteen rooms in individual 'cottages' surround a sandy yard shaded by palms, which make an excellent spot for dozing in the hammocks provided. The rooms are not luxurious, but what makes it worthwhile is the setting, facing the Caribbean Sea, and the mouth-watering seafood served in the restaurant. Diving and snorkel trips can be arranged, and sea kayaks are provided for guests.

Visiting St George's Caye is easy via the water taxi terminal in Belize City, and a one-way fare should cost BZ$10–25, depending on your bargaining skills. If you have a reservation with Cottage Colony, the hotel boat will pick you up from the Bellevue Hotel pier. The journey takes around half an hour each way, and the island can be thoroughly explored in an hour or so, since there really isn't anything much to see. The island is very much a retreat for a few wealthy Belizeans and those staying at Cottage Colony.

To play out your desert island fantasies you really want to invest in a day-trip to Sargeant's Caye, which is just a mound of sand with four palm trees on it, miraculously rising from the sea in the middle of 'nowhere'. In fact, the island lies on the sea route plied by all craft heading for Turneffe Atoll, but once your water taxi has dropped you off for the day, you'll certainly feel very solitary. Bring a picnic, plenty to drink, and your snorkelling gear, and this can prove a wonderful respite from Belize City. (Don't forget your sun lotion).

Alternatively, you could also visit the Cayes from Spanish Lookout Caye, which lie about 16 km outside the city, close to Sargeant's Caye. This is home to the **Spanish Bay Resort** ✆ 02 77288, ✉ 02 72797, which has ten rooms built in cabins over the water, and has a very fine wood-panelled bar overlooking the sea. Meals served here are highly recommended and, although the mangroves mean there is no beach, you can have a great time fishing.

English Caye, and neighbouring Goff's Caye, are about 16km southeast of Belize City, and lie along the main entrance lane for ships coming in from the Caribbean. The sandy beaches here make these two a favourite weekend spot, and this is the most likely time you will find day charters leaving from the city's piers. For an organized day trip, enquire at the larger hotels. Transport can easily be arranged either via the water taxi terminal in Belize City or as part of an organized tour run by local operators. Visit the tourist office to find out about the latest options.

Finally there is Caye Chapel which is a tiny, privately-owned island, just south of Caye Caulker, dedicated to luxury tourism, with a resort hotel and all the trappings you would expect at the **Pyramid Island Resort**, ✆ 02 44409, ✉ 02 32405. The bar is a popular weekend destination for many. Get there either by plane or charter a boat from Caye Caulker or Belize City.

The Cayes

Ambergris Caye	92
Caye Caulker	106
Other Cayes	114
Turneffe Islands	115
Lighthouse Reef	116
Glover's Reef	117
Bluefield Range	119
Tobacco Reef	119

Snorkelling or diving, all you can hear is your own breathing, all you can feel is the water washing over your body, but what you see is electrifying : monstrous coral with a texture that looks like brains, razor-edged orange branches, countless tentacles swaying in the currents; while all around flit a kaleidoscope of fish, so close you think you could reach out and touch them. Shoals of tiny fluorescent neon tetras open up to let you pass, while barracuda just stare indifferently and orange starfish ignore you altogether, slowly wending their way across the seabed. Few other natural environments will allow you to feel quite so close to its inhabitants.

296km long, the Belize Barrier Reef is a giant wall of limestone and coral that has taken millennia to form, harbouring some of the most extraordinary plants and animals on the planet. It is also the second largest Barrier Reef in the world. The hundreds of islands (cayes) and atolls are just the crest of this underwater wonderland, and make for excellent bases from which to explore. Traditionally inhabited by fishermen, the atmosphere on the islands is relaxed, and even the most commercial places are tempered by Caribbean ease. The perfect time to be here is from April to June, when the sea tends to be calm. The hurricane season is from June to November, and although Belize is rarely hit, this is the time when rough weather might pose a problem.

Taking a boat trip, you often find yourself being followed by dolphins dancing in the waves and, if you are really lucky, you might even see a giant turtle. Out on the reef, you can reasonably expect to see conch and starfishes, as well as countless tropical fish, such as barracuda, jacks, parrotfish, angelfish, and grunts, while the deeper waters are favoured by the harmless nurse sharks. Naturally, the fishing is excellent, and the most common catches include grouper, snapper and jewfish. To find out more about the sea creatures here, see *A Guide to Corals and Fishes of Florida, The Bahamas, and Caribbean* (Seahawk Press), by I. and J. Greenberg.

The most developed diving resort is San Pedro, on Ambergris Caye, with a full range of hotel accommodation, from budget to luxury, and offering any kind of watersport you could possibly wish for (*see* pp.96–106). Neighbouring Caye Caulker is a much less commercial place, favoured by young and budget travellers. The other main groups of islands, such as Turneffe Islands (protective mangroves here make for a great fish variety), Lighthouse Reef and Glover's Reef (interesting for underwater limestone formations, especially the Great Blue Hole), all have their own character, and you can visit them, either on a day charter, or by staying in the up-market resorts that hide there. Diving and fishing tours are offered by most of the hotels, ranging from day trips, to 'live-aboard' excursions lasting as long as you wish. Diving certification courses are available in San Pedro and Caye Caulker, as well as at the top resort hotels. *See* the Diving section in **Practical A–Z** pp.28–31 and Life on the Reef and A Short Note on Reef Hazards in **Natural Belize**, pp.62–64.

1997 International Year of the Reef

1997 was appointed Year of the Reef by the World Heritage Bureau. *Geographical Magazine* warned that approximately 60% of the world's coral reefs have already been destroyed, or are in imminent danger. The rest are believed by scientists to be set for extinction within the next fifty years, if nothing is done to protect them. These shocking statistics mean that an international effort to publicise the important role reefs play is all the more timely and welcome.

For visitors the Belizean Reef is first and foremost a leisure resource: a fantastic place for diving, snorkelling and fishing, not forgetting swimming. Yet for the local population the reef has always been a major source of food—now rapidly dwindling due to the pressures of over-fishing in order to supply a lucrative export and tourism trade. It has also provided a natural defence against the threat of hurricanes and associated tidal waves, bearing the full brunt of bad weather before it reaches the mainland coast. Its mangrove forests have created additional stability, the tangle of roots adding strength to fragile islands and flat coastlines. Without them, many more islands and beaches would have been eroded and swept away by now. Finally, the coral reef, mangroves and shallow lagoons are vital breeding grounds, where juvenile fish, lobster and conch can flourish in relative safety and contribute towards healthy levels of marine populations.

The Belizean Reef, and others around the world, are therefore not only vital and unique biospheres, but also important natural protectors of adjacent mainlands and an essential economic resource for the human population. In recognition of this, the World Heritage Bureau officially declared the protected areas of the Belize Barrier Reef a World Heritage Site in 1996, which should act as encouragement for the Belize government to not only support sustainable coastal management in its official laws and regulations, but also most importantly to enforce them. The reef is being threatened by pollution and the uncontrolled deforestation which is being undertaken to make way for mainland agriculture and coastal tourism developments. The Heritage Site consists of Hol Chan Marine Reserve, Glover's Reef Marine Reserve, Half Moon Caye Natural Monument, Bacalar Chico National Park and Marine Reserve, South Water Caye, Laughing Bird Caye and the Sapodilla Cayes. All can be visited on day or overnight charters.

Diving Equipment

Almost all equipment can be hired locally, though the experienced diver should note that firms often only provide cylinder and air without a backpack or harness. They do provide weightbelt and weights. The best kind of clothing for diving in these parts is a lightweight, lycra body suit, and if snorkelling, you might want to bring surf shoes to protect against cuts from the hard edges of the coral.

safety precautions and diving code

It is unsafe to fly directly after a dive, because the change in pressure can induce the 'bends'. As a general rule, you should not fly for a period of 24 hrs after a dive. When snorkelling, it is worth wearing shorts and a T-shirt, because you can get very badly sunburnt without feeling it while in the water. Note that the only recompression chamber in Belize is in San Pedro, Ambergris Caye and should be used by experienced divers only.

There are no official rules for divers, but there is a voluntary code, which is designed to protect the reef. Please avoid:

- Walking on or damaging the coral.
- Collecting shells or coral.
- Using spearguns or supporting speargun-fishing operations.
- Diving near working fishermen.
- Hand-feeding fish.
- Allowing anchors to drag over the coral.

Ambergris Caye

Ambergris is the largest of the reef islands, a jagged slither of land 40km long and characterized by swampy mangroves, innumerable lagoons and a beautiful stretch of sandy beaches facing the Barrier Reef, which lies just a short boat-ride away. Walking along the Caribbean shore you can easily recognize the reef by the white surf continuously cresting on the coral. Located 58km north of Belize City, and a spectacular short plane ride away, it is the country's most visited attraction. San Pedro, the only town on any of the cayes, caters to the tourist who wants to be

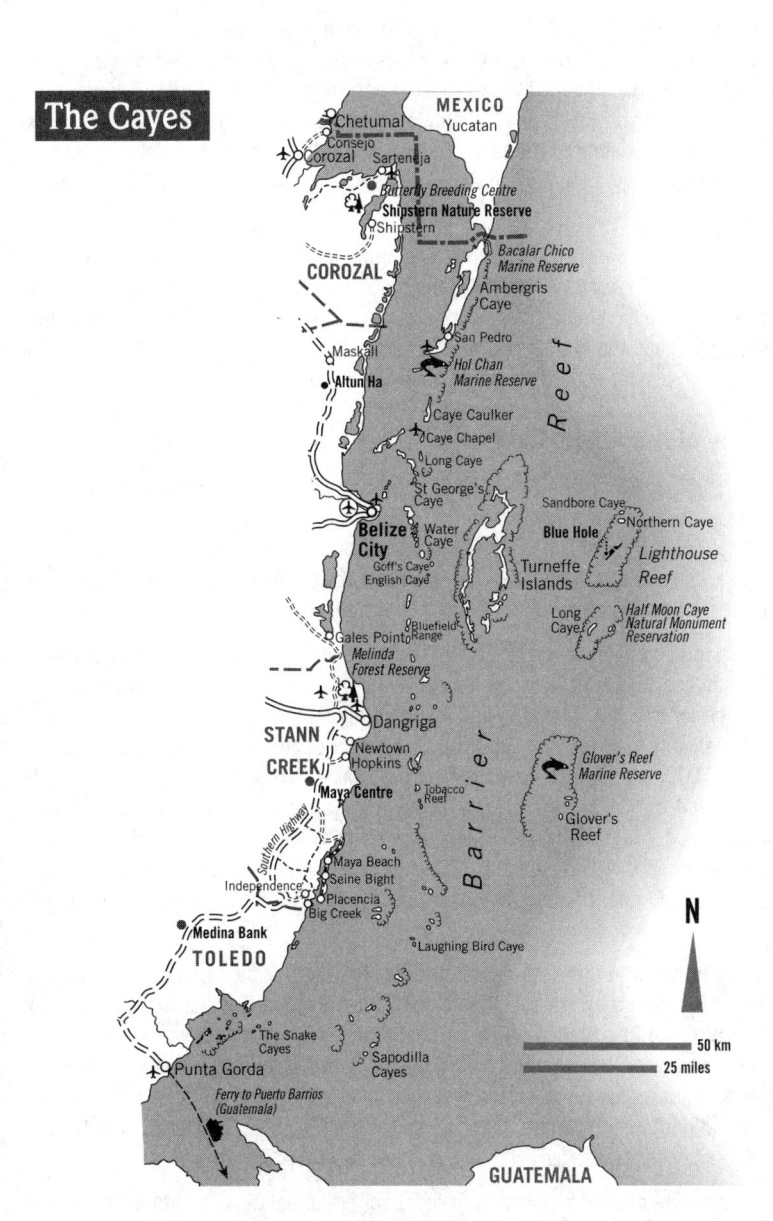

The Cayes

entertained. Most of its 4000 residents are involved in some aspect of the travel trade, with the result that the place is somewhat tacky with beachwear shops crowding into every space available. San Pedro was originally a tiny fishing community of wooden houses and, in spite of the dizzy pace of development, there is still an intimate feeling to the place. It has to be admitted that San Pedro's charms are limited but if you are here to explore the reef, you will find the widest range of opportunities.

Restaurants and bars are expensive, and unfortunately the prices are often not matched by good service. However, the hotels do their best to offer every kind of diversion a tropical holiday can provide, from beach games, to sailing, windsurfing, diving, snorkelling and deep-sea fishing. There is never a shortage of things to do and alfresco bars provide the main focus for socializing in the evenings.

History of Ambergris Caye

Belize's largest island is strictly speaking not an island at all, but a section of the Mexican Xcalac peninsula cut adrift by the Bacalar Chico channel. The Maya dug this channel in the 7th century AD to give their ocean-going trading canoes an entry to the calmer waters between the reef and the mainland, and many important trading settlements once existed along the western shores of Ambergris.

Closest to the channel, at the north-western end of the island, is **Chac Balam**, where archaeologists have found a great many Maya trade goods, such as obsidian, jade, pottery and salt. This site, and eighteen others, were inhabited from the Late Pre-Classic onwards (300 BC–AD 250), with the last dated monument recording the year AD 1000. A few sites, however, such as **Marco Gonzalez**, at the southern tip of the island, appear to have been inhabited right up to the 13th century, long after the Lowland Maya collapse. The theory is that the island's strategic trading importance, and Marco Gonzalez' close association with inland Lamanai, meant that continued occupation was made possible for as long as Lamanai continued to thrive.

But the island's golden era under the Maya was during the Late Classic (AD 600–900), when their trading canoes plied the seas all the way from the Mexican Yucatán to the Bay Islands off Honduras. Situated roughly half way between the two extremes, Ambergris Caye was their most important staging post in the maritime trade, not only for the crew and merchants plying this route, but also for the routes inland, to important mercantile centres, such as Lamanai, which also exported goods from as far away as the Guatemalan Pacific coast.

Many more people are believed to have inhabited Ambergris Caye at that time than at present. The island's pivotal role as a trading centre only declined in the 13th century, when Putún Maya from the Mexican Tabasco coast took control of the Lowland Maya sea routes and consolidated around new centres, such as Tulúm, further north. Although a great deal of excavation has been undertaken on Ambergris, the remaining mounds of Maya sites are not very interesting for the general visitor because little is visible above ground. Not only that, but the swampy, mosquito-infested land makes journeys to these remote sites almost unbearable.

Long after the Maya officially disappeared, the first Spanish contact came at the beginning of the 16th century and, by 1565, it is likely that the colonial authorities were exploiting the local lagoons for salt production. Missionaries soon followed, working among the remaining Maya communities living in the northern part of the island, at a site now known as **Basil Jones**, after a former lease holder of the land.

The channel that separates Ambergris from Mexico continued to be of vital importance throughout history. The Dutch, English and French pirates who settled here in the early 17th century used it to slip their raiding vessels into safe waters, beyond the reach of heavy galleons, while the Mexicans dug the channel wider and deeper in 1899, to allow their warships to pass through. And everyone, from the Maya onwards, used the island as a vital base for provisions. The shallow waters of the reef offered excellent seafood, including the tasty flesh of manatee and turtle, while the land offered good hunting for game animals, such as deer, peccary and small rodents, as well as the tasty land crab.

The British first made their mark on the island in the 1820s, when they imposed their laws on the mestizo fishing communities that lived along its beaches. But, in general, the English colonial presence was not strongly felt on Ambergris. The foundation of the island's only town, for example, was affected by Mexican refugees from the Caste Wars, in 1848, and the cultural traditions of San Pedro have much stronger latin roots than creole ones, although the two traditions have very much blended now.

In the 20th century, the island's fate has been determined by a succession of economic booms and busts, beginning with logwood extraction for dyes, followed by chicle extraction for chewing gum and the exploitation of coconut plantations, and ending with the fishing industry, which has virtually come to a standstill since the early 1980s. The latest boom is, of course, the tourism industry, and almost all of San Pedro's fishermen have become professional fishing and diving guides, converting their boats to the more lucrative trade that is dominating the island now. How long the present boom will last is anyone's guess, but the strains of overdevelopment are already there for all to see and a long-term solution is the single most important issue facing islanders today.

Getting to Ambergris Caye

by air

The fastest way to reach the island is to fly from the international or municipal airports in Belize City. If coming from Mexico, you can also fly directly from Corozal, in northern Belize. Flights are daily and frequent, so you should have no trouble making a connection without prior bookings. You can walk to most hotels in less than ten minutes from the airport. The more distant and exclusive resort hotels will pick you up on arrival.

by boat

Use the regular connections between Ambergris Caye and Caye Caulker; many smaller islands near the city are also connected. Matters have been hugely simplified by the completion of the Water Taxi Terminal (✆ 02 31969), on North Front Street, across from the post office. Times and prices are clearly advertised and maintained, all tickets bought from the central booth. A café, toilets, payphone and gift shops surround the seated waiting area, so it is now safe and convenient to kill some time here while waiting for transport. There is also a baggage lock-up—ask at the ticket booth for details.

If it is raining or the sea is rough, you may prefer to travel by covered boat, however. In which case you need to head for the Courthouse Wharf, the other side of the river, where the 'Triple-J' leaves daily for San Pedro (& Caye Caulker by request) at 3pm. The 'Yara Andrea' departs Mon–Sat at 3pm, calling at Caye Caulker and then San Pedro. Returns from San Pedro at 7am. Prices are the same as the Water Taxi Association boats. Note that these covered boats take at least half an hour longer to reach their destinations because they also carry cargo.

From Caye Caulker, you can always find someone to take you to San Pedro if you ask around near the main pier. The fare should not be more than US$8 per person.

Boats to Caye Caulker and Belize City leave from the Texaco pier in San Pedro, Mon–Fri at 7am and 2pm, Sat at 8am and 2pm. Get to the Texaco pier early to ensure a seat as no tickets are sold in advance. Alternatively, hire someone to take you, but this will prove expensive. Please note that schedules change, so always check them before travelling.

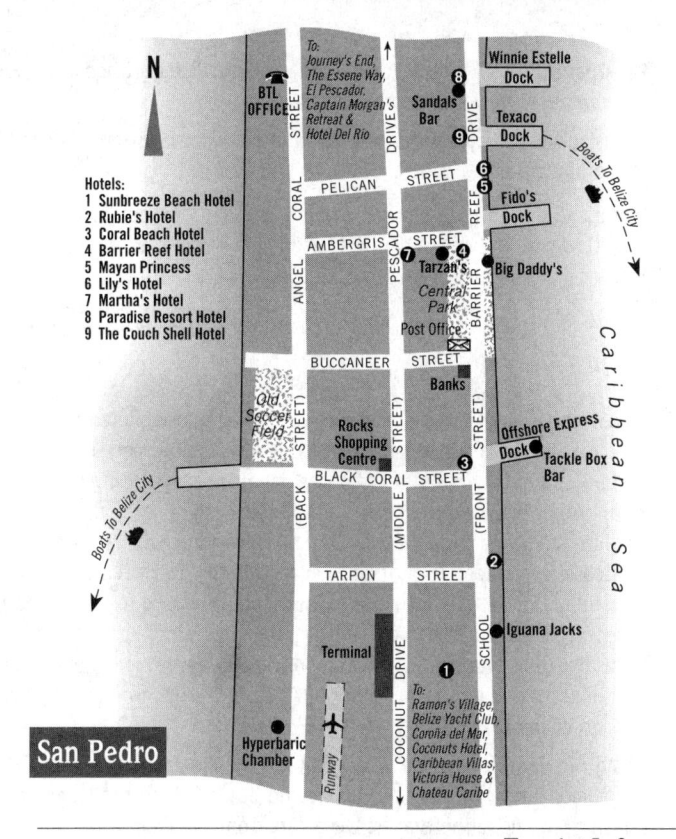

Tourist Information

Unbelievably, for the country's foremost tourist destination, San Pedro has no official tourist information centre. Instead you have to rely on private outfits, which invariably have vested interests. Having said that, competition is keen, so you will soon get a good idea of the prices for tours. The best policy is always to go by the recommendation of other travellers. For exchange there are two **bank**s in San Pedro, and you can generally also change cash or travellers' cheques in shops and hotels. Atlantic Bank, Front Street (*open Mon–Fri, 8–noon and 1–3 Wed 8–1, Sat, 8.30–noon*). Belize Bank, Front Street (*open Mon–Thurs, 8–1, Fri 8–4.30*).

The local **Belize Telecommunications Ltd** office is next to the power plant on Back Street. (*open Mon-Fri, 8–noon and 1–4. Sat, 8–noon*).

Laundry can be done at J's Laundromat, Middle Street (*open Mon, Tues, Thurs, Fri and Sat: 8–8; Wed, 8–6; Sun, 8–2*).

The **post office** is in the Alijua Building on Front Street.(*open Mon–Thurs, 8–noon and 1–5; Fri 8–noon and 1–4.30*).

The Island Photo shop are specialists in underwater **photography** and hire out equipment at good rates.

Motorised **beach buggies** can be hired by the hour, day or week, but at US$70 per hour, they are hardly a cheap option. They are also unnecessary as most hotels are within easy walking distance of the town centre.

Sports and Activities

archaeology

Two of the island's many archaeological sites are now offered as tour destinations. Neither is particularly interesting for the non-specialist, as there is nothing much to see, but a visit does entail seeing part of Ambergris you would otherwise never explore, and you just might see some of the rarer wildlife, especially birds. **Marco Gonzalez** was once a major trading post, located a few miles south of San Pedro, which can be reached either by mosquito infested trail or by boat. **Chac Balam** is close to the northern tip of the island, reached by boat only, which can include a visit to the new **Bacalar Chico National Park and Marine Reserve**, great for diving and snorkelling. (*See* pp.94–5 History of Ambergris, for more information on local archaeology).

Island Air also offer a day trip to **Tikal**, in Guatemala, which costs US$250 per person, including packed lunch and entry fees to the ruins, ground transfers, but not airport taxes. Departure from San Pedro is at 7am.

bird-watching

Surprising, you might think, with so many tourists around, but Ambergris is still a good place for spotting birds, and not just the large ocean birds either such as pelicans and frigate birds. Near the shoreline you might see a busy little spotted sandpiper, in the grassy shallows several species of heron hunt, while in the canopy of the littoral forest you might glimpse noisy Aztec parakeets, ospreys nesting and black hawks eyeing you back. In all, over 200 species of birds have been identified. The best months on the island are September to April, with October an ideal time to see many migratory birds that use the island as a resting place. An excellent base for bird watchers is the **Caribbean Villas Hotel** ✆ 026 2715, ℻ 026 2885, whose owner is a very keen twitcher and has built an observation tower to improve facilities.

diving

The main activity people come to San Pedro for is the diving, and there are more and more operators to choose from, of which the following are just a sample. As always, it is best to glean comments by word of mouth from others and shop around. The information available can be a little overwhelming if you are not sure what you want, so do take your time before making decisions. All operators hire out diving gear (usually at additional cost), although you should *see* pp. 28–31 for items best brought from home. Note that many hotels and resort hotels also offer diving packages, but they are usually more expensive.

Serious divers will want to visit the famous **Blue Hole**. But for most people the underwater wildlife elsewhere on the reef is more exciting and less daunting than the gloomy depths of the Hole, and that can be found at many dive sites closer to Ambergris. When considering day trips to the Blue Hole, remember that journey times are several hours each way, which can feel even longer if seas are rough.

In general, overnight tours are extremely good value as they give you plenty of time to enjoy being at sea, not just diving at a variety of sites, but also sunbathing, swimming, and eating and drinking. Trips that include the beautiful **Half Moon Caye** are highly recommended, especially around February and March, when the famous red boobies are tending their chicks. All dives are accompanied by a professional dive master, who will guide you to the best spots and ensure maximum safety. Finally, you don't have to be a diver to explore the reef, many operators now also take snorkellers. If you think you can master the technique sufficiently, you can record your dive and snorkel experience by hiring an underwater camera from **Joe Miller Photography** (✆ 026 2577), located on Middle Street near the airstrip, and also in Fido's Courtyard. **The Blue Hole Dive Centre** *see* p.100 also hires out cameras.

In case of emergencies related to diving accidents, the **Hyberbaric Recompression Chamber** is located at the northern end of the airstrip and is on standby 24 hours a day on radio frequency VHF 14.4600, or try ✆ 026 2851.

dive operators

Out Island Dives, (office at Coral Beach Hotel), ✆ 026 2013, ✉ 026 2864, e-mail: Forman@btl.net is owned by Allan Forman, who operates the 50-foot Offshore Express, which sleeps fifteen adults, although any group over twelve people would be very crowded. He is one of the very few who will allow infants and children on his boat, but parents should think carefully about taking very young children to sea who are unable to partake in the watersports the trips are designed for. (The minimum age for scuba diving is generally accepted to be twelve years). An overnight tour, taking in the **Blue Hole** and the **Half Moon Caye Natural Monument** —where you stay the night in tents on the island or in bunks on board — including all meals and five dives costs around US$250 per person. A four-day PADI course costs US$350.

The Blue Hole Dive Centre, ✆ 026 2982, ✉ 026 2981, e-mail: bluehole@btl.net is owned by Chris Allnatt, who runs a slick, professional outfit, which takes great pride in customer safety and satisfaction. He also takes reef etiquette seriously. His 50-foot Caye Explorer takes a maximum of twelve divers on day and overnight trips to the Blue Hole. 4-day PADI courses cost US$350 per person, less if there are 4–5 students.

The Flying Manta and **M.V. Manta IV** are speed boats that take a maximum of ten divers. The former has very powerful engines to speed up journey times to reach the Blue Hole, while the second boat is used for overnight trips that include the Blue Hole, Lighthouse Reef, and overnighting on Half Moon Caye. Day trips to the Blue Hole cost around US$185 per person, overnight trips cost US$250 for divers, US$200 for non-divers, and equipment is extra. The dock and office for both boats is located in front of the **Sun Breeze Hotel**. Advance reservations can be made via the US: ✆ 1 800 938 0860.

The Belize Dive Centre, located at the Belize Yacht Club, ✆ 026 2797, ✉ 026 2892 (US: 1 800 938 0860) is also worth investigating, as is the **Bottom Time Dive Shop**, at the San Pedro Hotel, ✆ 026 2437, ✉ 026 2766 (US: 1 800382 7776).

fishing

Fishing tours can be arranged by most of the hotels, in particular the **Coral Beach Hotel** ✆ 026 2013, ✉ 026 2864, **Ramon's Village Resort** ✆ 026 2071, ✉ 026 2214 and **Victoria House Hotel** ✆ 026 2067, ✉ 026 2429.

The one hotel on the island that caters specifically to sport fishing is the **El Pescador** (✆ 026 2398, ✉ 026 2977), on the beach north of San Pedro. For the most up-to-date list of registered fishing guides in San Pedro, don't forget to visit the Tourist Board in Belize City prior to arrival.

marine reserves

The Hol Chan Marine Reserve (small fee) is located about four miles south-east of San Pedro, which is an area of particularly beautiful corals, as well as plenty of fish, wonderful for snorkelling and diving too. A big attraction is also **Shark Ray Alley**, which is a shallow cut in the reef directly south of Hol Chan, where you are virtually guaranteed sightings of sharks and rays because captains regularly feed them, so be warned.

Founded in 1987, the **Hol Chan Marine Reserve** is marked out by buoys and covers just over five square miles characterized by three distinct areas. Zone A encompasses the reef, where visitors head for the fantastic array of coral and fish, especially around the natural cut in the reef, whose Maya description gave the reserve its name (hol chan meaning cut or break). But there is also Zone B, which encompasses a lagoon area with important seagrass beds. Zone C is where mangroves are left to grow undisturbed, acting as an important breeding ground for many underwater species.

Unfortunately, the daily groups of tourists that are brought here have taken their toll, and it is one of the most damaged areas of the entire reef. Great stumps of dead, white coral testify to thoughtless visitors, who touched the coral and thereby helped to destroy it. So please don't be one of them.

The country's newest marine reserve is the **Bacalar Chico National Park and Marine Reserve**, which is located at the northern tip of the island. In fact, the Bacalar Chico channel is the narrow water way that separates Ambergris Caye from Mexico, dug by the Maya a good fifteen hundred years ago. Much less visited, this area makes for more relaxed snorkelling and where the reef meets the island, at Rocky Point, you will find plenty of underwater life to marvel at.

snorkel and boat trips

Just walking along San Pedro's sandy streets, you will be inundated with boards advertising daily snorkel trips to the marine reserves, often including a visit to neighbouring Caye Caulker as well. Competition is fierce, so good deals are easy to find, including ones that offer snacks and drinks. Expect to pay around US$15 per person. One of the most popular snorkel trips is run by the captain of the **Winnie Estelle,** a 66-ft Island Trader moored at the Paradise Hotel pier, at the northern end of town. His full day trips cost nearer US$45 per person, but that does include free booze all day plus snacks!

A popular boat trip from Ambergris is to visit the manatees hiding around quiet cayes and in the Southern Lagoon, near Gales Point. Remember, however, these shy animals rarely stick more than their nostrils above water, so you are likely to see very little of their giant bodies. *See* pp. 150–51. If a barbecue on lovely Goff's Caye is included in the trip, however, that will provide some distraction.

Increasingly, tour operators are also taking boats to the mainland to visit Maya sites, such as Altun Ha, which makes for an interesting day trip if you have not already visited these by land from Belize City.

shopping

One of the most original shops you will find in Belize is **Iguana Jack's**, next to the Sun Breeze Hotel, on Front Street. Prices, even for the smallest item, start in the hundreds of US dollars, but it is still worth a visit simply to see the inventive ways that the artist finds to incorporate iguanas into his decorative plates, vases and bowls.

Best of Belize, on Middle Street near the airstrip, is the best place to find quality hand-made furniture from exotic wood, as well as a great many wooden kitchen tools, original carvings and ceramics.

Fido's Courtyard Art Gallery is always an interesting place to browse, even though most of the art comes from other parts of Central America, most notably Mexico. You will find anything here, from Guatemalan worry dolls to Nicaraguan painting, silver jewellery to painted pillow covers.

There are also at least half a dozen shops selling original T-shirts, jewellery, ziricote wood carvings, postcards and trinkets.

For groceries, your best option is **Rocks' Shopping Centre**, which sells everything from frozen chickens to hairspray.

Where to Stay

Being the country's top tourist resort, prices tend to increase regularly and vary according to season. Always ask for the latest price list, not forgetting three crucial questions: Which currency is being quoted? Are prices per person? Are all taxes included? Unlike the rest of the country, prices often relate to each individual, which can come as a nasty surprise to couples. The following is just a selection of the best choices, and there are many more places to stay. Prices have been listed in detail to indicate that they do not fall into the categories normally used in the book and are often substantially higher. **Note** that prices listed below are without tax. If you cannot contact a particular hotel, you can always book via the tourist office in Belize City.

South along the Beach

Closest to the airstrip, the southern end of San Pedro has quite a few pleasant hotels. Virtually next to the airport is the **Sunbreeze Beach Hotel**, P.O. Box 14, ✆ 026 2191, ✉ 026 2346. Spotless rooms and friendly service with air-conditioning, are offered around a small garden and private beach. Singles US$90–US$125, doubles US$100–US$135, triples US$125–140.

The top resort-hotel along here is **Ramon's Village Resort**, ✆ 026 2071, ✉ 026 2214, which has a collection of beach cabañas that look rustic on the outside, but inside are first-class, with fans or air-conditioning. There is a private beach, as well as a pool, bar and restaurant. Prices are US$135–US$320 per person, depending on the standard required.

The Belize Yacht Club Hotel, ✆ 026 2777, ✉ 026 2768, has no beach but a delightful pool and attractive modern rooms in small villas. Singles or doubles US$198–300, depending on standard. **Hotel Playador**, ✆ 026 2870, ✉ 026 2871, looks similar to Ramon's Village, but the rustic exterior is matched by a rather basic interior. They do have a lovely beach, though, and a popular but overpriced bar. Singles or doubles US$95-105. **Corona del Mar**, ✆ 026 2055, ✉ 026 2461, offers simple self-catering apartments, right on the beach. The convivial American owners can arrange all diving and fishing trips. Singles or doubles US$75–110.

Coconuts Caribbean Hotel, ✆ 026 3500, ✉ 026 3501, has attractive modern rooms with fan and private bath and its own, private beach. Prices include a delicious breakfast, and a bar is open during the evenings. Singles US$95, doubles US$105. **Caribbean Villas**, ✆ 026 2715, ✉ 026 2885, is a personal favourite: a small hotel with personal service and the winning combination of a lovely beach and self-catering apartments. Free bikes are available during the daytime for trips into town, and you will be picked up from the airport if you have a fixed booking. Singles or doubles US$150.

The Victoria House, ✆ 026 2067, ✉ 026 2429, is a luxurious place, expensive but good value if you're inclined to splash out. There is a choice of beach cabaña, suite, or rooms around a private beach, within walking distance of San Pedro. Singles are US$115–200, depending on room or suite, doubles are US$130–290. Finally, and not at walking distance from San Pedro, there is the **Chateau Caribe**, ✆ 026 3233, ✉ 026 3399, which has been recently completed and is worth considering.

In Downtown San Pedro and North along the Beach

Undoubtedly the best place to stay in the heart of San Pedro are the luxurious self-catering apartments called **The Mayan Princess**, ✆ 026 2778, ✉ 026 2784. Rooms are spacious, and each suite has its own ocean-view balcony. Facilities include everything from T.V. to fridge and air-conditioning. (Avoid the ground floor if the view is important to you). **The Barrier Reef Hotel**, ✆ 026 2075, ✉ 026 2719, is opposite Big Daddy's Disco, so perhaps a tad noisy in the evenings. Singles from US$40, doubles from US$48.

There are some less expensive hotels in San Pedro: just around the corner from the beachfront, **The San Pedrano**, ✆ 026 2054, is excellent value for money and friendly too. Singles US$25–US$30, doubles US$30–US$35, triples US$35–US$42. Self catering apartments here are also available from US$400 per week. **Martha's Hotel**, ✆ 026 2053, ✉ 026 2589, is the best of the budget hotels, and offers private bathrooms with all rooms. Singles are US$20–US$30, doubles US$30–US$40, and triples US$40–US$52. **Rubie's Hotel**, ✆ 026 2063, ✉ 026 2434, is right on the beach, nearest the airport. There is only one shower for all rooms, but it's an amiable place with a pleasant beachfront; US$15 per person. **The Coral Beach Hotel**, ✆ 026 2013, ✉ 026 2864 offers simple rooms with private bath, fan or air-conditioning, but is rather expensive for what you get. Singles are US$65, doubles US$100. Right on the beach, and operated by the same people who run the ferry to Belize City, **The Conch Shell Hotel** is by the Texaco pier. It is overpriced with singles at US$25–US$60, doubles US$35–US$60. Also worth checking are **Lily's Hotel**, ✆ 026 2059; and **Tomas Hotel**, ✆ 026 2061.

At the northern end of town, there is the **Paradise Resort Hotel**, ✆ 026 2083, ✉ 026 2232, which also has cabañas around a private sunbathing area, but no beach, plus restaurant and bar. Singles are US$70–100, doubles US$90–120. A good place for bargain conscious families or groups is the **Hotel del Rio**, ✆ or ✉ 026 2286, which is a short walk from town. The self-catering cabañas are excellent value at US$60 for 2–5 people, or US$40 for 2–3 people.

North of San Pedro: Accessible by Boat Only

If you want to be exclusive, then the following options may be for you. Farthest away of all (10 mins by boat), is **Journey's End Caribbean Club**, ✆ 026 2173, ✉ 026 2397. Described by the manager as 'Club Med without the hassle', this is a self-contained resort hotel, which unfortunately has no proper beach and not the most polite staff in the world. Guests however have free use of surfers and Hobie Cats, and there is a dive shop on site. The pool is the most elegant on the island, and sports a great poolside bar with the stools actually positioned in the water. Accommodation ranges from cabañas, to poolside rooms, to mangrove-lagoon-facing rooms, TVs in all but the cabañas. Singles US$200–240, doubles US$250–290. Air-conditioning is US$15 extra per day.

The nearest neighbour is the newly opened **Essene Way**, ✆ 026 2426, which offers 21 rooms in individual stone cottages with beautiful interiors of polished tropical woods and also a stunning luxury suite complete with sunken bathtub. It calls itself a 'non-denominational Christian Resort', so along with the usual beach activities, you can also make use of an extensive religious library and natural therapies, if you wish. Prices are available on request.

A short walk further south, **Captain Morgan's Retreat**, ✆ 026 2567, ✉ 026 2616, has rustic cabañas with fans only, on a private beach. There is a restaurant, and all watersports can be arranged. Singles are US$143, doubles US$187. Finally, **El Pescador**, ✆ 026 2975, ✉ 026 2398, is a family-run hotel in a traditional, wooden colonial building. Right on the beach, the rooms are nothing fancy, but all have private bathrooms, and a restaurant provides the meals. The hotel caters almost exclusively to deep-sea-fishing enthusiasts, though others are always welcome. Singles are US$120, doubles US$196, all meals included.

Eating Out

Eating out in San Pedro is one of its greatest pleasures, but it is expensive. Do not expect to get much for less than BZ$15, and get used to the idea of spending the best part of BZ$40 for most main dishes.

Apart from the numerous hotel restaurants, **Elvie's Kitchen**, on Middle Street, is one of the most popular eating places, a special attraction is its sandy floor and tree growing in the middle of the dining area. The tropical fruit juices are highly recommended.

Fido's Courtyard & Pier has **Mojo's Restaurant** downstairs, with delicious cheap snacks, such as a hummus platter, as well as dinner specials and good seafood. Upstairs is the **Reality Café**, which offers a pleasant location for breakfast and huge mugs of very good fresh coffee. You would expect the **Casa de Café**, on Front Street, to make decent coffee, but unfortunately it is disappointingly weak. The cinnamon rolls are good, though. For both delicious homemade pastries and good coffee, you should also try **Rubie's Café**, near the airstrip. **Celi's Restaurant** has a huge choice of meals on its menu, including imaginative fish dishes, such as grouper fillet stuffed with cheese. The delicatessen section, facing Front Street, also sells the best value take-away lunch snacks, such as burritos, tacos, sandwiches and delicious fruit juices. **Little Italy** is a firm favourite, offering delicious garlic bread with all meals. Excellent for pizza and pasta, but also for their Mexican lunchtime special, for just BZ$15.

Elvie's Kitchen is not the only restaurant on Middle Street. If you hanker after some Thai-style cooking, why not try the eclectic **Lagoon Restaurant**, which uses lots of satay sauces, but also offers Cajun lobster and *coq au vin*! Nearby, the Sunrise Restaurant does traditional Belizean dishes of rice and beans, as well as seafood dishes at reasonable prices. Not a restaurant, but a great shop for picking up fresh fruit and vegetables, is **Patty's**.

Heading past the airstrip, the **Bon Appetite Café** offers delicious banana bread and carrot cake, and lots of different rolls for breakfast. **Duke's Place**, further on, is the best place for lobster dinners, and daily specials come with free rum punch and dessert. Finally, about ten minutes walk further, you come to the **Jade Garden**, which is the long-standing Chinese restaurant on the island, offering delicious Cantonese meals, as well as steaks and poultry dishes.

There are three bars worth looking out for. The first is the **Sandals Bar**, in a new building at the end of Front Street. Best at night is the **Tackle Box**, on the beach, though they tend to charge an entrance fee after a certain hour. The bar at **Fido's** is also popular, and often has live music. The main disco is waterfront **Big Daddy's**, which raves to the sound of reggae each night. Across the street is **Tarzan's**, another popular nightclub.

Caye Caulker

Caye Caulker is changing, inevitably perhaps, as tourism gradually overtakes this island traditionally associated with lobster fishing. The small huddle of wooden houses that make up the sandy heart of Caye Caulker's only settlement have been joined by more substantial buildings made of stone, and a great many less substantial dwellings along the road to the airstrip, where squatters have settled in the hope of finding work.

Yet Caye Caulker's laid back atmosphere remains in tact, and for the visitor the increased tourism simply means there is now a better range of restaurants and accommodation to choose from. The commercial disneyland of San Pedro has so far been avoided, and Caye Caulker is still the favoured island for backpackers and a younger crowd of travellers, who are more interested in hanging out with the locals and are appreciative of the slightly cheaper prices.

Orientation is easy, as there are basically just three streets. Front Street runs almost the full length of the village, facing the reef, and is where most of the action is. Middle Street runs between the central football field and the southern end of the village. And Back Street runs from close to the back pier all the way to the airstrip. The latter is the least interesting route for visitors, with the only places you will want to visit the post office and Glenda's Restaurant.

Just south of Ambergris, Caye Caulker lies about 35km from Belize City and is a much smaller island, even more so since Hurricane Hattie sliced a hefty chunk off in 1961, at a place known as The Split. Activities on the island revolve around the reef, so there are quite a few diving and snorkelling operators, and you can also hire windsurfers. There is no beach as such, but most hotels have sunbathing areas and the northern end of the island, by The Split, has been turned into a popular tanning and socialising area, where swimming is also possible.

In recent years, the island has also become the focus of some dedicated naturalists, so you also have the opportunity to learn about reef ecology and the local bird population. You can't fail to notice the brown pelicans cruising the waves, or the huge frigate birds riding the air currents, but there are also plenty of smaller birds to discover, such as the cinnamon hummingbird and tropical mockingbird. In fact, over 140 species of birds have been sighted on the island.

Note that from December to February the sandflies can sometimes drive you crazy here, coming out whenever the breeze dies down. Insect repellent helps, but they are persistent creatures. Mosquitoes are ubiquitous, as elsewhere on the cayes.

Getting There

by air

Tropic Air and Island Air both fly to Caye Caulker. The journey takes around ten minutes from Belize City and costs BZ$73–84 one way from the International Airport and BZ$43–47 one way from the Municipal Airport. You can also fly between San Pedro and Caye Caulker, which costs BZ$43–47 one way. Tropic offers eleven flights daily, operating between 7.40am and 5.30pm. Island offers seven flights daily, between 7.40am and 5.15pm.

The airstrip on Caye Caulker is located at the southern end of the island, about twenty minutes walk from the centre of the village. Either wander down Back Street, which leads straight into the heart of the village, or you can walk directly to the shoreline footpath, at the eastern end of the airstrip, turn left, and walk into the village past all the beachfront accommodations. (This would be the quickest way to reach any of the following: Shirley's Guest House, Loraine's Guest House, Seaview Hotel, Tom's Hotel and Tree Tops Hotel).

If luggage and inclination make walking undesirable, there's always the golf cart taxi service waiting for your custom.

by boat

Boats for Caye Caulker regularly leave Belize City from the Marine Terminal (*see* p. 73) and the Courthouse Wharf, and the journey takes around 45 minutes (BZ$15 one way). From San Pedro, the daily 7 am boat leaving from the Texaco Pier will stop at Caye Caulker, as will all others on their way to Belize City.

The island has a front pier and a back pier. Whichever one you arrive at, you are no more than five minutes walk from the village centre and even the farthest flung hotel will take no more than twenty minutes by foot.

Tourist Information

There is no official tourist information on the island, although wherever you stay hosts will be able to advise you. As always, the best recommendations come from other travellers.

bakery

The best cinnamon rolls and bread are to be found at the **Caye Caulker Bakery** (*open Mon–Sat, 7.30–noon and 2–7*) on Middle Street, just past the supermarket.

bank

A branch of the Atlantic Bank (*open Mon–Fri 8–2, Sat 8.30–noon*) is on Middle Street, which changes cash and traveller's cheques, and advances cash on VISA cards only.

e-mail service

Cyber Services, at **Shirley's Guest Hous**e next to the airstrip, offer an e-mail service on (*open Mondays, Wednesdays and Fridays, 7–9pm*). To send one costs around BZ$18.

laundry

You will find a laundry service on Middle Street, close to the supermarket.

post office

This is located on Back Street, at the southern end of the village. (*open Mon–Fri, 8–noon and 1–5*).

shopping

Your best chance outside Belize City to find tapes of Belizean music is in the raised wooden house on Front Street, opposite Lena's Hotel. Feel free to browse, and make sure you have a look at the beautiful original T-shirts sold here.

telephones

BTL Office is located opposite the water taxi office, in the heart of the village on Front Street. (*open Mon–Fri, 8–noon and 1–4.30pm; Sat, 8–12.30pm*).

travel agents and tour operators

Hicaco Tours, on Front Street next to the Ocean Side Restaurant, ✆ 022 2174, ✉ 022 2239, is an informative place, where you can choose from a variety of daily snorkel and diving tours to all corners of the reef.

Chocolate's Tours & Gift Shop, at the northern end of Front Street, ✆ 022 2151, heading towards The Split, is highly recommended for the all-day manatee tour (BZ$55 per person, bring your own lunch), which includes an idyllic snorkel stop at either **Sargent's or Goff's Caye**.

A very knowledgeable rastafarian, **Ras Creek**, is recommended for good value snorkel trips (BZ$25 per person), which include a sandwich snack and a visit to the sting rays. Trips go daily, with up to eight people in his motorised dugout, and you can find Ras any morning before 11am at the **Castaways Restaurant**, on Front Street.

The only proper travel agent on the island is **Dolphin Bay Travel**, on Front Street, ✆ 022 2214, who can arrange flights and dives via any of the operators on Caye Caulker or San Pedro, and acts as booking agent for many tours. The only trouble is the office appears to be shut most of the time, so you'll have to pick your moment.

Water Taxi Association

Their office (*open daily 6–11 and 1.30–3 and 6.30–8pm*) is the small hut at the heart of the village, on Front Street as you come off the front pier. This is the best place to find out the latest boat schedules and prices for trips to San Pedro, Belize City and any of the smaller cayes you would like to visit. Opening hours are not cast in stone, but you should find someone here sooner or later. Tickets are sold in advance, so if you want to be sure of getting away on any of the early morning boats, get there a good half an hour before departure.

Sports and Activities

bird-watching and ecology

The best place for Belizean books, photos and postcards, as well as slide processing and information on local flora and fauna, is **Sea-ing is Belizing**, on Front Street (*open Tues–Sun, 9.30–2 and 5.30–7*). The owner, Dorothy Beveridge, also holds regular slide lectures on the island's birds, reef ecology and fish. Lectures start at 7 pm daily (BZ$5 per person).

Another useful source of information is the **Siwa-Ban Foundation**, on Front Street opposite the Tropical Paradise Hotel. The foundation was established in 1990, with the purpose of founding a marine reserve around the southern end of Caye Caulker, which was threatened by development. Sadly, the developers won and private homes are going up along the shore. Now efforts are concentrated on the northern part of Caye Caulker, which was cut off by Hurrican Hattie and remains uninhabited. The guiding light is Ellen McRae, whose house is not only home to the foundation, but also her **CariSearch** company, which offers naturalist slide lectures and escorted walking tours for bird watchers. Bring your own binoculars.

diving

There are two resident dive operators on the island, so you can easily visit both and choose the one you like best. A general observation is that diving from here is slightly cheaper and in smaller groups than out of San Pedro, but just as rewarding. You can visit the same sights, as well as unique local ones, such as underwater caves.

Belize Diving Services, © 022 2143, @ 022 2217, bzdiveserv@btl.net offers PADI instruction courses, night dives, charters to all parts of the reef, as well as day trips to the Blue Hole (US$165 per person, including meals). All equipment can be hired, which is well maintained. You will find the office located at the south-western edge of the football field.

Frenchie's Diving Service, © 022 2234, @ 022 2074, is Belizean owned and offers every kind of course and diving trip your heart might desire. If they don't offer the trip you want, they will put you in touch with

aboard dive boats based at San Pedro. A full open water diving course costs BZ$550, which is more expensive than elsewhere. Find them at the northern end of the football field.

sea kayaking and sailing

A quiet and enjoyable way to explore the reef on your own is by hiring a sea kayak, either from Ellen McRae at the Siwa Ban Foundation, or from **Daisy's Hotel** on Front Street. Prices start at around BZ$30 for half a day.

If you have the time and the constitution for it, sailing is the ideal way to visit the reef—no noise, no pollution, just the breeze and the waves. Recommended sailing trips are offered by **Sea-ing is Belizing** (*see* p.110), and also by Zuni Zaldivar, who offers full-day trips to the **Hol Chan Reserve** for a maximum of eight people (BZ$35 per person, including snorkel gear). You can find him after 7pm opposite the police station on Front Street.

Where to Stay

On the Seafront

All the properties listed under this heading are at or beyond the southern end of the village and can be reached by walking along the shoreline footpath, intermittently running below Front Street.

expensive

Beyond the southern end of the village, **Shirley's Guest House**, ℗ 022 2145, @ 022 2264 (no children), is a nice enough spot on the beach, but wrecked by the noise of incoming planes as the airstrip is right next door.

Much better value for money is the **Tropical Paradise Resort**, ℗ 022 2063, @ 022 2225, at the southern end of Front Street, which has air-conditioned rooms and an excellent restaurant.

moderate

Loraine's Guest House, ℗ 022 2002, a short walk past the southern end of the village, offers simple rooms with private bath, and its own beach, and is certainly one of the quieter places to stay. Be wary of **Ignacio Beach Huts**, next door, as the proprietors have serious attitude. The notice on their pier even threatens to 'run you off' if you so much as step on it, so tread carefully.

The Seaview Hotel, ✆ 022 2205, ✉ 022 2105 is run by a helpful couple, who offer clean rooms with private bath and cooling fans. A restful terrace faces directly onto the beach.

Not exactly on the beach, but still in view of it, the **Tree Tops Hotel**, ✆ 022 2008, ✉ 022 2115 offers spotlessly clean rooms, all with cable TV and fridge, which is quite a treat on this island. However, only one room has a private bath and there is no hot water (Be prepared for this, it's quite a common occurrence on the island).

At the lower end of the price range, virtually next door to Tree Tops, **Tom's Hotel**, ✆ 022 2102, is a long-standing favourite among backpackers, which has huts with private baths, as well as just rooms.

cheap

Lena's Hotel, ✆ 022 2106, nicely catches the breeze coming off the sea and offers a central location for a very good price.

Along Front Street

moderate

At the southern end of the village, **Vega's Inn & Gardens**, ✆ 022 2142, ✉ 022 2269, is just past the police station, facing the sea. All rooms share the bathroom, but there is also a private hut with own bathroom available, and camping in the garden is sometimes permitted. **The Rainbow Hotel**, ✆ 022 2123, ✉ 022 2172 is close to the front pier, a two-storey building offering small rooms facing the sea.

Much better value is **Sobre Las Olas**, ✆ 022 2243, at the northern end of the village, which also has a breezy balcony from which you can watch the world go by.

One of the best places for breakfast, the **Island Sun Guest House**, ✆ 022 2215, is a little further towards The Split, and also one of the few places where you can trade and buy books.

cheap

Daisy's Hotel, ✆ 022 2150, offers simple rooms in traditional wooden buildings raised high above the ground, at the southern end of Front Street. **Edith's Hotel**, ✆ 022 2161, is popular because it has hot water, and is also at the southern end of Front Street. Right in the heart of the village, above the restaurant, **Castaways**, ✆ 022-2294 is another popular budget hotel, and the **Mira Mar Hotel**, ✆ 022 2157 is another, offering basic wooden rooms with shared bathroom facilities.

Barbara's Guest House, ✆ 022 2025, is left from Front Street, just before you reach **The Split**, a quiet and friendly Canadian-run place.

Finally, if you are planning on staying long-term, you might want to check the houses and apartments to rent around the island. One of the oldest businesses for this is **M&N Apartments**, ✆ 022 2229, ✉ 022 2257, behind the Hotel Martinez, near the front pier.

Eating Out

The most popular restaurant on Caye Caulker is presently the **Sandbox**, close to the front pier on Front Street. Seating is available both indoors and alfresco, and best on the menu are the assortment of seafood dishes.

A close contender for top rating has to be **Castaways**, a short stroll further up Front Street, which also serves a delicious array of seafood and excellent, filling breakfasts.

When it comes to imaginative ways to cook lobster, you can't beat the **Tropical Paradise Hotel Restaurant**, which has the added bonus of being especially child friendly. For nightly barbecues and mouthwatering grilled seafood, make sure you head for **Sobre Las Olas**, at the northern end of Front Street. Alternatively, try **Syd's Bar and Restaurant**, which does seafood barbecues on friday nights and has a good bar. (In general, you can expect lobster dishes to cost around BZ$20, and other seafood around BZ$15).

A popular bar and restaurant to catch the breeze coming off the sea is the **Oceanside Restaurant**, on Front Street, which also serves breakfast. Probably the most popular place for breakfast, and always packed at this time, is **Glenda's**, on Back Street. The homemade cinnamon rolls are a treat, and there are plenty of healthy yoghurt and fruit dishes too.

In the evenings you will see **Damiano's Mobile Pizza Service** (✆ 022 2284), which he personally cycles around the village. Stop him wherever you see him and buy a slice of tasty pizza. For something completely different, you could also visit the island's only Chinese restaurant: **Chan's Garden**. The specialty of the house is the sizzling beef platter with lots of spicy vegetables.Finally, if you can't do without your Belizean rice and beans dish, best head for **Glenda's** or **Marin's**, at the southern end of Middle Street.

When it comes to drinking, many of the above restaurants are also popular for evening drinking. Of the bars, the **Reef Bar** on Front Street is one of the most enduring nightspots, while the three floors of **I&I's**, at the southern end of the village, go in and out of favour at regular intervals. Finally, **Patty's Bar**, up by The Split, is popular day or night, although it is rather a long dark walk back into the centre in the evenings.

Other Cayes

There are literally hundreds of islands (or cayes) off the Belizean coast, some just a speck of sand in the sea, others significant outcrops of the three major atolls. The vast majority are uninhabited, although the region is obviously well-known to local fishermen, who have been working the reef for hundreds of years. In fact, they were the very first divers to explore the reef, skin diving being the traditional way to catch lobster around here. Many still spend weeks at a time based at lonely fishing camps, even though the national fishing industry is in decline and several camps have been declared illegal, due to environmental concerns.

Even the smallest caye often supports all kinds of life, both above and below water. The littoral forests on the larger islands provide an excellent habitat for small mammals, such as deer, armadillo, gibnut and lizards. The forest canopies are favourite breeding or resting places for a variety of birds, most famously the red-footed booby on Half Moon Caye. Underwater, those islands protected by mangrove forests give shelter to thousands of juvenile fish, but also to saltwater crocodiles and the elusive manatee, and the beaches provide historic nesting sites for the country's three indigenous sea turtles.

The endangered green turtle used to grow to a substantial four foot in length, weighing up to 600 pounds. But over-hunting, entrapment in trawling nets, and the destruction of many seagrass beds has meant existing animals are substantially smaller and very rarely seen. The magnificent loggerhead turtle is also threatened, just like its smaller relative, the hawksbill, whose lovely shell has made it the target of trophy hunters and jewellery makers.

There are just seven atoll reefs in the entire Caribbean, and three are in Belizean waters, which makes this one of the most rewarding diving regions anywhere in the world. What is more, the relatively uninhabited nature of the Belizean Reef means that, in spite of environmental concerns, the coral and fish population is healthier and more varied compared to other parts of the Caribbean. These far-flung specks in the sea are therefore the highlight of any diving, snorkelling or fishing tour to Belize, and are not to be missed.

Whichever atoll you visit, you will find a necklace of islands embracing an aquamarine lagoon of calm waters, while all around the seaward rim, innumerable ledges and great walls encrusted with coral and teeming with marine life await exploration. The best way to visit a variety of dive sites is to invest in a live-aboard diving tour, which could take anything from two days to a week, depending on your purse and requirements. Virtually all of them visit the Blue Hole, made famous by the late Jacques Cousteau. Alternatively, there are several isolated resort hotels dotted around the reef, which offer week-long packages, including transfers, diving and meals—the ultimate option for enjoying the reef in splendid isolation. (Expect one week at any of these resort hotels to cost US$1500–2000 per person, which often includes flights from the US). Not all locations are exclusive, though. Accommodation on Tobacco Caye is within most people's reach.

getting to the other cayes

Unless you are on a pre-booked package to one of the island resort hotels, your only option is to join a diving tour, either by speed boat or sailing yacht. If you prefer not to join a group, you can easily arrange a private charter, although it will obviously cost you a great deal more. In all cases, contact the dive and tour operators listed for Belize City, San Pedro, and Caye Caulker. The exceptions to this general rule are Tobacco Caye and South Water Caye, which can be reached by daily water taxi from the southern town of Dangriga.

Turneffe Islands

About 40 km east of Belize City, this is the largest of the atolls, comprising over 200 little cayes covered in mangroves that form a great oblong shape, 48 km long. The eastern shore has a massive vertical reef descending into the sea, with giant horizontal ridges that make for fascinating diving. In fact, there are no less than seventy dive sites marked by permanent moorings around the atoll, ranging from shallow dives of 12–15 feet to ones around 35–45 feet, all the way to 60–150 feet dive sites. One of the most popular with advanced divers is a place known as **The Elbow**, at the southern end of the atoll, where substantial schools of large fish often congregate. Grunts, groupers, snappers and jacks are just some of the species regularly seen here. But there are plenty of options for the casual holiday diver too- dive sites with evocative names like **Hollywood** and **Jill's Thrill**.

The snorkelling is also wonderful, with a huge variety of small tropical fish in the shallow reef waters. Their bodies come in all shapes and sizes, displaying a seemingly endless variety of markings, from black and white stripes to fluorescent blue, from yellow and purple splashes to toady brown and burning red. Meanwhile Angelfish, Parrotfish, grunts and Moray Eels are just some of the medium sized fish you will see swimming around, often hovering close to the fantastic coral outcrops, such as giant brain corals and purple sea fans, towering Staghorn, thickets of Elkhorn and great Tube Sponges.

Where to Stay

The top resort hotel is the **Turneffe Island Lodge** ✆ & 📧 014 9564, in the US: ✆ (800) 874 0118 on **Caye Bokel**, which offers twelve luxury rooms with ocean view. A slightly cheaper option would be the **Turneffe Flats Lodge** ✆ 02 30319, 📧 021 2046, in the US: 📧 (605) 578 1304, which has eight double rooms on Northern Bogue island. Finally, you could also choose the more rustic environment of Blackbird Resort ✆ 02 32772, 📧 02 34449, in the US: ✆ (713) 658 1142, on Blackbird Caye.

Alternatively, if you have the time and money, you could also spend a couple of weeks on **Calabash Caye**, working for **Coral Caye Conservation**. For more information on this option, *see* pp.20–21.

Lighthouse Reef

About 113 km east of Belize City, this is the most distant atoll, situated on a separate ridge, with six cayes surrounding a shallow lagoon. Sandbore Caye, at the northern end, has a lighthouse and is home to a keeper and his family, while Half Moon Caye, to the south, has another lighthouse and is home to the Half Moon Caye Natural Monument. Made up by the entire caye of just 45 acres, it was established in 1982, and is administered by the Audubon Society.

Two separate ecosystems, of dense vegetation and open palm tree clusters, provide a home to countless bird species, among them the red-footed booby and great frigatebird with a seven-foot wing span. Lizards are also found here, with odd names like 'bamboo chicken' and 'wish willy'. And if you're lucky you might see the magnificent loggerhead and hawksbill turtles, both endangered species. Visitors must register with the lighthouse keeper, who is a mine of information and sells maps of the area. Camping is permitted, but you must bring all your own food and water, and pets are not allowed.

The best introduction to the island's wildlife is provided by following the **Bird Sanctuary Trail** (1 km), which leads to an observation tower right in the heart of the red-footed booby colony. Leaving the rickety pier, the trail leads off along the beach before heading into a palm grove knee-deep in fallen fronds and coconuts. Further on, you enter the gloomy world of a dense ziricote forest, where hermit crabs scuttle away at your approach, carrying their sea shells off into the undergrowth. Very soon you will find the observation tower and a quick climb up the ladder brings you out into the open, level with the forest canopy. Up here the forest is heaving, especially during the breeding season from February to June, with a dozen twiggy nests on every tree. Once the eggs hatch, each nest is filled with a squawky chick which is a greedy ball of white fluff. Look closely, and you will also spot tree-climbing rats in search of an unguarded egg. Back at the pier you will find a small visitor's centre and barbecue area, though no toilet. As often as not, the reserve guard is not around. But if he is, all visitors are supposed to pay BZ$10.

For divers, **The Great Blue Hole**, just off Half Moon Caye, is a 'once in a lifetime' treat. Located at the heart of Lighthouse Reef, this is a huge circular hole about 305 m wide and 145 m deep and was formed millions of years ago, when an earthquake caused the roof of an underground cave to collapse. Stalactites give vivid evidence of the catastrophe: those formed afterwards hang straight down. It is an eerie world that was first explored scientifically by the late Jacques Cousteau in 1972. Since then, an increasing number of commercial diving tours have followed, and today it features as the highlight of almost every overnight diving trip in Belize. Unlike Cousteau and his miniature submarines, however, visiting divers never descend beyond a depth of 230 feet, and then only if they are experts. For it is at this depth that a tunnel leads into a series of three caverns, where fine silt easily fogs up visibility in an already pitch black world. Turtle bones testify to the watery deaths of those who fail to find the way out.

None of the ordinary diving tours will risk visiting the caverns. Instead you are more likely to descend to around 165 feet, where sunlight still filters down and where you can swim amongst the first series of stalactites and columns that characterise this mysterious place. There is virtually no life down here, so you will see neither the coral forests nor the fish of other dives , but that is easily compensated by the extraordinary rock formations and the sheer thrill of perceived and actual danger. Don't worry if your dive master makes you sign a release form,-it is standard practice and a good opportunity to consider whether you feel confident enough to join the dive. Along with the Great Blue Hole, the **Half Moon Wall**, just off Half Moon Caye is rated as one of the most spectacular diving sites to be found anywhere in Belizean waters. Plunging to unknown depths, this sheer wall presents a magnificent panorama of the tropical sea, where virtually every kind of reef flora and fauna crowd into one place. From the tiniest neon tetra to the mighty sharks and elegant Spotted Eagle Rays, you will find them here. Barrel sponges vie for space with giant Plate Coral, and every nook and cranny is busy with the mysterious plants and creatures of this sea.

Where to Stay

The only resort hotel is the **Lighthouse Reef Resort** (✆ & ℻ 02 31205, in the US: (800) 423 3114 or (800) 304 3043), which is one of the country's most exclusive locations even boasting its own airstrip. Air-conditioned rooms are in individual wood chalets facing 'the best beach in Belize'.

Glover's Reef

Southeast of Belize City, this atoll is nearer Dangriga, in southern Belize, and the least visited of the lot. This is not a reflection on the diving opportunities, however and about 64km of reef await to be explored. In fact, **Glover's Reef** is the ideal location for the adventurous diver or snorkeller on a budget, as this is one of the few areas of the reef with easily affordable accomodation. If you want to get off the beaten track, this is the place for you, and the diving is some of the best on the entire reef.

What distinguishes Glover's Reef from other diving spots is the huge variety of marine life, and the superb opportunities for encounters with some of the larger species rarely seen elsewhere. For example between April and June you have a good chance of spotting the harmless Great Whale Shark, while during December and January the spectacular phenomenon of thousands of spawning Grouper can be found at **Grouper Point**, near the north-east corner of the atoll. In common with the other two atolls the underwater ledge and reef wall facing the open sea is the most dramatic, and good visibility all the way down to 150 feet is not uncommon. If the slightly wilder seas on the eastern seabord put you off, then the gentler diving along the western reef will not disappoint.

One of the most exciting dive sites, for example, is a spot called **Masada**, at the south-western end of Glover's Reef where the reef is punctuated by tunnels and caves spanning diving depths from 20–110 ft. In the shallower waters you will find the most colourful profusion of coral and smaller fish, while the deeper you go, the more likely the sight of Grouper, Jewfish and Sharks. All along the western reef you also have a very good chance of meeting turtles, which for some reason seem to like this region in particular.

An exhilarating dive site near Long Caye is **Long Caye Drift,** where you can safely ride the currents to cruise a dazzling landscape of corals. The variety of shapes and sizes matches the amazing range of colour, with startling shades of green, blue, red, yellow and purple seemingly competing with the equally exotic hues of fish. Whether you are an experienced diver or a novice, you are bound to enjoy Glover's Reef, and you could easily dive a different site every day for two weeks. Nor is the snorkeller excluded as there are plenty of patch reefs in the shallow waters of the lagoon, and also interesting sites along the western reef and at **Coral Cut**, at the southern tip of the atoll.

Where to Stay

The only resort hotel on Glover's Reef is the **Manta Resort** (✆ 02 32767, ✉ 02 32764, in the US: ✆ (800) 326 1724) on South Water Caye, which offers mahogany built beach cabañas for your base to fish, snorkel and dive to your heart's content. Much more rustic and affordable, you also have a choice of two other places to stay, both reached by weekly boat charter. The newest spot is on Long Caye, where **International Zoological Expeditions** ✆ 05 22214, in the US: ✆ (800) 548 5843, e-mail: ize2belize@aol.com have set up a comfortable campsite, as well as a few simple beach huts. A week long package, including boat transfers, meals and watersport facilities costs around US$335 per person, which is a bargain compared to most options.

Boats depart at 8 am every Saturday from outside the Riverside Restaurant in Dangriga (see also p.156), returning from Long Caye at 2 pm the following Saturday. At any other time a boat charter would set you back BZ$600 one-way. The journey takes 2–3 hours.

Or you could stay at **Glover's Atoll Resort** (✆ 05 23048), which offers a choice of rustic beach cabins or space for your own tent on Northeast Caye. Either way you have to bring all your own food and drink, and the means to cook it. Once you have made your reservations, you will need to make your way to the village of Sittee River, south of Dangriga (see p.159), where the weekly boat leaves on Sunday mornings, returning from Glover's Reef on Saturday afternoons.

Bluefield Range

A string of tiny inlands running parallel to the mainland, between Belize City and Dangriga, this is a remote area, where fishermen are better catered for than divers. There is just one place to stay, and that is on a working fishing camp called **Ricardo's Beach Huts**, ✆ 02 31609 contactable via 59 North Front Street, P.O. Box 55, Belize City, ✆ 02 44970; VHF Channel 68.

Tobacco Reef

Tobacco Reef is one of the more accessible regions of the reef, where you can also find a good selection of accommodation, from first class to basic. Located just off the mainland near the southern town of Dangriga, tiny **South Water Caye** marks the southern edge, where the best place to stay is **Leslie Cottages**, owned by the American company, International Zoological Expeditions (✆ 05 22214, in the US: ✆ (800) 548 5843, e-mail: ize2belize@aol.com).

Catering mostly to American student groups, anyone can stay here, although advance reservations are recommended. Each wooden cabaña is spacious with a private bath, while a large central building acts as dining room and study. A professional dive shop is also attached, **The Living Reef Dive Centre** (✆ 05 22214, e-mail: tread@btl.net), where you can take any kind of diving course as well as explore the reef on tours. Alternatively, you could stay at **Blue Marlin Lodge**, ✆ 05 22243, ✉ 05 22296, e-mail:marlin@btl.net, which offers a choice of concrete huts or beach cabañas and a fine restaurant, although the atmosphere is stilted. Maybe it has something to do with the reprimanding 'strictly no visitors' sign.

All watersports are also available. (If you are staying at the **Pelican Beach Hotel** in Dangriga, you could also enquire about their annexe on South Water Caye, which may or may not be operational).

Tobacco Caye

Tobacco Caye, at the northern end of Tobacco Reef, is just a short boat ride from its neighbour, but quite different. Just as small, the island has long catered for budget travellers, who crowd into any of the four options available, which cover the whole of the island.

Where to Stay

The nicest place to stay, with friendly staff and the best appointed rooms, is **Ocean's Edge Lodge** (✆ 05 22294, cellular phone: ✆ 0149633), which charges US$53 per person, all meals included. Not as attractive, but the best deal for what you get is **Reef's End Lodge** (✆ 014 7067 or 05 22419, ✉ 05 22828), which offers double rooms for US$65, cabañas for US$75, including all meals, coffee and juice. **Gaviota** (✆ 05 22085, ✉ 05 23477, cellular: ✆ 0149763) charges US$45 for two, including all meals. Not all rooms have fans, although the owner claims the sea breeze is constant. Snorkel rental costs BZ$15 per day. Next door is **Island Camps** (✆ 02 72109, ✉ 02 70350, cellular: 0147160), which is friendlier, and offers very simple beach huts for the same price, including meals. Tobacco Caye also has a resident dive shop, **Second Nature Divers**, ✆ 05 37038, ✉ 02 70350, which offers the cheapest diving course in Belize for US$225. This is excellent value.

Belmopan 124
San Ignacio 127

The West: Cayo District

Around San Ignacio	131
Branch Mouth	131
Cahal Pech	131
Xunantunich	132
El Pilar and Bullet Tree Falls	132
San Antonio and Pacbitun	133
Mountain Pine Ridge and Caracol	134
Macal River Trip	137
Caves	138
Jungle Lodges	140
To Guatemala	143

The western Cayo District is a place where black orchids (just one of 250 species) sprout from tropical pines, and waterfalls, pools and streams provide delicious swimming after a long day's hiking or horse-riding. Here the lowland savannah west of Belize City gradually gives way to a hilly landscape covered by humid forests which hide a number of Maya ceremonial centres. The magnificent remains of Caracol, deep in the Mountain Pine Ridge, are possibly more important than the famous ruins of Tikal in nearby Guatemala. The forest has hardly been cleared by the archaeologists, and huge buttress roots support towering trees festooned with epiphytes, parasitic plants that cling to their branches.

The slightly higher altitude of the region, rising to 1120 m, makes the country's heat more bearable, yet even here the temperatures can be limb-deadeningly hot. In San Ignacio, the district's friendly heart, the streets are often empty during mid-afternoons while the locals take their long siestas. It has a larger Spanish-speaking mestizo population than the rest of Belize, many of them originally refugees from Guatemala, but others descendants of the original loggers who used to search out valuable mahogany for export to Europe and North America.

The atmosphere in San Ignacio is relaxed, yet the evening nightlife can be as lively as in Belize City or the most popular cayes. Quite a few English and Americans have made their home here, so there are more bars and nightclubs than you would expect. By contrast, the country's official capital, Belmopan, has no nightlife at all and very little happening in the day.

Cayo is also the perfect place to escape into nature, staying at one of the many jungle lodges that hide in the forest along the Rivers Mopan and Macal. No other part of the country will give you such a good chance to glimpse the huge variety of Belizean birds, such as kiskadees, blue-crowned motmots, or vermilion flycatchers. If you're lucky, you might even see a jaguar, tapir or howler monkey drinking from the rivers at dawn and dusk. Certainly the noises of the forest will become familiar, the lone 'tock' of the toucan easy to distinguish among the sounds.

The Road to Belmopan

Heading west out of Belize City, the highway quickly takes you out into a swampy plain dotted with mosquito infested lagoons and cut by the Burdon Canal and Sibun River. Not a very appealing region at first sight, there are nevertheless a few places worth noting. If you head south at the village of Hattieville, you will find Canadian-run **River Haven** (✆ 01 49484, @ 02 70529) by the village of Freetown Sibun. Set on the banks of the river Sibun, this is the only place in the country where you can hire a houseboat and float down the river and lagoons. The waterways, mangroves and shrublands are home to a huge number of birds, including turkey vultures, kingfishers, herons, white ibis and the common black hawk. American crocodiles are also spotted regularly and if you travel as far as the Southern Lagoon, you will almost certainly see manatee, especially around their favourite warm water spring, just off Gales Point. (A less adventurous and quicker route to Southern Lagoon would be to stay at Gales Point village and take a tour from there, *see* p.149).

The next point of interest is the Belize Zoo (*see* p.85) and, if you wanted to travel to Gales Point and Dangriga on the old coastal road, you could turn left a short distance further on, at La Democracia junction. The road is unpaved, however, and best not attempted after the rains.

A shorter and more promising route would be to follow the sign left shortly afterwards, to the **Monkey Bay Wildlife Sanctuary** (Mile 31, Western Highway, ✆ 08 23180, @ 08 23361). A private property, the owner has developed a rustic camping and bunkhouse facility, along with an information centre about the resident howler and spider monkeys. About an hour-and-a-half out of Belize City, you reach the junction for Belmopan, which is also the entrance site to one of the country's smallest national parks, the **Guanacaste National Park** (*adm*). The park is named in honour of the solitary Guanacaste tree growing in the forest here, which is one of Central America's tallest tree species, growing over 130 feet.

Often supporting huge colonies of epiphytes clinging to its branches, this particular one is no exception nurturing many clusters of fragile orchids. Normally this kind of tree would have been felled to make dugout canoes from its exceptionally straight and hardwearing trunk. But nature saved the tree in this park by splitting the trunk three ways at the base, making it useless for human needs.

Short trails loop around the fifty acres of the park, and the visitor centre supplies a botanical leaflet which describes some of the many tree species found here including the ubiquitous Cohune Palm, the great Raintree, Cotton Tree and

Mammee Apple. There are even two rare Mahogany trees. Take a stroll early or late in the day, and you might even catch sight of the park's resident pair of blue-crowned motmots, but certainly some of the other bird species, such as woodpeckers, black-headed trogons, squirrel cuckoo and parrots.

Belmopan

> *The bus left the paved road and followed a gravel track to a parking area beside a tree... 'You looking at it,' the bus driver said when I asked where the town centre might be.*
>
> *Time Among the Maya*, R. Wright

Situated 80km west of Belize City, Belmopan is a kind of Brasília gone wrong: government buildings and a few hotels stand in what looks like an overgrown building site, and the visitor is left to imagine that there must be some mistake. Surely this can't be a capital city, and to all intents and purposes it isn't, because nobody wants to live here, and almost nobody works here, except the civil servants, who have no choice, many commuting from Belize City.

Few tourists visit unless they have official business at the two embassies (*see* pp. 15–16 for addresses). Anyone who does go to Belmopan may like to visit the **archaeological vault** in the **Department of Archaeology** on the Government Plaza. Guided tours are given on Mondays, Wednesdays, and Fridays, and you should make an appointment two days prior to arrival, by contacting ✆ 08 22106.

There are plenty of precious pottery objects and artefacts of obsidian and jade, and recent excavations in Caracol have unearthed a wealth of new treasures, including a priceless jade mask, that would make an impressive display in a proper museum. As it is, many objects are locked away for safekeeping.

There is one time in the year when it is worth making a visit to Belmopan, and that is for the country's largest fair, the **National Agricultural Show Weekend**, held every April. In a festive atmosphere you can also see the range of agricultural stands, including beautiful horses, and exhibitions from many aspects of Belizean life and culture.

If you haven't tasted creole cooking yet, you will find stands selling traditional fried chicken, as well as seaweed milk or plantain dishes. At night, the country's favourite bands come to play here, and large crowds dance the night away in huge tents. If you go please be careful. Crime is common at this time, and it is not a good idea to go out alone in the evenings.

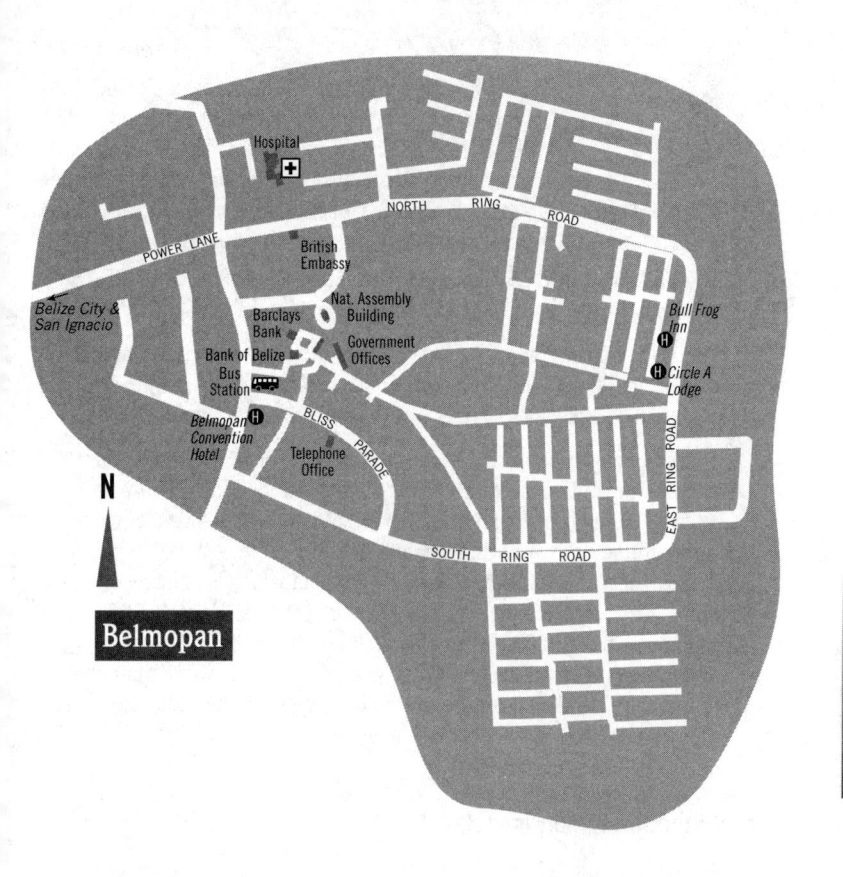

Getting to Belmopan

The journey takes about an hour from Belize City, taking any bus heading west, including buses for Dangriga, which all go via the capital. From Belmopan to San Ignacio takes another 45 minutes, to the border a further 20 minutes. Heading south, to Dangriga, takes around two hours along the Hummingbird Highway, as the dirt road is named. Wherever you are coming from or heading to, you will end up at the main bus terminal, which is the busiest spot in town.

Where to Stay

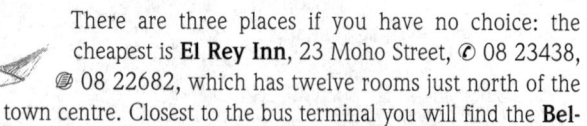

There are three places if you have no choice: the cheapest is **El Rey Inn**, 23 Moho Street, ✆ 08 23438, ✉ 08 22682, which has twelve rooms just north of the town centre. Closest to the bus terminal you will find the **Belmopan Hotel**, Col. Bliss Parade & Constitution Drive, ✆ 08 22130, ✉ 08 23066, which offers motel-type rooms in the expensive price range.

The **Bull Frog Inn**, 25 Halfmoon Avenue, ✆ 08 22111, ✉ 08 23155, at the eastern edge of town, has 23 decent rooms and a popular restaurant.

The best choice, however, is some way out of Belmopan. **Banana Bank Lodge**, ✆ 081 2020, e-mail: bbl@pobox.com. Private cabins with full breakfast at single rates start at BZ$95 up to cabins for five at $ 169.50.

This place enjoys one of the most scenic settings of any lodge in Belize, and must be the only one where you will find orchids growing in your bathroom. Built high above the Belize River, spacious lawns spread down to the bank, dotted with very comfortable thatched cabins, as well as the main dining hall. With 4000 acres to explore, half of which is primary rainforest, there is enough to keep you busy here for at least a week. Horses and canoes are available for hire, if you don't feel like walking. The owner, Carolyn Carr, has an art gallery where you can view her work and purchase prints, many of which feature the resident jaguar. (The sight of this beautiful animal kept in a shockingly small enclosure is the only blot on this otherwise lovely place).

From Belmopan to San Ignacio

Continuing west from the Belmopan junction you enter the lush green foothills of the Maya Mountains, a rich agricultural region, ever more densely populated. The road undulates up and around picturesque creole villages with names like **Teakettle** and **Mount Hope**, while the horizon to the south displays the mysterious contours of rainforest canopies and distant mountain tops. Turn left at Teakettle, and a bumpy but well posted dirt road takes you to one of the friendliest jungle lodges in the region: **Pook's Hill**, (*expensive*) ✆ 08 12017, ✉ 08 23361, e-mail: pookshill@pobox.com. From here you can explore an area of pristine jungle and swim in the beautiful waters of the Roaring River. Horse riding, mountain biking and tubing the river are all possible here, and simple rooms are offered in individual thatched stone cabañas, with private bath. Pook's Hill offers free transfers from Teakettle village which is passed by every bus heading for San Ignacio.

One of the advantages of staying at Pook's Hill is that the property is adjacent to the 6,741 acres of the **Tapir Mountain Nature Reserve**, which is normally only open to scientists. Since animals respect no man-made borders, however, you have an excellent opportunity to explore a section of tropical forest which is relatively undisturbed and rich in wildlife. The reserve is named after the Baird's Tapir, which is the largest terrestrial animal native to Belize, and one of its national symbols. A chunky mammal that can weigh up to 875 pounds, its features are a bizarre mixture: hooves indicate its equestrian heritage, short legs and stocky body resemble a miniature cow, while the elongated nose recalls an anteater. Popularly known as a 'mountain cow', the tapir is a shy herbivore, who only ventures from the undergrowth for its daily bath in the river.

Other animals resident here include a myriad of bird species and many small mammals, such as the handsome coatis, who resemble racoons and have a similarly stripey tail. Gibnut —the notorious 'royal rat' once served to the Queen—are also common, busily tucking seeds into their underground storage holes each day. Opossums, deer, kinkajous and armadillos, not to mention several species of snakes and iguanas are also found.

About half way between Belmopan and San Ignacio, you will pass **Caesar's Place**, ✆ 092 2341, @ 092 3449, which is a guest house, but primarily interesting for its café and gift shop. Stop here for a relaxing break if driving your own vehicle, and take a look at the locally made jewellery, wood carvings, and other craft products. (This is also a good spot for enquiries about staying at Caesar's remote **Black Rock Jungle Lodge**, *see* p.142).

Continuing westward, you pass ever more villages before reaching San Ignacio's opposite number, **Santa Elena**, on the east bank of the Macal River and finally reach San Ignacio itself by crossing the Hawksworth Bridge. This is the longest suspension bridge in the country, its metal sheets rattle fearsomely with every passing vehicle, effectively announcing new arrivals. Just wide enough for a single line of traffic, and no longer regulated by traffic lights, the noise is less worrying than drivers' brinkmanship as they speed to cross the river first.

San Ignacio

San Ignacio—always called Cayo—is a small town, 37km west of Belmopan, and just under 15km from the Guatemalan border. On first glance it is not immediately appealing, with a ragged collection of wooden buildings and rusty corrugated roofs mixing with rain-washed concrete buildings. It is San Ignacio's strategic position, at the confluence of the rivers Mopan and Macal, and close to the Mountain Pine Ridge Forest Reserve, which make it the ideal base for getting to know inland

Belize. A wealth of outdoor activities in a beautiful environment is complemented by some of the country's most unforgettable sights. You could easily spend a week here, discovering something new each day on your forays to the nearby attractions.

Getting to San Ignacio

Getting to San Ignacio is an easy journey from Belize City with the regular Batty or Novelo buses that plough this route daily. Coming from Dangriga, you need to change buses in Belmopan.

Tourist Information

There is no official tourist office in San Ignacio, but Bob Jones, who runs **Eva's Bar and Restaurant** on Burns Avenue, is an excellent source of information, and holds brochures and price lists for most of the surrounding lodges, as well as official taxi fares. Whether you want to book a tour or need a doctor, he can point you in the right direction.

There are two **banks** here: Atlantic Bank, near the police station, is best for credit card cash. (*open Mon, Tues, Thurs & Fri, 8–noon and 1–3; Wed, 8–1; Sat 8.30–noon*). Belize Bank is on Burns Avenue, (*open Mon–Thurs, 8–1; Fri, 8–4.30*).

There is no reliable **car rental** service in San Ignacio, so best make arrangements in Belize City.

The **post office** is above the police station, by the suspension bridge.

The local **Belize Telecommunications Limited** office (BTL) (*open Mon–Fri, 8–noon and 1–4; Sat, 8–noon*) is on the top end of Far West Street, on the second floor of the building housing the St Martin's Credit Union.

Sports and Activities

The range of things to do around San Ignacio increases every year, as more and more operators devise trips into a landscape rich in natural and manmade wonders. As always, the best place to look for inspiration, as well as prices and practical information is Eva's Bar.

archaeology

There are many Maya ruins in the region, including two of the most spectacular in Belize: Caracol and Xunantunich. *See* pp. 132–7. Right on the edge of San Ignacio itself, you will find the ruins of Cahal Pech, while El Pilar, beyond the village of Bullet Tree Falls, was once the administrative centre of the Maya in this area. *See* pp. 132–3.

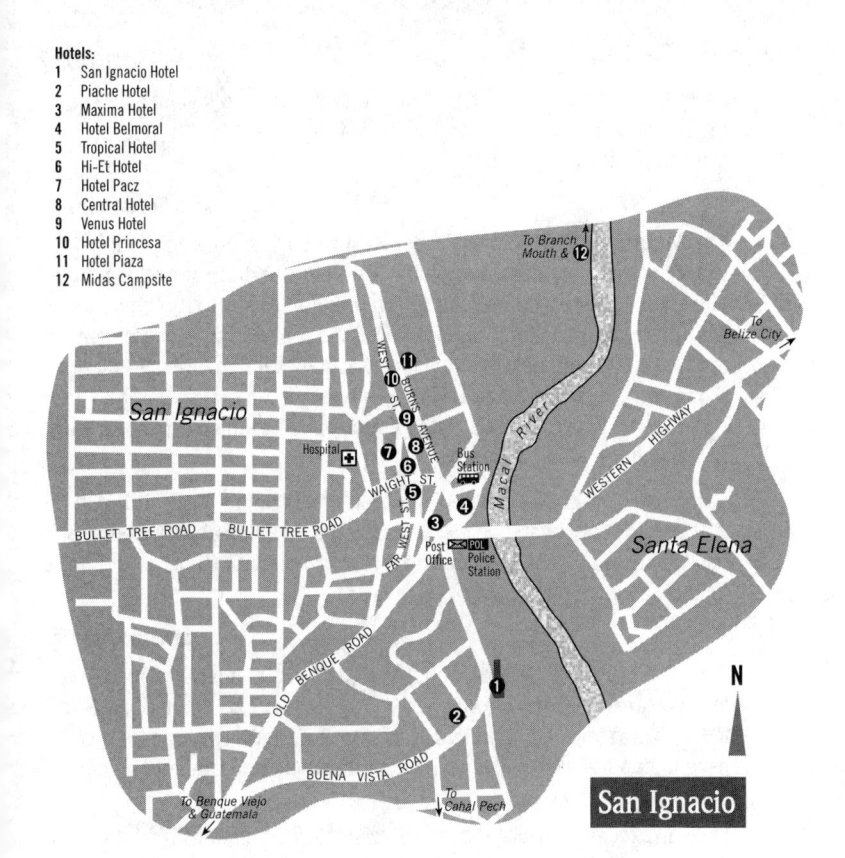

Hotels:
1. San Ignacio Hotel
2. Piache Hotel
3. Maxima Hotel
4. Hotel Belmoral
5. Tropical Hotel
6. Hi-Et Hotel
7. Hotel Pacz
8. Central Hotel
9. Venus Hotel
10. Hotel Princesa
11. Hotel Piaza
12. Midas Campsite

caving

Caving tours have now established themselves as one of the most exciting things you can do in Cayo, and some of the best are run by ex-British army soldier, Pete Zubrzycki, who also runs the PACZ hotel ✆ & 📧, 092 2210.

cycling

Mountain biking is a great way to explore the surrounding villages and Maya ruins under your own steam, and you will find a decent selection of bikes for hire at **B&M Mountain Bikes**, 23 Burns Avenue. Remember to check your choice carefully before setting off, and make sure you know what backup arrangements are in place in case of mechanical failure.

fishing

Terry Ryle, ✆ 092 3363 offers tours to the rivers and lagoons, all equipment and packed lunch included for around BZ$100 per person. (Maximum of three people).

horse riding

The **Mountain Pine Ridge Forest Reserve** offers wonderful opportunities for horseback riding, and many of the surrounding jungle lodges also offer riding tours. The only one specialising in this activity, however, is **Mountain Equestrian Trails** ✆ 092 3310, ✉ 082 3505, which is very much family orientated, with plenty of activities for children. A full day's riding will cost you close to US$100, and they also offer adventurous trips lasting several days to reach remote areas, such as the **Chiquibul Rainforest** and the ruins of Caracol.

Local operators are a good deal cheaper. For example, **Easy Rider** ✆ 09 23310, also contactable via Eva's, will take you along trails around San Ignacio and also to Maya ruins nearby for around US$40 per person for a full day, including lunch.

natural history

The ideal place to introduce yourself to Cayo's natural history is the excellent **Natural History Centre** (*open daily, 7–4; BZ$10*) at Chaa Creek lodge, which you can either reach by taxi or by your own transport, or by paddling up the Macal River on one of the wonderful canoe tours offered by Tony. (*See* Eva's Bar).

Several excellent displays cover diverse topics, ranging from the local geology of the Maya Mountains to the flora and fauna of the rainforest, and an added attraction is a visit to the adjacent butterfly breeding centre, where you can see hundreds of blue morphos, one of the most beautiful butterflies of the rainforest. If that were not enough, there are also some informative exhibits about Maya history and culture, with many items from everyday Maya life on display.

Adjacent to Chaa Creek, you can also visit the **Rainforest Medicine Trail** (US$5) at Rosita Arvigo's farm, where thirty-five useful and medicinal plants are featured along a self-guided trail. *See* p. 137 Macal River Trip.

Around San Ignacio

Of the Maya ruins, Caracol and Xunantunich are the highlights, while a visit to San Antonio is ideal to discover the traditional arts and crafts of the present-day Maya. Tours are available to just about everywhere, so there is no need to hike, paddle or ride, if you do not wish to. Best of all, perhaps, the region is dotted with some of the finest places to stay in the entire country, with quality and service a good deal better than almost anywhere else.

Branch Mouth

This is the point where the River Macal joins the Mopan, eventually to become the River Belize. It is a delightful, quiet spot, 30 minutes' walk outside San Ignacio. At weekends, it is popular for picnics and swimming. To get there, just walk along the dirt road that also passes the Midas Campsite.

Of the two rivers that join here, the Macal is the easier to explore, as there are a good many jungle lodges hidden along its banks, which also hire out canoes. Most commercial canoe trips from San Ignacio also seem to favour it.

The Mopan's emerald waters are just as beautiful, though, and two ideal places to base yourself near it are either Nabitunich Lodge, along the road for the Guatemalan border, or Parrot Nest just outside the village of Bullet Tree Falls, *see* pp. 132–3, 5 km from San Ignacio.

Cahal Pech

Its name meaning 'the place of ticks', this was an important site as early as 200 BC although habitation commenced as long ago as 1000 BC. Archaeologists believe it was the exclusive home of Maya nobles in the later, Classic period and you will find some excellent examples of the Maya's famous corbelled arch here.

Excavation work has only been carried out in recent years, but already many artefacts have been found here. The most intriguing of all is a large stone bench that still retains much of its original red colouring, as well as ancient graffiti. Perhaps it was a sleeping platform, but specialists are still undecided.

Situated on the hillside above San Ignacio, you can walk here in 20 minutes. Follow the road straight up to the thatched Cahal Pech bar, next to the radio station. Opposite the bar, turn left, and then first right, along a dirt road leading into the forest, where the site hides. (Small fee).

Xunantunich

Open daily, 8–5; adm.

Pronounced 'shoo-nan-too-nitch', this is a small Classic Maya site, with one of Belize's largest ancient pyramids, El Castillo, affording great views across the jungle canopy. About 40 m high, it was believed to be the highest building in Belize until the temples of Caracol were discovered. Only two plazas remain clearly visible, dotted by a few stelae, though a great deal of work has been done recently to reveal more. The location and the path leading to the site are stunning, and even when jungle mists obscure the view, the atmosphere is quite magical.

To get there, take any bus heading for Benque Viejo, and ask to be dropped off at the ferry, by the Maya village of Succotz. Here a hand-drawn ferry (free) takes vehicles and pedestrians over the Mopan river, from where a steep track leads 1 km through the forest and up to the ruins. Unfortunately, this track is notorious for robbers, so it's best not to go alone. Make sure you don't miss the last ferry crossing back at about 5pm.

El Pilar and Bullet Tree Falls

About five kilometres northwest of San Ignacio, the small village of Bullet Tree Falls is principally interesting because you can visit the charming property called Parrot Nest, where you can arrange to hire horses and a guide to visit the Maya ruins of El Pilar.

Once the most important administrative centres for the Classic Maya in the Belize River Valley, the site is in the process of being developed as part of the 2000-acre El Pilar Archaeological Reserve for Maya Flora and Fauna. An ambitious project, the idea is to establish an eco-tourism venture that will highlight the daily life of ordinary Maya, concentrating on their agricultural and domestic life. As yet, however, there is very little to see here and getting there on horseback is more interesting than arriving. This is bound to change in future, as preliminary archaeological work has already established that Pilar is one of the country's largest Classic Maya sites, stretching over an area of 50 acres.

At least fifteen plazas have been mapped so far, incorporating all the hallmarks of an important site: temples, palaces, and a ball court. The most mysterious feature is a man-high wall, which appears to run indefinitely west, perhaps an ancient link with Guatemala's Tikal.

Information on the ruins and the park can be obtained by writing to The El Pilar Program, CORI/Meso American Research Centre, University of California, Santa Barbara, CA 93106, USA or to the Belize Archaeological Settlement Survey/El Pilar Program, P.O. Box 5, Cayo, Belize, ℘ 092 3002.

San Antonio and Pacbitun

The village of San Antonio, which lies on the Cristo Rey Road to the Mountain Pine Ridge, is not immediately memorable. A ragtag of houses line the mud road for a while, and there is nothing much to see, except the inhabitants going about their business. Yet the village is significant, not only because it is one of the few that is almost exclusively inhabited by Yucatec Maya, but also because it is home to the García sisters and their **Tanah Art Museum and Community Collection** (*open daily, 8–5; adm*). Tanah is the people's own name for their village, and the sisters have become famous in Belize for producing some of the finest slate carving and sculpture to be found by contemporary Maya. Their style is simple— galleries would probably market it as 'primitive art'—yet they render the traditional symbols and images very well.

One of the more interesting pieces of jewellery that they make are small amulets carved with Maya astrological symbols, each one explained on a small piece of paper attached. But the sisters also produce large replicas of famous Maya pieces, such as the head of the Sun God (Kinich Ahau), found at Altun Ha. Equally interesting are their homemade herbal remedies, many of which were handed down by the revered local healer, Don Elijio Panti, who trained the American herbalist, Rosita Arvigo, who owns Ix Chel Farm next door to Chaa Creek.

There is another reason for Maya enthusiasts to visit San Antonio, and that is to get permission from Mr Tzul to visit **Pacbitun**, which is on his land. (He lives about one kilometre south of the village, at the turn-off for the ruins). As at Pilar, there are no visitor facilities at the site and you really need a guide to make your visit meaningful. Yet Pacbitun is significant, because it is one the most important Pre-

Classic sites in west Belize, which probably had close trading links with Mexican Teotihuacan. Archaeologists have found a great many artefacts here, as well as a high number of musical instruments, such as clay flutes, which leads them to believe that Pacbitun was not only an important trading centre, but also home to a powerful élite.

The Mountain Pine Ridge Forest Reserve and Caracol

The Mountain Pine Ridge includes some of the highest peaks found in the Maya Mountains, ranging from 860–1020 metres, which rise above a dramatic wilderness area, full of bubbling streams and tumbling waterfalls, deep gorges and empty plateaus. Most interestingly, the region also encompasses a surprising variety of vegetation and climate, which is due to its unique formation. The Ridge is, in fact, the oldest land surface in Central America, which millenia ago was a volcanic island surrounded by ocean.

Today, the granite rock that formed its core has been exposed by millions of years of erosion, leaving only a very thin layer of soil, which is why you find not only jungle, but also large areas of pine forest, and wind-swept hills with no trees at all, such as the appropriately named Mount Baldy (1020m). It seems unnatural at first, but these tropical pines and Alpine vistas are entirely indigenous and can also be found in other tropical countries, such as Thailand, wherever the geology and subsoil dictate it.

Much of the Moutain Pine Ridge Forest Reserve also encompasses the more familiar rainforests of Belize, which grow on the limestone skeleton that makes up the bulk of the Maya Mountains. You can find yourself gazing across deep chasms, one side cloaked in rainforest, the other in towering pines. Beneath the rainforest, meanwhile, a subterranean world of mysterious caves and rivers stretches endlessly in all directions. The most extensive cave system found so far is the **Chiquibul**, where some caverns tower hundreds of metres high and are among the five largest in the world.

From earliest times, these caves have provided sanctuary for all kinds of animal species as well as humans. The Maya believed caves were the natural entrances to the Underworld, *Xibalbá*, and used them for important ceremonial acts as well as burial places. Countless numbers of sacrificial offerings, ceramic artefacts and skeletons have been found in the region, and many can still be seen in their original resting places.

Exploring the Mountain Pine Ridge on foot, horseback or four-wheel drive is an exhilarating experience not to be missed. An opportunity not only to discover one of the country's great wildernesses, but also the Maya ruins and caves that hide within it. The finest ceremonial site of all is **Caracol**, in the far south west, but there are many smaller centres, some no doubt still undiscovered. Of the many waterfalls, 1000-ft Falls are the most famous, but the Butterfly Falls are more beautiful (on Hidden Valley Inn property).

If your budget allows it, you would ideally base yourself at one of the four lodges dotted around the reserve: Pine Ridge Lodge, Blancaneaux Lodge, Five Sisters Lodge or Hidden Valley Inn (*see* pp.141–3). Alternatively, Mountain Equestrian Trails (on the Chiquibul Road entrance route) or Maya Mountain Lodge (on the Cristo Rey entrance route) are very close. Note that tours around the Mountain Pine Ridge and to Caracol are much cheaper out of San Ignacio than most of those offered by the hotels and lodges in and around the reserve.

Getting to and around the Mountain Pine Ridge

There are two main entrance roads to the Mountain Pine Ridge, both unpaved and best negotiated by four-wheel drive. Closest to San Ignacio is the Cristo Rey Road, which turns south off the Western Highway in Santa Elena. A beautiful route, this takes you past Maya Mountain Lodge and San Antonio village before reaching the reserve entrance at the Mai Gate (Santa Elena to Mai Gate is 25.6km). This is where you normally pay a small entrance fee, although people on tours will find the price is usually included in their fee for the day.

The other entrance road to the reserve begins as a turn-off south at the village of Georgeville, 9.6km east of Santa Elena, on the Western Highway. The unpaved section of this route is almost ten kilometres shorter to Mai Gate and considered easier to drive, but it is less interesting, with nothing much to see along the way.

The road continues about six kilometres into the reserve before passing a turn-off for Cooma Cairn Road and Hidden Valley Inn to the south-east (about 7 km away). Not much later you also pass the Pine Ridge Lodge and turn-off for Blancaneaux and Five Sisters lodges to the west (about 5 km and 10 km away respectively). But the main track continues south, winding up and around to the lovely Rio On Falls and pools, a brilliant place for a swim.

Eventually, you reach **Douglas da Silva forestry station**, where camping is permitted, and you can visit the nearby Rio Frio Caves. Soon you're winding through the hills, passing a small collection of wooden buildings among the trees, where the families of the foresters live. The pine forest could almost be in North America, but look closely, and you will see orchids growing from niches in the trees. Further south still, the road gets progressively worse and more deeply rutted until, at last, you reach the archaeological ruins of **Caracol**, a good two hours after you passed Mai Gate. This is as far as members of the public can go, and it is recommended that you travel by tour, rather than in your own vehicle, as sign-posting is not comprehensive and you can easily get lost. If you don't have the time or money to visit Caracol, you can still visit the reserve, by taking a shorter Mountain Pine Ridge Tour, which will take in the 1000 ft Falls and the Río On pools, and possibly the Río Frío Cave. This costs around US$25 each, for a group of five people, and Bob Jones can help you arrange it. The journey to Caracol can only be attempted during the dry season, from January to June. It is a long trip and you should take along a packed picnic and water.

Caracol

Once past the reserve entrance, the road takes you through forests festooned with bromeliads, getting ever thicker and moister, until you find yourself surrounded by tall rainforest, hung with creeping vines and sprouting palms. The shadowy light filters through the canopy above, and the mud road is increasingly difficult.

Approaching the great city itself—which is estimated to cover a total area of 80 square kilometres, including its satellite communities—the jungle becomes especially striking, with huge buttress roots folding around giant trees. At the entrance, you pass Canaa Temple (Temple of the Sky), its huge limestone staircase gleaming white once more. This pyramid now holds claim to being the highest building in Belize, rising 42 m above the forest floor.

An archaeological team from Florida University works here every dry season, and members voluntarily take time out to show visitors around (a donation to the University project is appreciated). Caracol was only rediscovered in 1936, when chicle (gum) gatherers stumbled upon the site, and archaeological work is still in the very early stages; the Caracol Project was begun in 1985. Being shown around the temple structures, stelae, ball courts, tombs and living quarters by dedicated and enthusiastic professionals is a highly educational experience.

It is believed that at the height of its era as many as 300,000 people lived in the city and its surrounding territory—which is more than the entire population of Belize today—though others argue for lower estimates of around 180,000 people. What is known for sure is that the site was occupied from Pre-Classic to Classic times, and in AD 563 its rulers defeated nearby Tikal, rising to great power and influence, which is reflected in increased building after this period.

Magnificent tombs have been uncovered here, and as recently as 1991, the second largest jade mask found in Belize was retrieved from one of the temples. Eventually, Caracol may well emerge as the most important Maya city in the Guatemala and Belize region, overshadowing Tikal as the major tourist attraction, just as it once defeated its neighbour in war. Note that tours to Caracol are only possible during the dry season (roughly January–June) and will cost around US $50 per person for a full day's travelling by a four-wheel drive vehicle.

Bring your own lunch and something to drink, as well as swimming gear for a dip in the Rio On. Day trips to Tikal, in Guatemala, are also possible and cost about US$75 per person.

About 13 km south of Caracol, an outstanding natural phenomenon is the **Chiquibul Cave System**, which is the longest in Central America, and has the largest cave room in the Western Hemisphere. Unfortunately, however, these caves are inaccessible to all but the expert caver and guide.On the return journey, the driver should be willing to stop for a swim at the **Río On**.

This is a gorgeous place for a cool swim, where the river flows over limestone rocks to form a succession of pools, their waters fragrant with the scent of pine. If you head for the top pool, you will also find a natural jacuzzi, where boulders squeeze the water into a churning tub, just big enough for four people.

Macal River Trip

This is an excellent excursion by canoe, taking in a few swimming stops, as well as an optional visit to the Rainforest Medicine Trail (US$5), next to Chaa Creek Cottages, where you stop for lunch. (A Natural History Centre has also been established at Chaa Creek recently (*open daily 8–5; US$5*). Along the way you'll see a tremendous variety of birds, such as egrets, pygmy kingfishers, toucans, cormorants, herons, kiskadees, kite hawks and vultures.

Most startling are the huge iguanas sunning themselves on rocks or branches, their prehistoric-looking spikes giving them a terrifying appearance. Specimens of 4ft and over are quite common. You will also pass a colony of tiny fruit bats, sleeping upside down on the roof of a limestone ridge, overhanging the water.

The Rainforest Medicine Trail is an interesting opportunity to learn about the forest's medicinal qualities, and a marked trail tells you about which plants take care of what, ranging from contraception, headaches and upset stomachs, to malaria or headlice.The best person to take you on this trip is the rastafarian Tony (*see above*), who does most of the work paddling you in his canoe, though it helps if you offer to paddle too. He's immensely knowledgeable about the river's wildlife, and you won't see half the birds and animals without his expert eyes and ears to point them out. Contact him via Eva's restaurant.

Caves

Of the countless caves to be found in the region, there are presently four that can easily be visited by tour, and many more that local guides would be willing to show you. In all cases, it is a good idea to use a guide, as it is easy to get lost. If you have a torch, remember to bring it along, and do wear sturdy shoes and carry a long-sleeved top, as it can be damp and chilly underground. Bringing some drinking water is also a good idea. For the latest options and prices check the notices at Eva's Bar or see Pete Zubrzycki at the Pacz Hotel.

The most commonly visited caverns in the region are the **Rio Frio Caves**, which are just a short drive away from the Rio On Pools, in the Mountain Pine Ridge Forest Reserve. The roof of the cave rises up to 65 feet and the Rio Frio runs straight through it, past striking rock formations and dripping stalactites. When the river is low, you can walk almost one kilometre along the sandy river bed, and out into sunshine the other end. In the distant south of the region, **Vaca Cave**, hides within the **Vaca Plateau**, and was once an important burial site for the Maya. Close to the Guatemalan border, near Benque Viejo del Carmen, one of the most exciting caves to visit is **Che Chem Hah** (*BZ$50 entrance fee for 1–3 people*), where you slither down narrow passages and climb rope ladders to enter pitch black catacombs littered with large Maya vases, once used for food storage. Some are believed to be up to two thousand years old.

In certain places the walls are blackened from the fires of ancient ceremonies, and you really feel as if you are stepping back in time, to an era when these caves were the domain of priests and secret rituals. In the largest cavern found so far, there are also traces of wall paintings, further evidence of the great significance the ancient Maya attached to this place. (Note that a certain degree of fitness is required for visiting this cave, as there is a strenuous uphill path to negotiate that takes about twenty minutes to walk. Last, but not least, you could spend an adventurous afternoon visiting **Barton Creek Cave** by canoe. Accessed by river beyond the Mennonite settlement of Barton Creek, visitors are taken deep into the gaping jaws of the cave, which has an atmosphere, due to the many Maya burial sites.

Where to Stay

There are plenty of places to stay, in town or in one of the many lodges in the surrounding countryside, *see* pp.140–43.

San Ignacio

expensive

The top hotel in town, which prides itself in having looked after the Queen on her last visit, is the **San Ignacio Hote**l, P.O. Box 33, © 092

2034/2125/2220, ◉ 2134. The location, perched on the steep hill above the town centre, makes for great views, and the pool is a popular place for evening drinks.

moderate

A bit further up the road is the **Piache Hotel**, ✆ 092 2032, which has a lovely garden and fine hilltop views. Rooms are simple and have private baths. Right up by the Cahal Pech ruins, **Rose's Guest House**, ✆ & ◉ 092 2282, offers simple rooms with fan and spotless bathrooms but it's a long hot walk from the centre. In the town centre, your best option in this range is the **Hotel Plaza**, 4 Burns Avenue, ✆ 092 3332. If that's full, try the Maxima Hotel, Hudson Street, ✆ 092 2265, ◉ 092 2225.

cheap

In the town centre hotels are very affordable and the **Central Hotel**, 24 Burns Avenue, ✆ 092 2253, is the best value. Rooms are clean, all have fans, and there are two bathrooms. If that is full, why not try the **Hotel Pacz**, 2 Far West Street, ✆ 092 2110, ◉ 092 2972, which offers guests discounts on tours to the surrounding region. An excellent place to stay is **Martha's Guest House**, 10 West Street, ✆ 092 2101, which only has two rooms, along with use of a kitchen and lounge. Book ahead if you want to be sure of staying here. **The Venus Hotel**, 29 Burns Avenue, ✆ 092 2186, has clean, simple rooms with fans. **Hotel Princesa**, 3 Burns Avenue, is a decent budget choice, all rooms with fan and private bath. The **Hi-Et Hotel**, 12 West Street, is a pleasant family house, offering basic rooms with shared bathroom. The recently refurbished **Hotel Belmoral**, 17 Burns Avenue, ✆ 092 2024, is now also a decent choice.

Camping

Camping is only permitted in two places: either at the Mai Gate entrance to the **Mountain Pine Ridge Forest Reserve**, or at its forestry station, **Douglas da Silva**, right in the heart of the reserve. There is no public transport to get there and you have to bring all your own provisions and equipment, so they don't make it easy for you. You also need to get permission from the Forestry Officer, either at the entrance or at the forestry station. Much easier, although much more expensive too, is to stay in one of several lodges dotted around the reserve and listed in the text below. If you prefer to go it alone, remember that a good map (and possibly a compass) are essential, since no one will come looking for you if you get lost.

The most detailed maps are available at Stanfords in London, *see* p.36, or directly from the Survey Department at the Ministry of Natural Resources in Belmopan, which is also much cheaper. The most useful sheets are numbers 24, 28 and 29. There is a campsite on the edge of San Ignacio on private land, however, where you can either pitch your own or use the owner's tents. A good option if you are on a really tight budget: **Midas Campsite**, © 0923172, @ 02 3845, is on the banks of the River Mopan, along the dirt track that begins at the bus depot. There are also thatched huts by the river, with a nice beach.

Eating Out and Nightlife

Serendib, Burns Avenue serves good curries and creole dishes, worth the slightly higher prices. The restaurant of the **San Ignacio Hotel** is highly recommended, and not as expensive as you might expect. Make sure you try their fruit juices. There are also a few ice-cream parlours and snack shacks, which you will easily find dotted around the centre of town. A welcome addition to the town's eating venues is the **Mystic Moon Country Kitchen** at 5 Mossiah Street, which concentrates on pasta dishes and offers a large choice of fruit juices and milk shakes.

One of the most popular rendezvous in town is **Eva's Restaurant**, run by Bob Jones, an Englishman who decided to stay on after serving here in the British Army. Meals, including breakfast, are simple and filling, and prices are reasonable. Other than Eva's, which closes early, there are three bars/nightclubs.

The Blue Angel, in the centre of town, is always packed at weekends, and is the most popular place. Up on the hill, the **Cahal Pech**, is a large thatched venue, which regularly has live music. This is a good place for dancing as it is open to the night breeze. On Sundays, when things are pretty dead around here, the most lively place is the **Central American Art Centre**, opposite the bus depot. There is nothing noticeably arty here, but there is usually a local band playing.

Jungle Lodges Near San Ignacio

Lodges do not offer transport from San Ignacio. All guests must take a taxi from Ignacio if without their own transport. Guests with advance reservations can be picked up from the international airport, for which they will be charged US $30–100 per person, depending on their numbers. All of these lodges are relatively expensive, and few can be reached by public transport, which makes them great hideaways, but not necessarily convenient without your own vehicle. (If you decide to take a taxi, remember to check the official rate at Eva's Restaurant first.) However, most lodges arrange tours and excursions, though they are rather expensive, to the surrounding countryside and Maya ruins.

luxury

Blancaneaux Lodge, ✆ 092 3878, ✉ 092 3919 was once film-maker Francis Ford Coppola's very own retreat, deep in the heart of the Mountain Pine Ridge. Now it is one of the most luxurious places you can stay in, with prices to match. Everything, from the landscaped gardens to the exquisite guest rooms, exudes designer elegance and the setting is magnificent. Almost all rooms look onto Privassion Creek, its waters tumbling in a series of small waterfalls, and the interior decor is characterised by hand-picked artefacts and weaving from Guatemala and Mexico. Only problem is there is nothing particularly Belizean about this lodge, nor is it in the jungle. Surrounded by the characteristic pine forest of the Mountain Pine Ridge, it could be almost anywhere with similar scenery—California even.

Chaa Creek Cottages, ✆ 0922037, ✉ 0922501, e-mail: chaacreek@btl.net is the luxury jungle lodge that sets the standard for all others. Find it on a rough turnoff along the road to Benque Viejo. The place is simply a dream, where you can indulge yourself close to the forest. By some miraculous quirk there are no bugs here, so no need for screens or nets, but plenty of tropical birds and beautiful flowers. Set on a huge slope descending to the Macal River, the property is mostly forested and offers a great many activities, including swimming, canoeing, bird and nature trails, horse riding and tours throughout the region.

The ambience at the lodge is sophisticated without being elitist, and even travellers on a tight budget can afford to treat themselves to **Chaa Creek's Macal River Camp Site**, a short distance downstream from the hotel area. Spacious tents are permanently fixed on raised platforms, each with an additional roof, and the bathroom facilities are the cleanest and most modern you will ever find at a camp site. (around US$40 per person, including 3 meals cooked for you at the campsite).

A short distance upriver is **DuPlooy's** ✆ 092 3101, ✉ 3301, which is less exclusive, but extremely beautiful, with an intimate, family-run atmosphere. The best feature is the bar, which is on a high platform, with great vistas of the surrounding jungle and river below. Full board is in the luxury category but bed and breakfast is cheaper. Children under 6 years are charged at around 15% the adult fee.

Ek'Tun Hotel ✆ 092 2881, offers just two rooms in traditional thatched cottages, set on a grassy bank above the Macal River beyond DuPlooy's. Much of the forest has been cleared away here, but the setting is still beautiful and the narrowing valley offers a wealth of spectacular hiking trails.

Hidden Valley Inn, ✆ 08 23320, ✉ 08 23334, is set in 18,000 acres of private land in the Mountain Pine Ridge area, and offers twelve cottages with their own fire-places, great meals and plenty of exploring. This really is the ideal base for hiking, with well-maintained trails to many of the famous waterfalls, including 1000-foot Falls.

expensive

Nabitunich, ✆ 093 2096, ✉ 093 3096 is halfway between San Ignacio and the Maya ruins of Xunantunich. In fact, on a clear day you can see the tip of the main pyramid rising above the jungle. This is one of the easiest lodges to reach by public transport, close to the Mopan river, just off the main road to Benque Viejo. Excellent value for money, even though 18% tax is added.

Windy Hill Cottages, ✆ 092 2017, ✉ 092 3080 on the main road to Benque Viejo, about 2 kms outside town, has the advantage of a pool and easy access, but is neither near the river nor in the forest. 15% tax added.

In complete contrast, **Black Rock Jungle River Lodge**, ✆ 092 2341, ✉ 092 3449, is one of the best places to stay if you really want to get away from it all. Situated in a remote gorge, the lodge is perched on a promontory high above the Macal river, with spectacular views from its restaurant terrace. The atmosphere is friendly, the rooms are in individual cottages with private bath (cheaper rooms available without private bathrooms, at US$42 for a double). A superb place to relax, but also ideal for hiking, horseback riding, swimming in the river, or tubing.

Maya Mountain Lodge, ✆ 092 2164, ✉ 092 2029, e-mail: maya_mt@btl.net, is an ideal jungle lodge for families, with plenty of activities for everyone, including story-telling, hiking, horseback riding and canoeing. Situated on the Cristo Rey road leading to the Mountain Pine Ridge, the lodge is near San Ignacio (2 km), yet the tropical gardens and surrounding forest give you a strong sense of being close to nature. Rooms are in individual stone and thatch cottages, all with private bathroom, and meals are delicious. The owners, Bart and Suzi Mickler, are dedicated educationalists, and know a great deal about the region's natural history and local cultures, both historic and modern. A reference library is also available for guests.

Mountain Equestrian Trails, ✆ 092 3310, ✉ 082 3235 specialises in horseback riding holidays and is especially happy to cater to children. Located on the Chiquibul Road leading into the Mountain Pine Ridge, the lodge is very close to the forest reserve and offers a wealth of hiking and riding trails to keep you busy. Rooms are in thatched cabañas, or you could stay at their tented camp, where each tent is set on a wooden platform.

If you would rather stay in the Mountain Pine Ridge itself, one of the best value accommodations is the **Five Sisters Lodge**, ✆ & ✉ 091 2005, on Privassion Creek beyond Blancaneaux Lodge, which takes its name from the Five Sisters waterfalls. Six thatch-roof cabañas are perched dramatically above five waterfalls, cascading 300 feet to join into one great pool, wonderful for swimming.

Alternatively, you could stay at the **Pine Ridge Lodge**, ✆ 092 3310, ✉ 092 2267, which is the first place you see after the Main Entrance Gate of the forest reserve. Rooms are set in eight tiled stone cottages, and delicious meals are served in the hotel's central restaurant building. Plenty of trails lead off into the forest, and you can also join tours to many of the sights around the reserve.

moderate

A popular lodge, close to the ruins of Xunantunich, is **Rancho Los Amigos**, ✆ 093 2483, which is well-known for its vegetarian meals. To get there take any bus heading for Benque Viejo, and get off at the village of San José Succotz. Excellent value and not too far from San Ignacio, the **Parrot Nest**, ✆ 092 3702, offers four thatched cabins, above the Mopan River bank, set in a beautiful tropical garden.

To Guatemala

The last town before the Guatemalan border is **Benque Viejo**. There is nothing to see here, and if coming from Guatemala, you should try to make it as far as San Ignacio. The only place remotely worth visiting is the local art centre, where you can buy hand-painted T-shirts. If you do get stuck in Benque Viejo, the best place to stay is **Maxim's Palace Hotel**, 41 Church Hill Street, ✆ 093 2360, ✉ 093 2259. Buses connect Benque Viejo with San Ignacio regularly, but you can always find a taxi too.

If heading for Guatemala, your best bet is to catch a bus that leaves San Ignacio and goes all the way to the border, a few kilometres beyond Benque Viejo.

The border is open from 6am–8pm. If travelling by public transport, you will need to be on the Guatemalan side of the border in time for either of the morning buses to Flores, either at 9 or 10am. Sometimes there is also a bus around midday, but do not count on it. The journey to Flores takes around three hours along an unpaved road. If you miss the buses from Melchor de Menchos, which always stop at the border post for passengers, you can also travel by one of the waiting minivans, which depart whenever they are full. Finally, an expensive alternative is to travel on one of the private tourist buses that regularly ply this route. These are obviously faster and more comfortable than the Guatemalan 'chickenbuses'. Before you discount local transport, however, consider two things: the private buses are much more expensive (at least US$30 per person, compared to around US$2), and local bandits are notorious for picking on the tourist buses along this route.

The South: Stann Creek and Toledo

Dangriga	151
Placencia	159
Around Placencia	163
Punta Gorda	164
Around Punta Gorda	170

If western Belize is interesting for its tropical landscape and wildlife, then southern Belize is interesting for its diversity of people and cultures. As you head south on the Hummingbird Highway, you cross over the furthest outcrops of the western highlands before heading out into the open plains. Here you are surrounded by huge citrus plantations and row upon row of orange trees that stretch into the far distance.

The first town on the coastal plain is Dangriga, 'capital' of the Garifuna people and the country's second largest town. Descendants of African slaves and Carib Indians, the Garifuna are part of the same group that inhabit many settlements along the Gulf of Honduras, in Belize, Guatemala, Honduras and Nicaragua. To the outsider they look indistinguishable from other Belizeans. Their culture and original language, however, are quite different and in the small fishing villages further south, the people are as likely to use a traditional healer as a modern doctor.

Beyond Dangriga, the pace of life really slows down. From here onwards the traveller follows a route between the contours of the western Maya Mountains and the coast. Almost no one lives beside the Southern Highway and so there is a tantalizing sense of emptiness. Sometimes you wonder if there are any people here at all. Yet the intensely farmed countryside tells you villages cannot be far, and small tracks lead off towards the jungle-covered mountains or the sea, inviting you to break your journey and follow your curiosity. Independent transport is essential if you want to make these kind of detours, since no public buses leave the highway. If you can overcome this inconvenience, you will find few tourists and a pleasing sense of discovery as you explore rarely visited places.

You will find the most beautiful mainland beaches on the thin peninsula that culminates in the lovely village of Placencia, which is rapidly becoming a popular holiday resort. Here you can walk for ages and ages along white sand lapped gently by the sea, and the chances are you will meet nobody along the way. Shrubs and the occasional cluster of palm trees line the shore, and there are plenty of places to play out your Robinson Crusoe fantasies.

In the country's remote Toledo District, Mopan and Kekchi Mayas live in traditional villages embraced by the thick forests near the

Guatemalan border. Their homes are made to the ancient designs of their forebears: square or oblong wood constructions, sometimes raised slightly off the ground, and covered by a thatched roof made of palm leaves.

The strong Maya heritage of the region can also be seen at three small but interesting sites: Lubaantun, Nim Li Punit and Uxbenka. Out on the coast, the small town of Punta Gorda is the main centre of population, where Garifuna mix with Creoles, while surrounding areas are settled by East Indians, descendants of American Confederates, German Mennonites, and other foreigners. In fact, walking down the street in Punta Gorda, you are quite as likely to meet a Rastafarian as a dungaree-clad Mennonite, an East Indian worker or a Kekchi Indian farmer.

Although the south has this varied cultural mix, it is sparsely populated and substantial areas are still untouched by human hand. This is especially true of the Maya Mountains which trace the border with Guatemala and, with a bit of initiative, you can find yourself deep in the ancient forests that cover the region. An ideal introduction to this kind of environment is in the Cockscomb Range, where you will find the world's only jaguar reserve and one of the country's highest mountains, Victoria Peak. Solitary mahogany and ceiba trees tower above the jungle canopy, while marked trails take you through the hidden world below.

Hummingbird or Manatee: the Roads to Dangriga

By paved road, the 168km journey from Belize City to Dangriga takes three hours, first heading west to Belmopan, and then southeast on the Hummingbird Highway a route as beautiful as its name implies. Beyond the capital, you enter a thickly forested region rich in natural wonders, the first of which is **St Herman's Cave** (small fee), near Caves Branch. Unfortunately, the trail leading to the cave is notorious for robberies and worse, so you should never go alone, and ideally always go with a guide.

The best place to make enquiries is at the visitor's centre or Ian Anderson's **Cave Branch Jungle River Camp**, ✆ & ✉ 08 22800, clearly sign-posted from the road. Alternatively, you can also visit on a tour from San Ignacio (*see* pp.127–30). A short drive further along the road is **The Blue Hole National Park** (*open daily, 8–4; adm*), where you can swim either in the Siburn river or the Blue Hole itself, a karst sinkhole filled with water from the river, to form a perfect swimming pool.

Continuing along the highway, you travel through magnificently fertile countryside, where lush forests eventually give way to large citrus plantations. Before you reach them, however, a good place to stop over is the **Over the Top** restaurant and bar, where you can eat the 'best food on the highway'. (All buses will stop here if you ask the driver).

St. Margaret's village is the best place to find transport to and information about the **Five Blues Lake National Park**, located just over six kilometres east of the main road. Named for the changing shades of the local lake, the park is very much in the initial stages of development and is rarely visited. If you have time, though, a visit is worthwhile, because you will almost certainly have the nature trails, bathing spots and for-hire canoes to yourself. The lake is surrounded by forest, wildlife is abundant, and there are also many caves in the vicinity.

Once past Over the Top, the Hummingbird Highway descends into the Stann Creek valley and huge citrus farms, where line after line of orange trees head endlessly into the distance. The basis for one of the country's most successful export industries, the road is frequently lined by the shacks of plantation workers, many of them immigrants from El Salvador, Honduras and Guatemala, grateful to work for a pittance in return for a peaceful life.

Where to Stay

Even though the local attractions are so far neglected by most visitors, there are a number of places to stay. Top of the list is undoubtedly, **Tamandua**, ✆ 08 23182, ✉ 08 22458, which is an integrated fruit farm and wildlife sanctuary close to the National Park, where you can wander in the jungle to your heart's content and recover in refreshing plunge pools outside your cabin. **Palacio's Mountain Retreat** is directly on the highway and offers simple cabañas and traditional cooking, or you could try your luck with the **village bed & breakfast initiative**.

To find out more, stop off at Over the Top or try ✆ 08 12005. If you succeed in finding a room with a local creole family, expect humble conditions, which are more than offset by the warm welcome.

The Old Coastal Highway

If you could head straight along the coast, the distance from Belize City to seaside Dangriga would only be around 58km. In fact, if you have the time, you might consider hiring a boat, which could take you along the Burdon Canal and through several lagoons before cruising out to sea and into Dangriga harbour. More straight-

completely, the British punishment was harsh: deportation to the Honduran island of Roatán, where many starved or died of disease. This deportation was also tactical, since the British hoped the Garifuna would repel any Spanish claims to Roatán. But the Garifuna handed the island to the Spanish forces based on the Honduran mainland, in return for their freedom and being shipped to the mainland, where they thrived once more as free labourers and fishermen. The first settlement was in Trujillo, but small groups of Garifuna soon dispersed along the entire Bay of Honduras, many becoming expert smugglers on the Belize coast, where they traded contraband with the British. They also found work in the burgeoning logging trade and, in the early 19th and 20th century, in the banana plantations. But primarily they were fishermen and sailors, and even today many Garifuna men work in sea-related trades. Their traditional homes are always by the sea, hence the coastal settlements of today, although large numbers of Belizean Garifuna have emigrated to the United States, where an estimated 25,000 live in New York and Los Angeles. 80% of all Garifuna live in Honduras.

Getting to and from Dangriga

If at all possible, it is highly recommended that you have your own transport for southern Belize, since there are few buses, and journeys are arduous because of the unpaved roads. (Car rental is available in Punta Gorda.) There is almost no public transport to the coastal villages or inland regions, and you will find it very difficult to visit any of the Maya ruins or other interesting places. You could always try hitchhiking, but there are very few vehicles on the country roads, and a better, if more expensive, option would be to go on one of the organized tours that leave from Dangriga, Placencia or Punta Gorda.

by air

Since the bus journey is only 3 hours long it hardly seems worth flying. However, there are daily flights from Belize City to Dangriga, which is a stopover on the way to Placencia and Punta Gorda. If you wish to book flight tickets from Dangriga, you can do it at the **Pelican Beach Resort hotel** or at **Treasured Trave**l, Commerce St, ✆ 05 22578, ℻ 05 23481.

by sea

Coming from Belize City, you could hire someone to take you south, which will be expensive but a novel way to travel. Get advice from the tourist office before striking a deal with the local boatmen, and remember never to pay the full fee before the journey is completed.

by bus

There are regular daily buses run by Z-Line, between Belize City and Dangriga (3 hrs), at least two of which travel via the old coastal route and the lagoons. Coming from San Ignacio, you need to change buses in Belmopan, where all buses from Belize City pass by. Coming from the south, there are direct buses from Punta Gorda, also run by Z-Line. (From Dangriga buses leave for Punta Gorda daily at noon, 4 and 7pm). The ticket office is on the main entrance road to town, where the new terminal is, and if you want to be sure of getting on the bus, you should buy your ticket in advance.

There is also a direct bus connecting Placencia with Dangriga. The Promised Land buses leave Dangriga daily at 12.30pm, travelling via Hopkins village and Sittee River (returning from Placencia at 6am).The journey can take up to 3 hrs. Z-Line buses also follow this route, departing Dangriga daily at 11 am for Placencia via Hopkins village, and at at 1 pm for Placencia direct.

A new service is offered by Ritchies Bus Service, which travels between Belize City and Dangriga, via the coastal highway. Departs Mon–Sat from Pound Yard Bridge in Belize City at 2.15pm and 4.30pm (the first continues all the way to Placencia); departs Dangriga at 5.15am and 8.30am. Sundays only the 2.15pm goes from the city, and the 8.30am from Dangriga. They also run buses between Dangriga and Placencia, Mon–Sat, departing at 11.30am and 4.30pm, via Hopkins and Sittee River villages. Returning from Placencia at 5.15am and 6am.

Tourist Information

There is no official tourist information in Dangriga, but you can get lots of information on tours and transport to the nearby islands of Tobacco Caye and South Water Caye (*see* p.120) at the New River Café, right in the middle of town. If you are looking for some professional diving instruction or tours, the best person to speak to is Tony Read, who runs **The Living Reef Dive Centre** on South Water Caye, ✆ 05 22214.

Travel information is best gathered at the bus terminal, at the entrance to town.There is a Barclays Bank (*open Mon–Fri, 8–1*) and Novia Scotia Bank (*open Mon–Thurs 8–1; Fridays 8–4.30*) on Commerce Street, which is north of the river.

The **post office** is at Caney Street, south of the river, around the corner from the Bonefish Hotel (*open Mon–Thurs, 8–noon and 1–4.30; Fri, 8–noon and 1–4*).

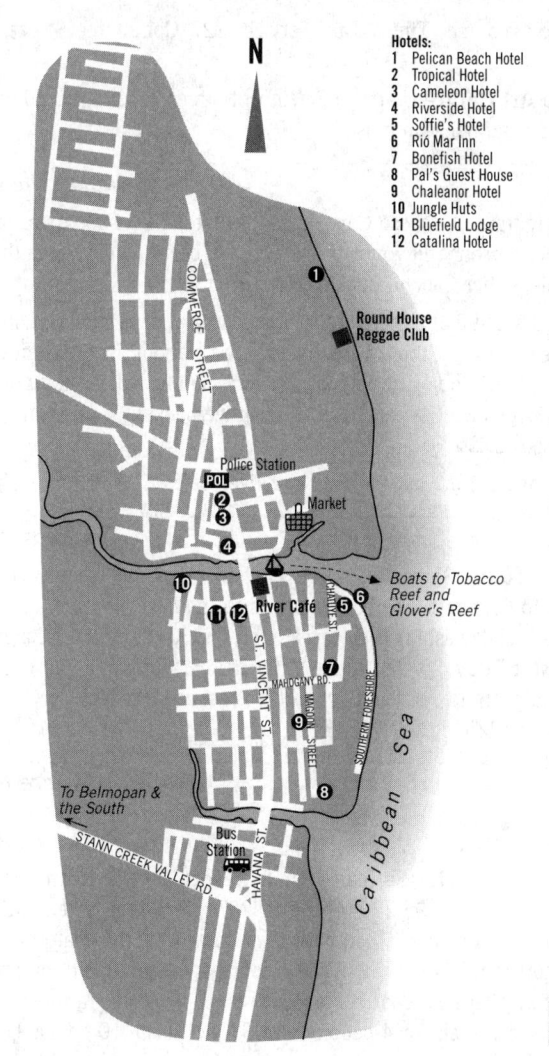

Hotels:
1. Pelican Beach Hotel
2. Tropical Hotel
3. Cameleon Hotel
4. Riverside Hotel
5. Soffie's Hotel
6. Rió Mar Inn
7. Bonefish Hotel
8. Pal's Guest House
9. Chaleanor Hotel
10. Jungle Huts
11. Bluefield Lodge
12. Catalina Hotel

Dangriga

Across the street from the post office is **Sharlis Copy & Computer Services**, Sharp St #1, ✆ & ✉ 05 23324 or 22346, where you should be able to send both faxes and e-mails. The building also houses **Val's Laundry**, which charges around BZ$9 for washing and drying one load.

For a **taxi**, contact Tino's Taxi Service, 127 Commerce Street, ✆ 05 22438.

Dangriga **Art Centre** is at 174 St Vincent Street, recommended for local handicrafts and Belizean music.

Boats to the Cayes

A one-way trip to Tobacco Caye or South Water Caye should cost around BZ$30 per person, and you can contact two reliable captains via the New River Café, either Captain Buck or Norlan Lamb.

On Saturdays, at 8 am, there is also a regular boat departure for Long Caye on Glover's Reef, for those with advance reservations for the campsite run by International Zoological Expeditions (*see* p.119). Note that if not travelling to Glover's Reef as part of an all-inclusive booking, a one-way trip will set you back BZ$600.

All boats depart from outside the New River Café.

Tour Agents

Rosado's Tours, 35 Lemon Street, ✆ 05 22119, is the place to go for car and van tours, as well as boat charters to the cayes for snorkelling and fishing. An all-day fishing trip costs around US$50 per person for a group of four. **Lester Eiley**, 25 Oak Street, ✆ 05 22113, works as a tour guide, and offers boat charters. For flight tickets try **Treasured Travel**, on Commerce Street, ✆ 05 22578, ✉ 05 23481.

Where to Stay

expensive

The Pelican Beach Resort, P.O. Box 14, Dangriga, ✆ 05 22044, ✉ 05 22570, is the top hotel, but there's not much competition. Located on the seafront, on the northern edge of town, the colonial-style house is clean and very quiet. They offer boat charters for up to 8 people costing around US$145 per day; van rentals for 4 people are US$150, for 5–10 people US$170. The hotel also rents out holiday cottages on Southwater Caye. At the lower end of this price category, the **Bonefish Hotel**, 15 Mahogany Road, ✆ 05 22165, ✉ 05 22296, is a friendly, small hotel with excellent meals in the restaurant. All rooms have private bathrooms and televisions. Tours can also be arranged.

moderate

The best place to stay in this category is easily the **Chaleanor Hotel**, 35 Magoon St, ✆ 05 22587, @ 05 23038, which offers clean, modern rooms with private bath, and a roof top terrace with the best views in town. The owners are also extremely helpful, and can advise on all aspects of travel in the region. A little out of the way, but very pleasant, are **Jungle Huts**, Ecumenical Drive, ✆ 05 22142, @ 05 23038, which are best reached by following the river inland from the central bridge, on the south side, or taking a taxi. Spacious polished wood cabañas await, each with private bath and fan. **Soffie's Hotel**, 970 Chatuye Street, ✆ 05 22789, is a friendly and clean place, with meals available, just south of the river mouth, in the centre of town. Soffie's is particularly recommended for single women travellers. Facing the sea, across the road, is the **Rio Mar Inn**, 977 Southern Foreshore, ✆ 05 22201, also with restaurant.

cheap

The best in this category is **Bluefield Lodge**, 6 Bluefield Rd, ✆ 05 22742. Clean, friendly and central, rooms either share a bathroom or have their own, all with fan. If you prefer to be near the sea, your best option is **Pal's Guest House**, 868 'A' Magoon St, ✆ 05 22095. The **Riverside Hotel**, 135 Commerce Street, ✆ 05 22168, on the northside of the river, does not have very nice rooms, but compensates with a cool and spacious guest lounge. Finally, very simple rooms at rock bottom prices can be found at the **Catalina Hotel**, 37 Cedar St, ✆ 05 22390.

Eating Out

The best and most expensive meals in town are to be had at the **Pelican Beach Resort**, a 10-minute walk from the town centre. In 'downtown' Dangriga, the **Riverside Café** has established itself as a favourite meeting place for travellers, although the food is unremarkable. Further along the street, at **Soffie's**, you can eat good traditional meals, and **Pola's Kitchen**, on St Vincent Street, specialises in local Garifuna dishes. Filling meals are also offered by **Burger King**, on Commercial Street, whose name has nothing to do with the better-known restaurant chain. They may do burgers'n'fries but they also do wholesome Belizean favourites such as rice'n' beans.

Entertainment and Nightlife

The entertainment options are rather limited, apart from getting wrecked in the local pool bars —take a walk along St Vincent and Commercial

Streets, and you will easily find these places. At weekends, you could check out The **Round House**, situated on the beach near the **Pelican Beach Resort**, which often has live bands playing punta rock and the latest reggae favourites. But remember to take a taxi to be on the safe side.

Around Dangriga: Out to Sea and South along the Coast

Dangriga is an excellent base from which to visit **Tobacco Caye** and **South Water Caye**, which are the few places on the reef that are easily accessible, yet off the beaten track. (For detailed information about facilities and accommodation on the islands *see* p. 120). The first place of interest south of Dangriga is the coastal village of **Hopkins**, founded in 1937, by the surviving women and children of Garifuna men massacred by the authorities in Honduras, because they were suspected of supporting the Liberals.

The country's newest Garifuna settlement, it is also ironically the one where ancient traditions, including the language, are most vibrant, and you have anexcellent opportunity to learn more from the women's co-operative, which runs **Sandy Beach Lodge**, ✆ 05 22033.

A branch road (7km) connects the Southern Highway with the village, where you will find a jumble of traditional pole and thatch homes, wooden houses and modern concrete ones, all spread along a magnificent white sandy beach, lined with coconut palms.

The village itself is not especially picturesque, but the beach and the interesting local heritage easily make up for that, which is why Hopkins is slowly but surely becoming popular with tourists. A sure sign of this is the increased range of places to stay.

Where to Stay

Where once the only choice was Sandy Beach Lodge, you now find a variety of places, from the expensive **Jaguar Reef Lodge**, ✆ & ✉ 02 12041, on its own beach just south of the village, to several budget options, of which **Ransoms Beachside Garden**, ✆ 05 22889, ✉ 05 22038, is the best. In the moderate price category, your best bet is **Hopkins Inn**, ✆ 05 37013, which offers stone cabañas, right on the beach, and can also arrange tours inland and out to sea. A good place to eat and drink is **Swinging Armadillos Hammock Lounge**, at the northern end of the village, where you can also learn about tours around the region. If you want something more indulgent, try the 'gourmet' restaurant at the Jaguar Reef Lodge. The lodge also has its own dive shop, and offers sea and land tours.If you continue along the bumpy beach road south, you eventually reach Sittee River village, at the mouth of the river, which is an extremely verdant and quiet place. Not much happens here, and the only visitors to get off the bus are normally those heading for Glover's Reef. Yet the village is an excellent base from which to explore upriver as well. A good place to stay if you want to do a bit of quiet animal spotting or fishing are the moderately priced **Sittee River Lodge**, ✆ 05 22006, or **Toucan Sittee** (no phone). All buses from Dangriga or Placencia that stop in Hopkins also stop at Sittee River.

Placencia

Placencia is the kind of place you come to see for a few days and end up staying a few months. This is the real thing: white sandy beaches, palm trees fringing the shoreline, and creaky wooden houses on stilts, hiding in the shade. The village is small and the people say 'hello' to each other when passing. Great mounds of conch shells pile up by the village path, their pinkness gleaming in the sun. In fact, there is such an abundance of these lovely shells that they are just tossed away or used for building fill.

San Pedro, on Ambergris Caye, was probably once like this, and the people of Placencia village are aware of how much they have to lose. Already there are more foreign-owned businesses than local ones, but the pace is still very relaxed. Originally a fishing village, many inhabitants still make a good living this way, and are loathe to sell themselves or their land to tourism. One can only hope that they can maintain their stance. You will not, therefore, find a resort with people, eager to fulfil your every wish but you will find a beautiful place, genuine locals, and accommodation ranging from luxurious hideaways to simple rooms.

Getting to Placencia

by air

You can now fly direct to Placencia, coming from the north or south of Belize. The airstrip is very close to the village, so you can either walk or take a taxi, if it is too hot. There is really no reason to fly to mainland Mango Creek, but if you do, there should be boatmen at the airstrip to take you to Placencia. Alternatively phone the post office in Placencia, ✆ 06 2946, and a boat will come and collect you. The fare should not be more than BZ$40 (US$20). If you have booked accommodation in advance, your hotel will send someone to pick you up.

by bus

From Belize City, you need to take a bus to Dangriga, and change there for a direct bus to Placencia (75km), which leaves daily at 11am (via Hopkins) and 1pm (direct). Coming from northern or western Belize, you can change buses for Dangriga in Belmopan. The bus departs from Placencia at 6 am, on the same days. Coming from Punta Gorda, in the south, you can take any bus heading north, and get off at Mango Creek. Here you should walk to the waterside, and ask around for a boatman to take you to Placencia. The journey takes about 25 minutes, and you should not have to pay more than BZ$40 (US$20), whether there is one passenger or three.

Tourist Information

There is no official tourist office, but then there are few things you will need to know. The handful of resort hotels offer their guests every kind of land or sea tour, while other visitors will always find a group to join if they make themselves known to the local tour operators advertising in and around the village.

The nearest **bank** is in Mango Creek, (*open Friday mornings, 9–noon*). However most hotels and shops in Placencia should change traveller's cheques or cash.

Flight tickets can be booked at **Sonny's Restaurant**, who can arrange transportation to the airstrip as well. Mango Creek also has the nearest immigration office at the police station, where you can get extensions for your visitor's permit, or an exit stamp.

If you're self-catering, the **market store** is at the entrance to the village, on the dirt road, and the only place to buy groceries.

For additional information try the **Orange Peel Shop**, ✆ 06 23184.

For photographic needs, visit Wade Bevier at **Rum Point Inn**, who also runs photographic tours.

Sports and Activities

For diving and snorkelling trips, see the **Placencia Dive Shop**, ✆ 062 3313, ℻ 062 3226 (*open daily 7.30–noon and 3–6*). A full PADI Certification course costs US$350, snorkel trips (including gear, lunch box and water) cost US$40 per person. Always shop around, though, because there are plenty of others offering the same trips.

Sailing charters start at US $40 per person, for a group of four. You can also arrange fishing trips from here, and the following can help you, specializing in fly and sport fishing: **Blue Runner Guiding** (Julian Cabral, ✆ 06 23130); **Kingfisher Sports** (Charles Leslie, ✆ 06 23175, ℻ 06 23204); **Westby Sportsfishing** (Joel & David Westby, ✆ 06 23234).

Where to Stay

With the increasing popularity of the village, more and more places are opening up all the time. Most are within easy walking distance of the village, so if you find something you like better, it's easy to pack up and move.

Up-market Beach Hotels

As in San Pedro on Ambergris Caye, accommodation prices outstrip the usual categories used in the guide, especially at the top end of the market. Prices have therefore been listed as a general guideline.

Furthest away from the village (30 mins walk) is **Rum Point Inn**, ✆ 06 23239, ℻ 06 23240. It is also the most expensive. There are five concrete cabañas that look like they have just landed from outer space, while the main house is a more traditional wooden structure, with a good bar and library. Singles are US$140, doubles US$165, plus US$50 for an extra person, all meals included.

A short walk further south (15 mins walk from the village) is **Kitty's Place**, P.O. Box 528, Belize City, ✆ 06 23227, ℻ 06 23226, which is a delightful small hotel, with a choice of rooms, either in the main house, in beach cabañas, or two-room apartments. The bar and restaurant are a great place to socialise, and there is a good library too. They also have their own dive Shop with a diving instructor, and bicycle rental. (Diving certification courses cost around US$325.) The cheapest rooms are around US$25 singles, US$35 doubles, sharing the bathroom; while the two-person apartment is around US$75. 15% tax is added to bills.

The Turtle Inn, ✆ 06 22069, @ 06 23202, is a beautiful spot, with six thatched cottages looking out to sea. Total capacity is twenty people, so this is the place if you want peace and quiet; and personal service from the friendly proprietors is assured. Meals are served family style at one table. There is a bar and lending library. Prices include all meals: singles US$72, doubles US$123, plus US$35 for an extra person. A fully equipped beach house for two people is US$400 per week.

Not convenient without your own transport, but a decent choice otherwise, is the **Serenity Resort**, ✆ 06 23232, @ 06 23231, located on the peninsula road leading to Placencia.

Seine Bight

Seine Bight is rapidly challenging Placencia as the prime tourist destination on the peninsula, so there are quite a few guest houses springing up here. Offering free mopeds, the **Nautical Inn**, ✆ & @ 06 22310 is one of the most beautiful lodges on the beach. The best place to stay in the village is the expensive **Hotel Seine Bight**, ✆ 06 22491, which also has a popular restaurant. If that is full, you could try the **French Quarter Belize**, ✆ & @ 06 22472. A popular, gregarious place is the **Kulsha Shack Inn**, ✆ 06 22015, where you can eat, drink and occasionally enjoy some vibrant Garifuna drumming and dancing.

In Placencia Village

expensive

Beautiful beach cabañas are for rent for around US$54 per person, per day, the best being those at the far end of the beach, around the corner from the dock, owned by Janice Romero Leslie. Contact **Trade Winds Hotel**, ✆ 06 23122, @ 06 23201). **Sonny's Resort**, ✆ 06 23103, in the middle of the village, has a mediocre restaurant and unhelpful staff. Far better stay at the small **Westwind Hotel**, ✆ & @ 06 23255, located on the beach nearby.

moderate

A decent hotel is **Julia's Budget Hotel**, ✆ 06 23185, which has pleasant wooden rooms, raised slightly off the beach. Next to the best bar, at the southern end of the village, is the **Paradise Vacation Hotel**, ✆ and @ 06 23179, which is plain with an inviting atmosphere. Alternatively, try the **Traveller's Inn**, ✆ 06 23190, in the centre of the village.

If you want to stay long-term, you can rent fully furnished houses (daily, monthly and yearly) from **Ted's Rentals**, ✆ 06 23172.

cheap

Ran's Travel Lodge, ✆ 06 22027, is a good budget choice. There are also plenty of families renting out rooms, and one of the best is **Conrad and Lydia's Rooms**, ✆ & ✉ 06 23117. Conrad can also take you on boat trips. Rooms are basic but clean with a shared bathroom.

Eating Out

The best restaurant in the village is the **Kingfisher** (*open 6–midnight only*), right on the beach, which offers tasty seafood at reasonable prices. **The Tentacles Bar/Restaurant** is good but pricey, more popular for drinking than eating. **The Stone Crab** is also excellent and good value for money, while **Sonny's** is not. Home cooking is offered by **Jaimie's** and **BJ.'s**, as well as **Brenda's** (on the way to Tentacles) and **Omar's Diner**, in the middle of the village. An increasingly popular restaurant is also **The Galley**, right beside the football pitch.

Entertainment and Nightlife

While all the restaurants in the village double up as drinking spots, some of the nicest places to drink are the beachside bars of the hotels outside the village. The **Turtle Inn** bar is recommended, and **Kitty's Place** is always full. The main disco is the **Cozy Corner Disco**, which is right on the beach, in the village, blasting reggae music out to sea. Try also **Mike's Caribbean Club**, next to the dock.

Around Placencia

Cockscomb Basin Jaguar Reserve

An interesting inland excursion is to visit the **Cockscomb Basin Jaguar Reserve**. It can be reached by a one-hour bus journey from Placencia, to the village of Maya Centre, on the way to Dangriga. Unfortunately there is still no transport provided into the reserve so you have a hot 8-km walk ahead of you, which takes 2 hours (remember that you have to be back at Maya Centre by 3, if you want to catch the bus back to Placencia). Tours to the reserve are also offered, which is an expensive option, but perhaps more convenient.

The Cockscomb Basin is one of the most dramatic natural locations you can visit in Belize. Bordered on three sides by high mountains, the basin is in a remote world of its own, where a great many of the country's animal and plant species thrive in good numbers. All five of the famous felines inhabit the Reserve, even the rare puma, although you are unlikely to see any of them on a short visit. If you stay overnight, you might hear the occasional roar, but it is more likely to come from the recently reintroduced troops of howler monkeys. Yet a visit is extremely worthwhile for the chance to walk on well-maintained paths through beautiful primary and secondary rainforest, thick with dramatic vines and giant ferns, exotic epiphytes, including orchids, and a myriad of tropical trees. These precious woods once brought loggers to the area. Of course they had a much harder time of it than modern visitors, and the map testifies to their feelings with names like 'Go-to-Hell Camp' and '*Sale si puedes*' (leave if you can). Bring your swimming gear, and you can take a wonderful cooling dip in one of the rivers.

Covering an area of 100,000 acres, the reserve is a haven not only for mammals, including Baird's Tapir, anteaters and armadillos, but also almost 300 bird species, of which the endangered scarlet macaw is the most colourful. But you might also spot the Great Curassow, Keel-billed Toucan or King Vulture, and dozens of smaller birds. The permanent exhibition at the visitor's centre will give you a good introduction to all these and more, and if you contact the Audubon Society in advance, you can also arrange to stay at the campsite or cabins here. There are no provisions available, so you should bring all your own food and drink. If you plan to hike as far as Victoria Peak (1120 m), you must obtain a permit before arrival from the Audubon Society. Remember also that you will need a good map for this tough hike, and it is strongly recommended to hire a local Maya guide from the village of Maya Centre, at the entrance road to the reserve.

Punta Gorda

Punta Gorda, or P.G., as it is generally known, is a quiet little town at the end of the Southern Highway, with just over 3000 inhabitants. A handful of roads, lined by dilapidated buildings, give the place a pleasant atmosphere of a forgotten film set, and nothing happens very quickly here. Most days the heat is freshened by a sea breeze, but to be in a room without a fan is almost unbearable. Being so far from the rest of Belize, P.G. never gets many visitors, and those that do pass this way are usually on their way somewhere else, only stepping off the ferry from Guatemala and onto a bus heading north. It is nevertheless a useful base from which to see interesting destinations inland, most of them relating to the Maya heritage, past and present.

In an effort to vitalize the tourist trade, and more importantly, help the Maya (and Garifuna) population share in the profits, a highly innovative programme has been developed, which should be fully operational by the time you read this. The **Toledo Eco-Tourism Association** has helped 13 villages in the region, one of which is Garifuna, to build guest houses, so that tourists can get the best out of visiting their traditional communities. The idea is that visitors sleep in the village guest house, but eat each meal with a different family, thus getting an excellent opportunity to meet the local inhabitants and learn about their culture. Local guides are provided to take a maximum of four people at a time along trails in the surrounding jungle. Profits go into a central fund, helping to improve the living standards and opportunities of the communities. To find out more, contact Chet Schmidt at **Nature's Way Guest House**, 65 Front Street, ✆ 07 2119. Transport to these remote villages is somewhat difficult without your own vehicle, so you might want to hire one from Alistair King, at the Texaco petrol station (about BZ$200, including petrol, for overnight hire). Otherwise the best day to arrive in P.G. is Tuesday or Friday, which gives you time to sort things out at Nature's Way Guest House in time for catching the buses which run on Saturdays and Wednesdays, to take villagers to market. Each village guest house sleeps eight people in single bunks fitted with mosquito nets, and basic facilities include drop toilet and washing out of a bucket. The cost is US$42 per person, which includes registration, three meals a day, and two tours.

In the meantime, there is also a private project being run by Alfredo Villoria, called the **Indigenous Experience**. On payment of a registration fee he will put you in touch with a host family. You can contact him at his information booth at the town dock, daily except Thursday and Sunday, 8–noon. It is an unfortunate aspect of increased tourism opportunities that two competing operations are under way. This threatens to split local communities since they cannot belong to both. The idea behind this programme is to bring foreigners and Maya together, but the project is potentially damaging. The Indian households who have been chosen as suitable hosts are paid directly by the guests, thus giving them a lucrative income over others in the village, which will undoubtedly lead to bitter friction and undermine traditional communal systems. Not only that, but chosen families do not necessarily have the resources to host foreigners, whose expectations of bathroom facilities may not match the hole in the ground they are bound to find. Nor does a family always have space for an extra person, resulting in a member of the family having to give up their sleeping place for the guest. This is wrong, and potentially embarrassing for the visitor, who would not wish to impose to such an extent.

Whichever programme you choose to use, the experience of staying in a Mopan or Kekchi Maya village is a memorable one. An unusual aspect of meeting these people is that they speak English and if you have just arrived from Guatemala, you will find it very odd to hear soft, Belizean creole coming from an Indian mouth. In fact, a 'traditional' Maya community in Belize is very different from its Guatemalan equivalent. Here, many of the communities developed from refugees fleeing from persecution or slavery in Guatemala, and although they have maintained their traditional architecture and cooking, their language and dress have often been lost. Only in recent years has there been any effort to regain old traditions. The children go to English-speaking schools, and many never learn their Maya language. Equally, the famous Maya weaving and embroidery is not to be found here. Instead, the most rewarding thing about visiting these villages is meeting modern, Belizean Mayas, who have a unique knowledge of the surrounding forest flora and fauna, which they are happy to share.

Getting to and from Punta Gorda

by air

There are several daily flights from Belize City, which stop at all main towns along the southern coast. A one-way ticket costs around US$65. Tropic Air flies from P.G. to Belize City, Mon-Sat, 7, 9.30, noon and 2.30pm. Sun at 7am. Maya Airways flies out daily, at 9.55am and 3.35pm. You can also fly to and from Puerto Barrios in Guatemala with Maya Airways, which costs around US$70 one-way for a minimum of 3 passengers. The **airport** is right in the town, so everything is within a short walking distance. **Pennel & Son**, 50 Main Street, ✆ 07 22014, is an agent for Tropic Air and Maya Airways.

by road

Since Punta Gorda is the end of the line for the Southern Highway, you cannot miss it. It is 171km from Dangriga, a hot and dusty journey along unpaved roads which takes 6 hours.

Coming from Belize, you can travel by comfortable Pullman **bus** with the James Bus Line, and their ticket office in P.G. is the small hut opposite the police station. Travelling from P.G. north, James buses leave at 4.30am on Mondays and Saturdays, and 11 am on Tuesdays and Fridays; 6am on Sundays. The Z-Line company also runs buses, which leave P.G. daily at 5am, 9 & noon. On Fridays there is an additional bus at 3.30pm. The bus terminal is located opposite the army barracks in the southern part of town, on West Street. Local buses leave from the municipal park, at the junction of Main Street and Queen Street. **Cars** can be rented from the Texaco service station, ✆ 07 2126.

Punta Gorda

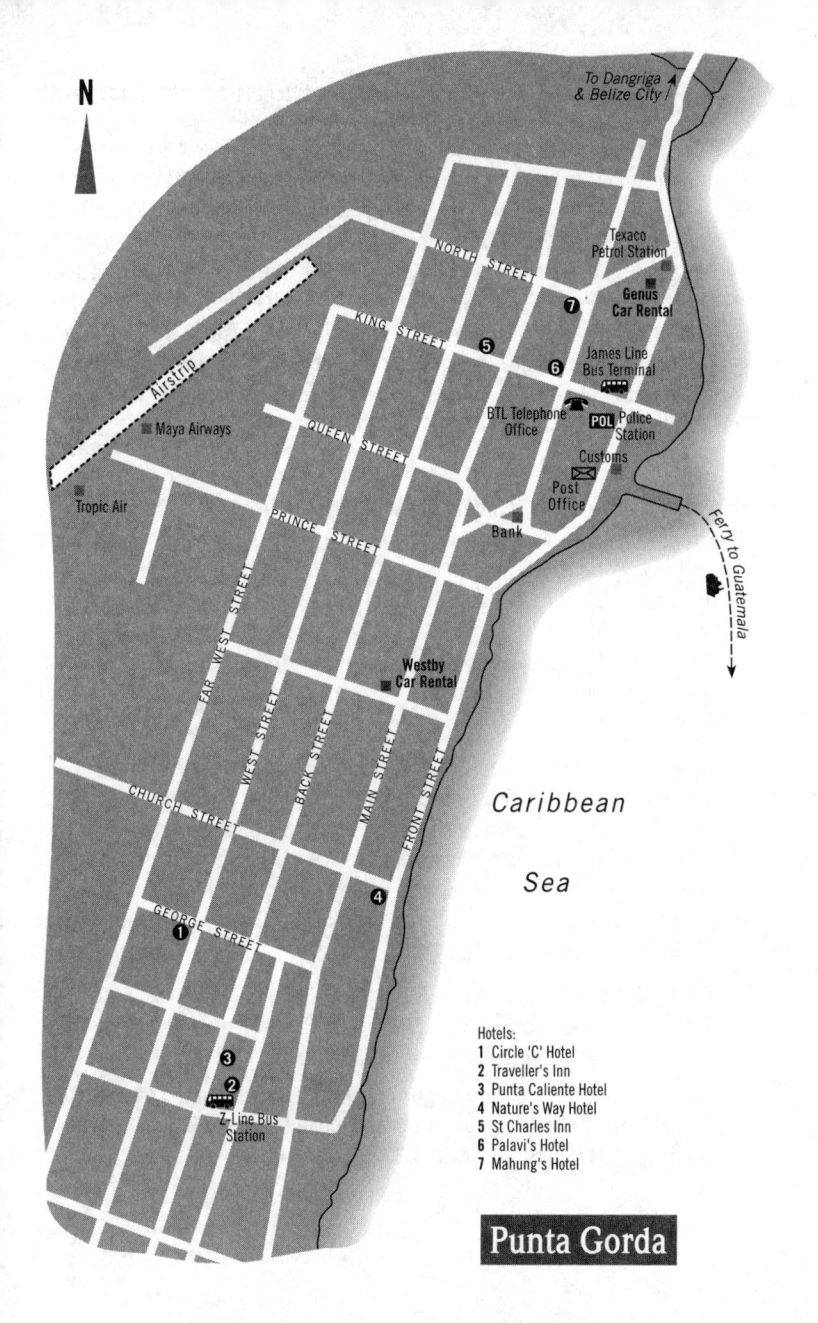

Hotels:
1. Circle 'C' Hotel
2. Traveller's Inn
3. Punta Caliente Hotel
4. Nature's Way Hotel
5. St Charles Inn
6. Palavi's Hotel
7. Mahung's Hotel

By Boat: to and from Guatemala

The ferry leaves Puerto Barrios, in Guatemala, at 7.30 am on Tuesdays and Fridays, and takes about two-and-a-half hours. Leaving Belize, the ferry also goes on Tuesdays and Fridays, leaving at noon. Tickets are US$8.50. The ticket office is at 24 Middle Street. Remember to take your passport for buying the ticket, and get your exit stamp at the police station (on Front Street) before you leave. Alternatively, you can go by charter in a speed boat, that only takes around fifty minutes, but could leave you very wet if conditions are rough or the weather turns bad. See **Requeña Charter**, at 12 Front Street, ✆ 07 22070. Boats leave daily at 9am and 2pm.

Tourist Information

There is a brand new **Government Tourist Office** ✆ 07 22531 on Front Street (opposite the Kowloon Restaurant), (*open Tues–Fri, 8–noon and 1–5; Sat 8–noon*). In addition, you will also find the privately operated **information booth** at the town dock, run by the friendly Alfredo Villoria, who can advise on tours or regional buses, and also keeps a selection of brochures. Another excellent source of information is Chet Schmidt at **Nature's Way Guest House**. Get there by walking south along Main Street, until you come to a small sign pointing left for the guest house.

Sadly, however, tourism development in P.G. has become mired in political in-fighting, so none of the above co-operate or acknowledge each other, with the result that visitors receive a very limited service. The best policy is not to take any information at face value, but to check it against several sources by word of mouth. To find out about adventurous journeys in the surrounding area, stop by at the **Toledo Explorers Club**, 46 José Maria Nuñez Street, ✆ 07 22986.

The **Belize Bank** is located on Main Street, near the municipal park (*open Mon–Thurs, 8–1; Fri 8–4.30*). The local BTL office in also on Main Street, (*open Mon–Fri, 8–noon and 1–4; Sat, 8–noon*).

There are a couple of **tour agencies**: Briceno Taxi and Tour Services, 6 Cemetery Lane and, for tours and boat charters, Julio and Placida Requena, 24 Front Street, ✆ 07 22070.

Where to Stay

expensive

Traveller's Inn ✆ 07 22568, ✉ 05 22814 above the bus terminal offers cool rooms with private bath and breakfast included. Recently constructed, facilities are as good as they get for P.G.

moderate

Right next to the bus terminal, the **Punta Caliente Hotel & Restaurant**, ✆ 07 22561, is a friendly place to stay, all rooms with fan and private bath. A short walk away, **Nature's Way Guest House**, 65 Front Street, ✆ 07 22119, is a beautiful house, cooled by sea breezes, with meals cooked to order. All rooms share the bathroom. At the other end of town, the **Charlton Inn**, ✆ 07 22471, on the corner of Main Street and North Street, has clean rooms, with fan and private bathroom.

Close by, **Mahung's Hotel**, ✆ & ✉ 07 22044, offers good rooms around the back of the hotel only. **Pallavi's Hotel**, 19 Main Street, ✆ 07 22414 is a reasonable budget hotel. **St Charles Inn**, 23 King Street, ✆ 07 22149, ✉ 07 22199 is respectable, but rather expensive for the town. The owners are delightful. However, be wary of **The Mira Mar**, 95 Front Street, as it is overpriced and unpleasant. **The Circle C Hotel**, 117 West Street, ✆ 07 22726, is not far from the bus terminal but is only worth staying at if everywhere else is full.

The newest addition to accommodation is **Tate's Guest House**, 34 Jose Maria Nuñez St, ✆ 07 22196, ✉ 07 22199, which offers clean rooms in a modern house.

Eating Out

A good place to sample the local seafood is the **Punta Caliente**, next to the bus terminal, which is also a good spot for breakfast. Another popular option for creole cooking is **Lucille's**, on Main Street. Get there early, since you usually have to wait a long time, which goes for all the eating houses in town. Another good creole restaurant is **Scheibers**, on Front Street. One of the more bizarre places to eat is the Bavarian-run **German Restaurant,** on the seashore, close to the Texaco Station. The menu is interesting including 'schnitzel', though sadly the owner-chef is often too drunk to come up with the goods.

More central for breakfast is **El Café**, at 5 North Street, which opens at 6 am, Mon–Sat, 7 am on Sundays. The cooked breakfast is the best in town, but they also offer straight toast and coffee.

Bobby's Restaurant Bar, on Main Street, is best for soups, and if you feel like a Chinese meal, head for the **Kowloon** restaurant.

Around Punta Gorda

Maya Ruins and Villages

Nearest to Punta Gorda is the Kekchi village of **San Pedro Columbia**, which you can reach by local bus, either direct to the village or by taking a bus to San Antonio and getting off at the appropriate junction. The second option involves a 3 km walk. Located about 20km northwest of Punta Gorda, the village is on a clearing in the forest, close to the emerald waters of the broad River Columbia. Houses are a variation on the pole and thatch design, and the people live from slash and burn agriculture, only venturing to town on market days.

The surrounding landscape, in the foothills of the Maya Mountains, is very attractive, and a walk of around 45 minutes will take you to the most important ruins in the region: **Lubaantun**. Two major pyramids remain, their most significant characteristic being that they were built without the use of mortar. Unfortunately, an English adventurer used dynamite to explore them in the early 20th century, so they now look like a giant has given them a good kick, causing them to cave in and tilt at odd angles. Stones litter the site, and looting has done its worst here.

The site's name, meaning 'Place of Fallen Stones' is therefore sadly apt. However, the location is beautiful, and certainly worth making an effort to see. Historically, Lubaantun flourished in the Classic Period, but only for a very short time, its occupation dated AD 730–890. Never a Maya centre of primary importance, it was nevertheless significant agriculturally, because it produced cacao beans, used all over Mesoamerica as currency. A sure sign that cacao was its most important trading item was found in the pottery discovered here a small figurine wearing a cacao-pod pendant. Perhaps more intriguing for the casual visitor, though, is the unresolved mystery of the Crystal Skull, which was discovered here by the North American, F.A. Mitchell Hedges, in 1926. He found the skull—which is perfectly shaped yet has no trace of tool marks on it—on his daughter's birthday. Some believe it was a hoax for her amusement, but she insists otherwise and still owns the skull today.

San Antonio village, about 5 km west of San Pedro Columbia, has a direct bus service from P.G., and also a hotel, which makes a good base from which to visit the **Uxbenka** ruins. Inhabited by Mopan Maya, this is a modern village, with a stone church built by resident American missionaries. The community has strong ties to its traditions, however, and the best time to see this is on 5 August, on San Luis Rey Day. The Uxbenka ruins are about 5 km away, just off the dirt track leading to Santa Cruz village. Situated on a small hilltop, the site was not officially discovered until 1984, and what you find is a small, unexcavated ceremonial centre, with good views over the surrounding jungle.

About 1 km further along the road, a small track leads off to the left to **New Falls**, which is a lovely place for a swim and picnic. The river broadens out into a wide pool under some waterfalls, embraced by thick jungle on both sides (if you reach St Elena village, you have gone too far).

The only place to stay in San Antonio is the basic **Bol's Hilltop Hotel**. Meals must be ordered in advance, and this is the only place to serve food in the village. If you would like to hire a guide for exploring the region, you could not do better than Matilde Kaal, who, in spite of his name, is male, and extremely knowledgeable and friendly. You will find his home by asking around in the nearby settlement of Crique Lagarto.

The Maya site of **Nim Li Punit** is not conveniently accessible by public transport, but if you have your own, the place is worth visiting for the terrific views across the coastal plain and nearby highlands. Its name means 'Big Hat', and it was only discovered in 1976, hiding on a small hilltop above some Indian homesteads. The best preserved details are the stelae, of which no fewer than 25 have been found, indicating that this was an important ceremonial centre. The site is near Indian Creek settlement, off the Southern Highway, 40km north of P.G.

Blue Creek

At the junction for San Pedro Columbia, where Roy's Coolspot offers snacks and cold drinks, there is a turning for **Blue Creek**, which is a beautiful place for tranquil swimming, huge trees shading the deep green water. You need your own transport to get here). Heading up the right-hand side of the river on foot you soon come to the lovely natural pool.

If you want to stay, one of the most interesting places nearby is the **Blue Creek Rainforest Station**, contact ✆ 05 22119, ✉ 05 23152 for information and reservations, not far from Blue Creek village. A major attraction is the canopy walkway, suspended 80ft above the ground, which affords a bird's eye view of life in the rainforest—the vast majority of which actually goes on in the tree tops, rather than on the ground.

Hidden in the depths of the jungle near the Guatemalan border, about 30 km beyond Blue Creek, are the Maya ruins of **Pusilhá**, which can be reached only by guided expedition.

Dem Dats Doin

For anyone interested in integrated farm systems, a visit to **Dem Dats Doin** is a must. Run by a Hawaiian couple, Alfredo and Yvonne Villoria, their farm is a delightful place, full of innovative and simple technology that anyone could use to create a self-sufficient, tropical farm. There are also a huge number of fruit trees, and a tour (US$5) around the farm is not only educational, but wonderfully scenic.

To get there, follow the road to San Pedro Columbia, and turn right where a wrecked car is parked, with the farm's name painted on its side. There is also one room available for overnight stays, moderately priced. To book the room or a tour ahead, contact Alfredo at his information booth in P.G., or via P.O. Box 73, Punta Gorda, Toledo District, Belize, ✆ 07 22470.

Northern Belize

Along the Northern Highway	175
Crooked Tree Wildlife Sanctuary	175
Orange Walk	176
Lamanai	180
Shipstern	182
Rio Bravo Conservation Area	183
Corozal	185

Much of northern Belize is flat and swampy, dotted by lagoons and marshes which make an ideal habitat for aquatic birds. The coastal lagoons stretch endlessly and are for the most part uninhabited, fishermen being the only regular visitors. In the western reaches of Orange Walk District, the landscape becomes hilly and is covered by thick tropical forests which are some of the least accessible and least explored in the country.

Exploring the region without your own transport is difficult although if you have the time and the money highlights include the ancient Maya ruins of Lamanai, the Crooked Tree Wildlife Sanctuary northwest of Belize City, the magical Rio Bravo Conservation Area in the far west and Shipstern Nature Reserve in the far northeast.

The paved Northern Highway cuts straight through the region, and travel from Belize City to Mexican Chetumal is just a matter of three or four hours. The only significant towns on the way are Orange Walk, once at the centre of a lucrative sugar-cane industry and, more recently, the country's marijuana growing capital, and Corozal, which nestles in a bay surrounded by small ancient and modern settlements, a short detour off the highway near the Mexican border.

Historically, northern Belize has often been a refuge for asylum seekers. Some of the earliest refugees were the Santa Cruz Maya of the Yucatán who came to Belize in 1901. They were a group of Mayas who had allied themselves with the British after defeat in the Caste Wars of 1847, during which the Spanish had violently put down an Indian uprising. The Santa Cruz Maya were among a larger group who formed independent Maya states in the Mexican region of Quintana Roo. However, the Mexican authorities could not allow separate Indian states in their country, and so they mounted another attack in 1901, which resulted in final and bloody victory. The Santa Cruz Maya fled to the lands of their former allies, to what was then British Honduras, and their descendants have remained.

Other groups that have come to the region include German Mennonite communities, who settled in Shipyard and Blue Creek; and Nicaraguan and Salvadorean refugees, squatting in various remote parts, including around the Maya site of Lamanai. The Spanish language predominates here, unlike in the rest of the country, and the closer you get to the Mexican border, the more likely you are to meet people who speak no English at all, being mestizos not creoles.

Along the Northern Highway

Crooked Tree Wildlife Sanctuary

Located about 53km northwest of Belize City, this reserve is the first point of interest beyond the close environs of the city. Established in 1984 and administered by the Audubon Society, the sanctuary's landscape is predominantly wetlands, which are the ideal home for all kinds of resident and migratory birds. In particular during the dry season, the place is a safe haven for thousands of birds, including many types of heron, two species of duck, egrets, kingfishers, ospreys, hawks, and many more, the largest of which is the Jabiru stork. The best time to see birds here is from November to May, and a visitor's centre is along the entrance road to the reserve, where you need to register and pay a small fee, if you wish to walk on one of the self-guided nature trails around the lagoons. This is also the place to enquire about hiring a canoe (US$15 per day for three people) or going on a guided motorboat tour (US$70 for 1–5 people). Basic provisions can be bought in the village and there is a restaurant, offering traditional rice 'n' beans type dishes.

Getting There

Crooked Tree can be reached by public transport from Belize City (see p.74), and the bus will drop you either by the Jex Store, by the main lagoon, or at Alice's Shop, which is closer to Sam Tillett's Hotel. Take one of the four daily buses to Crooked Tree from Belize City. Check the times first by calling ✆ 02 44101 or 44333.

Alternatively you can take a day trip from Belize City. Travel agents offer different deals.

Where to Stay

expensive

By far the best is the **Bird's Eye View Lodge**, ✆ 02 32040, ✉ 02 24869, run by the charming Verna Gillett-Samuels. Rooms look straight onto a large lagoon, and the hotel offers birding, boating, horse-riding and canoe rental. **The Crooked Tree Resort**, ✆ 02 77745, ✉ 02 31734, on the other hand, has little to recommend it, as it appears to be popular with the local drunks.

moderate

If the birds fascinate you enough, the best moderately priced accommodation is offered by **Sam Tillett's Hotel**, ✆ & ✉ 02 12026, in the village of Crooked Tree. Rooms are rustic, but the reception is friendly and relaxed.

cheap

Your only option is the local bed and breakfast initiative, which you can find out about at the Visitor Information Centre or the Audubon Society in Belize City, *see* p.78.

Orange Walk

86 km north of Belize City, the town of Orange Walk is a scruffy place that holds no attraction for the tourist in itself, but can act as a starting point for visits to the Maya site of **Lamanai**, as well as to the **Rio Bravo Conservation Area**. Originally a timber camp, the town became an important centre for sugar cane and citrus production, and is still predominantly a market town for the surrounding farms. The continuing recession means that the illicit cultivation of marijuana, popularly known as 'Belize Breeze', still goes on, but nothing like on the scale it used to, when local drug barons lived behind fortified houses around here. Spotter planes loaned from the American Drug Enforcement Agency helped to destroy that trade, however, and Belize is no longer a significant drug exporter, though perhaps it is still an important stopover point for cocaine aircraft travelling between South and North America.

But Orange Walk has always had a slightly wild side to it, and was the scene of gory battles in the 19th century, when the local Indian population regularly attacked settlers. The last battle was in 1872, and the ruins of Fort Cairns and Mundy are a legacy of the time when Orange Walk was frequently besieged and needed military protection.

Wandering around today, you will find little evidence of the town's turbulent past, and the most intriguing sight will be the Mennonite farmers going about their business dressed in regulation dungarees and straw hat.

Getting to Orange Walk

Buses arrive at Queen Victoria Avenue, always known as the Belize–Corozal road. Buses leave both north and south bound every half an hour. Local buses on their way to nearby villages leave from near the crossroads in the middle of town.

Orange Walk

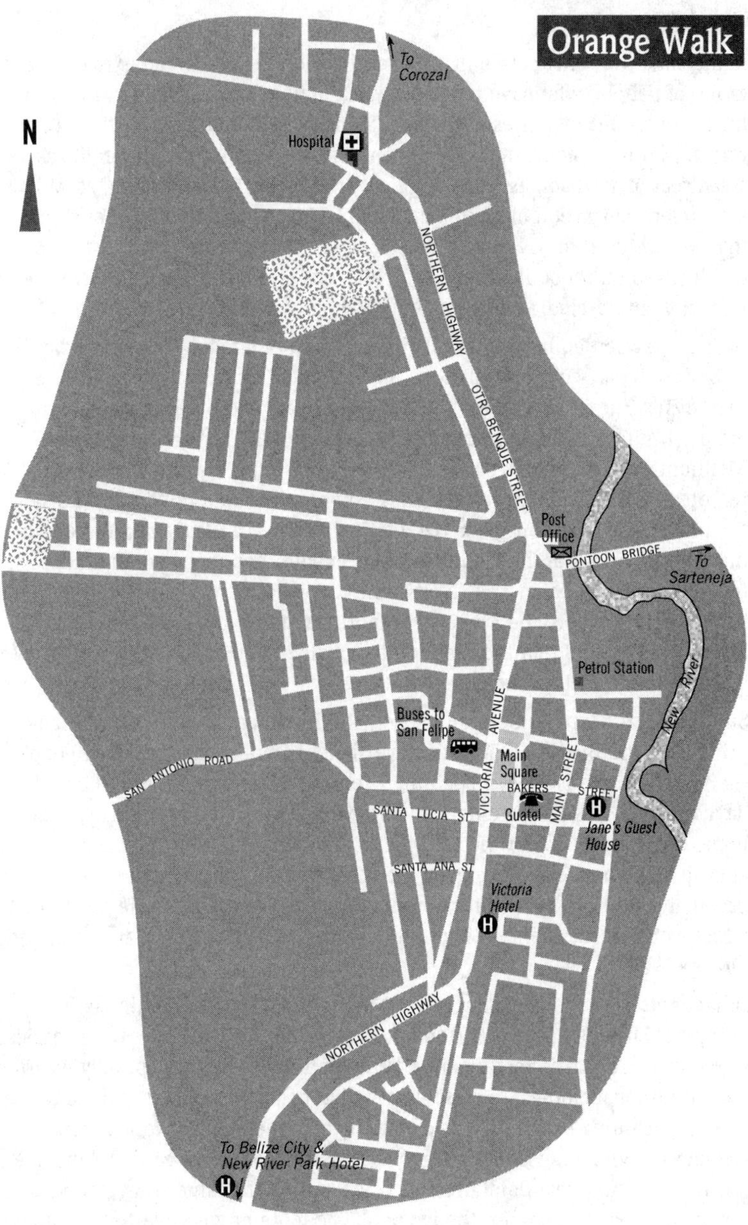
N
To Corozal
Hospital
NORTHERN HIGHWAY
OTRO BENQUE STREET
Post Office
PONTOON BRIDGE
To Sarteneja
Petrol Station
New River
VICTORIA AVENUE
Buses to San Felipe
Main Square
SAN ANTONIO ROAD
BAKERS STREET
MAIN STREET
SANTA LUCIA ST
Guatel
Jane's Guest House
SANTA ANA ST
Victoria Hotel
NORTHERN HIGHWAY
To Belize City & New River Park Hotel

The Mennonites

Rather like the Amish of Pennsylvania, the Mennonites are an extraordinary group of people, who have tenaciously maintained their beliefs and way of life for over four centuries. Originally founded in Switzerland by the Dutch priest, Menno Simons, in the 16th century, the Mennonites began life as a small sect of Anabaptists, adhering to a strict principle of pacifism, as well as a complete separation of church and state. This meant, among other things, that they refused to pay certain taxes or use the state's financial institutions, and insisted on schooling their own children. This guaranteed a hefty dose of suspicion and prejudice would fall upon them wherever they went.

At first they settled in northern Germany, but militaristic Prussia was hardly a comfortable place for pacifists, so they migrated to Russia instead. But by the 1870's Europe was gearing up for major wars and the Russian government withdrew that crucial exemption from military service, forcing the Mennonites to migrate even further afield. This time they moved to the remote wastes of Canada, establishing communities on the windy planes of the prairies, in Manitoba, Alberta and Saskatchewan. Alas, anti-German feelings after World War One led to another exodus, and many communities travelled south to begin new lives in the highlands of Mexico. Yet it was only a few decades before the Mexican authorities moved too close for comfort, and it was in 1958 that the Mennonites finally found their latest resting place in Belize, then British Honduras.

Still speaking a type of German dialect, still insisting on all their traditional principles, the British authorities nevertheless granted these distinct people their wishes because they hoped their renowned farming skills would help develop what was an extremely underdeveloped agricultural industry. Their hopes were granted—for the six Mennonite communities of Belize have almost single handedly developed the country's dairy industry, as well as producing all of Belize's poultry products and the best handmade furniture, which you can see them selling in the markets of Belize City, San Ignacio and Orange Walk.

Inhabitants of the most conservative Mennonite communities, living in Shipyard, Little Belize and Barton Creek (outside San Ignacio), are the easiest to recognize, because they retain a 19th-century way of life, not only wearing their traditional clothes, but also eschewing modern machines and technology, including basics such as electricity and telephones. Notice their arrival in town by horse and buggy wearing the distinctive garb of dungarees for the men, and neat floral dresses, black aprons and large straw hats tied down with black ribbon for the women. The more progressive communities of Blue Creek, Progreso, and Spanish Lookout (near San Ignacio), however, have chosen to adopt some 20th century innovations, such as tractors, fertiliser and electricity, which have not only allowed them to become efficient and wealthy farmers, but also to enjoy music and receive news of the outside world on the radio.

The easiest conservative Mennonite settlement to reach from Orange Walk is Shipyard, which you can either get to by road or via the New River, which passes nearby, on its way to the Maya ruins of Lamanai. Note, however, that these people are shy of outsiders and take particular offence to being photographed. Communication is also difficult, as the most conservative do not even speak English, let alone Spanish. It is an insularity that is coming under increasing pressure, not least because their tiny gene pool is resulting in serious and frequent birth defects.

Tourist Information

The **Belize Bank**, on the corner of Main Street and Market Lane (*open Mon–Thurs, 8–1; Fri, 8–4.30*) changes both cash and traveller's cheques, as well as advancing cash on VISA and Mastercard.

The **post office** (*open Mon–Thurs, 8.30–noon and 1–4; Fri, 8.30–noon and 1–3.30*) is right by the Police Station, off the main road, confusingly called the 'Sub-Treasury'. The local **BTL** Office (*open Mon–Fri, 8–noon and 1–4; Sat 8–noon*) is on the main square, above the photo store.

Where to Stay

expensive

The best place to stay is actually some way outside Orange Walk, on the banks of the New River: **New River Park Hotel**, ✆ & ✉ 03 23987. The advantage of staying here is that it is almost opposite the spot where tours for Lamanai depart, and also has the best restaurant around here. All buses travelling between Belize City and the north pass the hotel, so just ask to be dropped off if you are without your own transport. (Getting in and out of Orange Walk is easy in the daytime).

moderate

In Orange Walk itself there is just one hotel these days, which is rather grubby and not great: **Victoria Hotel**, 40 Belize-Corozal Road, ✆ 03 22518, ✉ 03 22847.

cheap

Jane's Guest House, 2 Baker Street, ✆ 03 22473 (on the street leading down to the river from the Belize Bank), offers very basic rooms with fan and shared bathroom.

Eating Out

Other than heading out to the **New River Inn**, part of the New River Park Hotel, the best place to eat in Orange Walk is **The Diner**, 37 Clark Street, up past the hospital at the northern edge of town. (Half an hour's walk from the centre of town, or take any bus heading for Corozal and get off at the hospital).

For ordinary creole food, served with no frills at decent prices, head for **Juanita's**, 8 Santa Ana Street, which opens for breakfast as early as 6am. Right by the main square, you could also try the **Lover's Restaurant**, 20 Lover's Lane, which serves typical mestizo and creole dishes, such as relleno or rice and beans.

Finally, if you want to sample the local nightlife over the weekend, head for **Mi Amor Disco & Lounge**, 119 Belize Corozal Road, which boasts 'space age lights' and the latest hits.

Maya Sites Around Orange Walk: Lamanai

A tour to **Lamanai** is undoubtedly one of the highlights of any journey to Belize, not only because of the ruins themselves, but also because of the wonderful rivertrip you have to make to reach the site. You travel almost thirty miles by boat along the New River, which is a great opportunity to see a huge variety of birdlife, such as snail hawks, herons, and spoonbills, not to mention crocodiles and turtles. Your guide should be prepared to slow down occasionally to point these out to you, as well as stop for photo calls. About half way along, you reach the Mennonite village of **Shipyard**, founded in 1960 and renowned for the distinctive mahogany furniture made by the men. One of the small delights of this journey is scanning the riverbanks, which are lined by the ivory blossoms of waterlily. At last, after a good hour-and-a-half, you reach the ruins themselves, situated right on the New River Lagoon, where beautiful trails lead off through jungle, taking you not only into the heart of Lamanai, but also into the hidden sanctum of the yellow-breasted toucan (the country's national bird) and troops of rowdy howler monkeys.

Getting to Lamanai

To reach Lamanai, your best bet is to go on a tour from Orange Walk (Lamanai Maya Tours, Tower Hill, ✆ 03 23839 or Mr Godoy, 4 Trial Farm, ✆ 03 22969) or from Belize City (*see* pp.9–10 for tour companies). Note that all tours coming from Belize City can be joined at the New River dock, so there is no need to travel all the way to Belize City, if you are coming from the north. Just make your arrangements by telephone.

In theory you could also make your way to the villages of Guinea Grass or Shipyard (closer), from where you could hire a boatman to take you south along the New River. However this would certainly be a more expensive option and there are no guarantees that anyone would be found to take you when you wish to travel.

The Site

On arrival you can visit a small site museum which houses an impressive collection of artefacts found here, divided into shelves of Pre-Classic, Classic and post-Classic objects. The most impressive work comes from the final era, and you will see a marvellous array of finely decorated tripod bowls. The most extraordinary exhibit is a small, zoomorphic figurine, which shows a human face emerging from a crocodile's mouth, while its tail represents the fearsome jaws of a shark. (Toilets and picnic facilities are available at the entrance to the ruins.)

Lamanai was an important site during Maya times, and it is estimated that in the 6th century, it was home to around 20,000 people. The earliest inhabitants came here in 1500 BC and this site has one of the longest records of occupation, long before it became a Maya ceremonial centre. The earliest stone architecture appeared in the 9th century BC, and the largest Pre-Classic structure in the Maya territory is to be found here, a pyramid rising 33m above the surrounding forest and savannah, whose earliest building phase dates back to 100 BC.

The site's name is the original Maya one, and means 'Submerged Crocodile', and images of crocodiles appear frequently amongst the carvings found here. (Another theory has it that this name is actually a mistranslation by the Spanish missionaries, who came here in 1544, and that the proper name should be 'Drowned Insect', which doesn't have quite the same ring to it, though).

Maya descendants were living here as late as the 16th century and the Spanish duly built a mission church to Christianize them. The results were poor, however, and the Indians burnt the place down in 1640. In the 19th century the British built a sugar mill nearby but this failed too, when the manager died of a fever and the ruins have been left in peace, the surrounding area sparsely populated, until this day. Tourism may yet change that, however, and there is already one luxury hotel on the New River Lagoon you could stay at **The Lamanai Outpost Lodge**, ✆ & ✉ 02 33578).

Other Maya Sites

Strictly for enthusiasts, there are two minor archaeological ruins easily reached by taxi from Orange Walk. The closest is **Cuello**, just off the road to Yo Creek village, which is actually one of the earliest known Maya sites, with an occupation record stretching right back to 2500 BC. Sadly, the site has been extensively damaged by agricultural activities and is now reduced to a few mounds in a cattle pasture. The property on which the site lies belongs to the Cuello Distillery, and permission to visit must be obtained by telephoning ✆ 03 22141.

Possibly a more interesting destination is the ceremonial centre of **Nohmul**, which lies about 15 km north of Orange Walk, west of the village of San Pablo. Situated on a ridge among some sugar cane fields, the main temple platform rises just eight metres above the ground, yet it is the highest landmark in this flat and swampy region. Nohmul's earliest occupation dates back to the Late Formative Period (300 BC–AD 150), but the site appears to have been insignificant for most of its history, only bursting into significance in the Late Classic Period, around AD 900 , shortly before the Lowland Maya mysteriously disappeared. In fact, it has been suggested that this late flowering was due to invading Yucatec Maya, who took the site over as their new administrative centre for the region.

Shipstern Reserve

Entrance fee US$5; self-catering accommodation US$10 per person.

This reserve is in a remote region northeast of Orange Walk, near the village of **Sarteneja**, about an hour's drive from the town along a dirt road. Getting to Shipstern is best in your own vehicle, though there is a daily bus connection, leaving Orange Walk around midday and returning from Sarteneja village at 6 am. Ask to be dropped off at the reserve entrance and remember to bring all your own food and drink if you plan on staying overnight.

Reservations can be made via the Belize Audubon Society (*see* pp 78). There is an efficient visitor's centre where you can arrange for a guided tour around the reserve which covers 31 square miles and a variety of habitats, ranging from the shallow Shipstern Lagoon to savannah and forests.

One of the most interesting trails is the **Chiclero Botanical Trail** (approximately 45 minutes), where you can learn about the uses for many of the trees. Almost all the species of animal found in Belize are found in this region, including the jaguar.

Over 60 kinds of reptiles and amphibians have been recorded here, and a staggering 220 species of birds. The trail is a must for all wildlife enthusiasts.

A special attraction is also the **Butterfly Breeding Centre**. Visit on a sunny day, and you will have the best chance to see some of the 200 species of butterflies. Note that mosquitos can be a real menace here, so insect repellent and long sleeves are essential for any visit to the reserve. Just don't spray your repellent anywhere near the butterflies!

Río Bravo Conservation Area

The Rio Bravo Conservation Area represents a substantial chunk of north-western Belize, and a visit there is probably the best chance you will ever have of experiencing life in the local rainforest. Based at the working research station, where you share very comfortable, but simple, accommodation and meals with the resident scientists and labourers, trained guides take you on daily trips into the forest. A self-guided trail has also been cut into the forest if you prefer, but whichever way you choose to explore, you will soon find yourself in a fascinating twilight world, where giant blue morpho butterflies dance in search of moist resting places, while nuts and fruit dropping from high above indicate monkeys or even the shy coatimundi—a type of possum.

Watch your step as you gaze above, though, because the rotting foliage beneath your feet hides many other creatures, including the deadly fer-de-lance snake. (Your guide should see both the dangers and the thrills long before you do, however, so there is no real reason to worry). Even in the open clearing of the camp itself you will see several exotic sights, such as ocellated turkeys that shriek indignantly whenever you disturb their grubbing, or perhaps a shy toucan hiding high up in the trees.

If you go out on a night drive, you might see anything from a prowling jaguar or a tiny marguey to a red-eyed tree frog clinging to the reeds in some swampy patch. Or you might see nothing but the glinting eyes of spiders. Either way exploring the natural wonderland around here is an unforgettable experience.

Belize is littered with ruins left by the Maya, and the Rio Bravo area is no exception. In fact, the nearby **La Milpa** ruins are the third largest in the country and are believed to encompass the greatest plaza in the Maya world: almost 20,000 square metres. Lost from 1939 to 1985, the ceremonial platforms were rediscovered by marijuana growers, and have not yet been cleared or excavated on a large scale, though the University of Boston has now established a long-term survey project.

It is believed that La Milpa was founded in the Late Pre-Classic (around 400 BC), though its Golden Age appears to have been in the 5th Century AD, with a resurgence in the 8th Century AD, the period from which most of the visible architecture dates.

The Rio Bravo Conservation Area is managed by **Programme for Belize**, which is a non-profit organisation, founded in 1988, dedicated to the promotion of economically sound conservation and sustainable tourism. This means that a great deal of research is going into discovering long-term solutions, and all money earnt from commercial tourism to the property goes towards supporting that effort.

Getting to the Rio Bravo

Visits are arranged by Ava Davis at the head office in Belize City: Programme for Belize, 2 South Park Street, (P.O.Box 749), Belize City,

✆ 02 75616, ✉ 02 75635. Transport is extra, and costs US$120 each way from Belize City, though only US$20 each way from San Felipe village, which you can reach using a local bus from Orange Walk.

You can visit the reserve in your own four-wheel-drive (a must) vehicle, and detailed instructions are available from the office in Belize City.

Where to Stay

Accommodation is either in a private wooden cabaña (US$80 per person, including all meals), or in a dormitory, sharing a bathroom (US$65 per person, including all meals). Prices also include two excursions per day, and there are at least eight different options to keep you busy. Facilities include a gift shop and a small but useful library.

Chan Chich Lodge

Neighbouring the property of the Rio Bravo Conservation Area is the private estate of Mr. Barry Bowen, which is home to his **Chan Chich Lodge**, ✆ 02 75634, ✉ 02 75635 northern Belize's most exotic resort hotel. The lodge is a superb place for bird watchers, and they can search out some of the hundreds of species that have been recorded around here, as well as enjoy the comforts of rustic luxury. To get there either charter a plane to Gallon Jug airstrip or, during the dry season, take a four-wheel-drive vehicle via Orange Walk, San Felipe and Blue Creek.

Corozal

Of all the northern settlements, this is the most pleasant to visit, facing out to the turquoise seas of Corozal Bay, 134 km north of Belize City and 14 km from the Mexican border. **Corozal** was badly damaged by Hurricane Janet in 1955, however, and so it does have a somewhat empty feeling to it. Like Orange Walk, the town has suffered from the decline of the sugar industry, and employment is scarce. Bored youths hang around street corners and there isn't very much to do for the visitor either. But it is a good spot to break the journey to or from Mexico. There are also flights to Ambergris Caye from here.

If you do find yourself with time to kill, you could hire a taxi to visit the Maya ruins of **Santa Rita**, on the northern edge of town, which are believed to be the remnants of the ancient Maya city of **Chetumal**. Sadly, most of the site has been covered by the modern town of Corozal, so there is not much to see. Nevertheless, the ruins are of great significance in Maya history, representing the remains of a major trading centre, once at the heart of maritime trade routes.

The most important trade good grown locally was the cacao bean, but honey and vanilla were also produced, along with rich harvests from the rivers and ocean. Evidence of Santa Rita's trading pre-eminence was found in the burial site of a Maya warlord, dated AD 500 , which contained several artefacts made after the fashion prevailing in distant centres, such as Kaminaljuyú in Guatemala, and Teotihuacán in Mexico. Some pottery finds are even believed to have originated from as far away as Peru.

Across the Bay of Corozal lies the Maya site of **Cerros**, which you can only conveniently reach by boat. (Enquire about guided tours at the Caribbean Village). Another important trading post, its strategic location gave it ideal access to the maritime routes, especially for jade and obsidian, although shifting trade connections caused the site to lose out early on.Therefore, even though it flourished during the Late Pre-Classic (400 BC–AD 250), there are no recorded structures or habitation records dating any later. Visible remains include two badly eroded pyramid structures, whose fine masks have been covered with plaster to protect them from the harsh sea air.

Getting to Corozal

by air

Corozal's landing strip is set amongst fields but there's always a cab or two ready to meet arrivals. For flight tickets from Corozal contact **Menzies Travel**, Ranchito village, ✆ 04 22725 or 23414, and they will send someone to pick you up free of charge. Alternatively contact them via the Caribbean Village campsite on South Road.

by bus

Batty buses stop at 4 Park Street North, and Venus buses stop at 7th Avenue. You should have no problem travelling to and from Corozal by public transport, as all buses between Belize City and Chetumal/Mexico stop here. (The journey from Chetumal to Corozal takes about half an hour, including border formalities). There is also a daily bus connection between Corozal and Sarteneja, departing Corozal at 2.30pm (rtn 6am), a journey of about three hours.

Tourist Information

There are three **banks** in Corozal: Atlantic Bank, 1 Park Street South (*open Mon–Fri, 8–2*); Belize Bank, on the main square, (*open Mon–Thurs, 8–1; Fri, 8–4.30*); and Scotiabank, just off the main square (*open Mon–Thurs, 8–1; Fri, 8–4.30*).

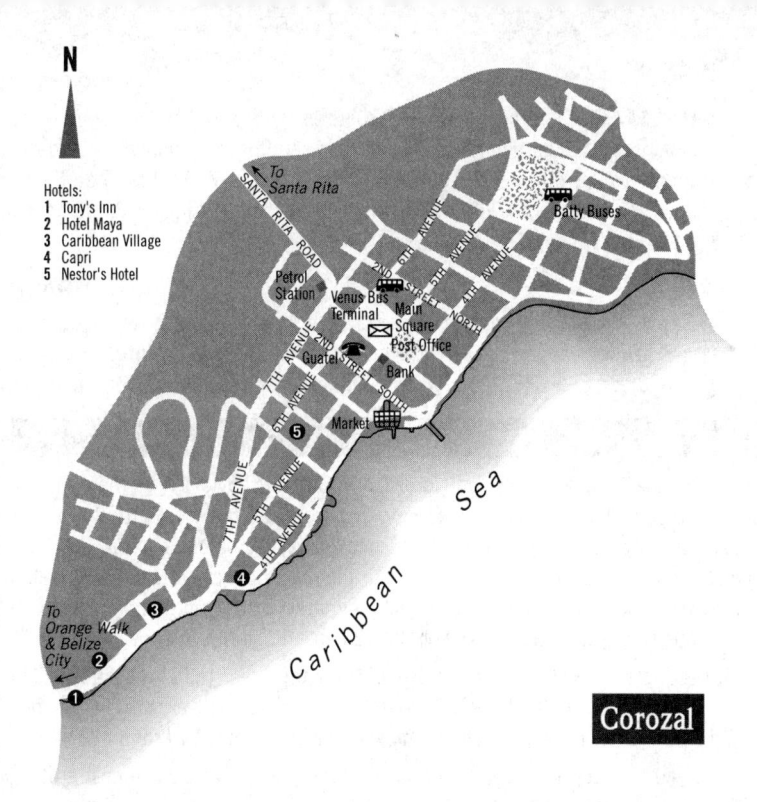

Hotels:
1 Tony's Inn
2 Hotel Maya
3 Caribbean Village
4 Capri
5 Nestor's Hotel

The local **BTL** office for phone calls and faxes is on Park Street South (*open Mon–Fri, 8–noon and 1–4; Sat, 8–noon*). The **post office** is located in the green building on the main square (*open Mon–Thurs, 8.30–noon and 1–4.30; Fri 8.30–noon and 1–4*).

Where to Stay

expensive

The top place to stay is the attractive **Tony's Inn**, at South End, ✆ 04 22055, ℻ 04 22829, which is right by the sea. Rooms have a fan or air-conditioning and TV.

Outside Corozal, near the village of Consejo, you will find the reasonably up-market **Adventure Inn**, P.O. Box 35, Corozal Town, ✆ 04 22187, ℻ 04 22243. Overlooking the bay, the hotel is made up of a main lodge and 14 cabins, and all watersports, especially fishing, are catered for.

moderate

Hotel Maya, South End, ✆ 04 22082, is clean and simple. Rooms with fan and private bath are available. A good spot for campers, which also has simple rooms on offer, is the **Caribbean Village**, ✆ 04 22725 on South Road. The adjacent **Hailey's Restaurant** is worth visiting for dinner, even if you don't stay here.

cheap

Capri, ✆ 04 22042, on the corner of 14th Avenue and 4th Avenue is loud and grubby, and the best budget choice is **Nestor's Hotel**, 123 5th Avenue, ✆ & ✉ 04 22354, which also has a good restaurant and cable TV.

On to Mexico

There is regular transport between Corozal and Chetumal/Mexico, as the former is one of the stops for all buses travelling to and from Belize City. Batty Buses and Venus Buses ply this route, and you can also take a taxi across the border. There are regular departures to and from Cancún from the main bus terminal in Chetumal, a journey that takes five or six hours, depending on whether you go first or second-class. A one-way ticket costs US$10 or US$12 depending on your choice.

If you need to stay in Cancún, the most convenient place is the **Novotel**, Avenida Tulúm y Azucenas, ✆ 98 842999, ✉ 98 843162. It is located very close to the bus terminal, and offers clean and safe rooms with a private bath, for around US$20.

If you need to reach the airport, a taxi is the only way, which will cost around US$8. Strangely, arriving at the airport, you are offered a ride in an airport bus, which drops you at whichever hotel you have chosen. (US$5). Unfortunately it does not operate in the other direction.

Please note: for simplicity's sake the country is referred to throughout as Belize, even though its historic lack of formal recognition as a territory or country meant it was actually known by a variety of names, the last of which was 'British Honduras', in use from 1862 to 1973.

11,000–2000 BC	Small populations of hunter-gatherers lived throughout the Americas
2000 BC–250 AD	Pre-Classic Maya civilisation evolved during this time, one of the earliest cultures being the Ocos one along the Pacific coast of Guatemala. Important later sites were Kaminaljuyú, now smothered by Guatemala City, and Lamanai in Belize, where the largest Pre-Classic structure was built.
250–900 AD	The Classic Period was the Golden Age for the Maya civilisation, when sites such as Caracol (Belize), Tikal (Guatemala), Copán (Honduras) and Quiriguá (Guatemala) reached their zenith.
900–1530	The Post Classic Period began after the Lowland Maya civilisation mysteriously vanished, between 790 AD and 889 AD. Highland Maya civilisation (in Guatemala) survived much longer, however, with the Quiché, Mam and Cakchiquel kingdoms still powerful when the Spanish arrived.
1523	Spanish forces arrive in Guatemala and begin a brutal and swift conquest, aided by disunity among Maya tribes
1527	The first Spanish capital is founded in Guatemala
1541	The hated conquistador, Pedro de Alvarado, dies
1650s	British buccaneers and adventurers settle on the Belize coast
1676	Foundation of Central America's first university in Guatemala City: University of San Carlos

Chronology

1697	Defeat of the last independent Maya at Tayasal on Lake Petén Itzá/Guatemala
1763	Treaty of Paris signed, which grants Spanish sovereignty over Belize, but allows the British to cut and export logwood
1779	The Spanish attack British settlers for the time since 1717 and take captive Baymen and their families to Mexico, then Cuba
1783	Treaty of Versailles signed, which is similar to the Treaty of Paris, but with stricter demarcations

1784	Captured Baymen and their families return to Belize
1786	Convention of London signed, which grants the Baymen logging rights without the right to build permanent fortifications, grow food, or establish a government over the territory.
1787	Over 2000 people are evacuated from the Honduran Mosquito Coast and shipped to Belize, as part of the British settlement with Spain. (People later known as 'Shoremen' to distinguish them from the local 'Baymen', whom they vastly outnumbered).
1798	A motley army of Baymen, Shoremen, slaves and British forces defeat the Spanish at the Battle of St George's Caye
1802	150 Garifuna settle at Stann Creek
1817	British Superintendent declares authority to grant land titles in Belize
1821	Central American regions declare independence from Spain
1822	Annexation to Mexico
1823	Independence from Mexico and declaration of the United Provinces of Central America
1824	There are still around 2300 slaves in Belize
1826	Outbreak of Civil War throughout Central America
1830	Morazán takes Guatemala City and becomes president of the United Provinces of Central America
1831	Free Coloureds are granted civil rights
1832	Mass arrival of Garifuna in Belize (which is still celebrated today)
1834	Abolition of slavery
1839	Central American federation collapses, Guatemala claims sovereign rights over Belize
1840	British Law is declared in force in Belize, unopposed by the Spanish
1847	Caste Wars in the Mexican Yucatán result in thousands of refugees coming to Belize
1850	US–British Treaty whereby Britain agrees to refrain from occupying, fortifying or colonizing any part of Central America. Britain claims Belize is excepted because of being settled already
1854	Belize adopts a formal Constitution and a Legislative Assembly
1859	Guatemala signs treaty recognising British sovereignty over Belize, on the understanding that a road is built connecting

	Guatemala City, the Petén and the Caribbean coast.
1862	Belize is officially declared a colony and recognized as part of the British Commonwealth, and becomes known as British Honduras
1871	British Honduras becomes a Crown Colony under the Governor of Jamaica
1884	Guatemala threatens to cancel the Treaty of 1859
1919	Blacks protest white rule in Ex-Servicemen's Riot
1936	Constitution and limited suffrage is granted. (Property, income and literacy requirements exclude many from the vote).
1945	Belize is listed as the 23rd department in Guatemala's new Constitution
1950	Minimum age for female voters is lowered from 30 to 21
1954	The new constitution grants universal suffrage to all over 18 years old
1955	People's United Party (PUP) successfully dominates elections for the next thirty years
1958	Formation of the first opposition party to PUP, the National Independence Party (NIP)
1961	Hurricane Hattie destroys Belize City
1964	Local government control passes to Belize, but Britain retains control over defence, foreign affairs, internal security, and terms and conditions of public service
1972	Guatemala threatens war and Britain sends navy and army troops to Belize
1973	The country officially becomes known as Belize and Belmopan is designated capital. Formation of the United Democratic Party (UDP)
1975	Belize gains control over its foreign affairs. United Nations votes to support Belize' right to self-determination, the US abstains from the vote
1978	Formation of the Belize Defense Force
1979	Refugees from Guatemala and El Salvador begin arriving in Belize
1980	The United Nations passes a resolution demanding Belize's right to independence is settled within a year
1981	Belize gets a new constitution and becomes a fully independent member of the Commonwealth of Nations. Independence is

	declared on 21 September and George Price of the PUP becomes the country's first prime minister. Belize joins the United Nations
1984	The United Democratic Party (UDP) enjoy a landslide victory and Manuel Esquivel becomes prime minister. The following year he signs an economic stabilisation agreement with the US Agency for International Development (AID), which dictactes an open economy and the privatisation of public sector agencies
1989	PUP and George Price are returned to power by a narrow margin
1991	Guatemala officially recognises Belize as an independent state, but disputes continue
1993	The British government announces withdrawal of its troops from Belize
1993	Long-term opposition party, the United Democratic Party (UDP) win the elections on a wave of popular protest against the People's United Party (PUP), which is blamed for the withdrawal of British troops from Belize at a time of great political turmoil in Guatemala. Manuel Esquivel becomes prime minister
1994	British troops complete their withdrawal, but retain tropical training camps

The majority speak English in Belize, but Spanish is widely used as are many Maya Indian languages. There are at least ten major language groups for the Maya people across Central America and among those the variety of dialects is staggering. Even communication from one region to the next can be impossible, and foreigners cannot hope to learn about the indigenous linguistic complexities on a short visit. Suffice it to say that most Maya can speak Spanish, and only in very remote areas will you find villagers unable to use it. Few people have a working knowledge of English or other European languages, and your visit will be immeasurably improved if you can at least communicate in basic Spanish. There are plenty of language schools in Central America and many travellers find that even one or two weeks of tuition makes all the difference. The courses are also much cheaper here than in the West, and tuition is generally one-to-one, making your advance very rapid. One week of daily four-hour sessions can cost you as little as US$45 or around US$120, depending on which language school you choose.

Formal Greetings

Buenos días	Good morning
Buenas tardes	Good afternoon
Buenas noches	Good evening
Buenos días, don (doña)...	Good morning Mr (Mrs)...
Señor!	Sir/Madam (applied to both)
Como está (usted)?	How are you?
Adiós	Goodbye

Informal Greetings

Hola!	Hello!
Qué tal?	How's it going?

Language

Adiós	Hello (in passing)
Hasta pronto	See you soon
Que te vaya bien	Stay well
Dios te cuida	May God keep you

Travel

Disculpe	Excuse me/sorry
Lo siento	Sorry
Habla inglés?	Do you speak English?
Dónde está...?	Where is?
Terminal de buses	Bus station
Camioneta	Bus
Estación de tren	Train station
Aeropuerto	Airport
Parada	Bus stop
Barco	Boat
Puerto	Port
Aduana	Customs
Cuánto cuesta...	How much?
A qué hora sale el bus?	What time does the bus depart?
Cuándo sale el próximo?	When does the next one leave?
De dónde?	From where?
Cuánto es el pasaje?	How much is the bus fare?
El boleto	Ticket
Ida y vuelta	Return ticket
Solo ida	Just one way
Hasta dónde?	Where to?
Hasta Antigua	To Antigua
Asiento	Seat
Lleno	Full
Atrás hay lugares	There are seats at the back
Buen viaje!	Have a good trip!
Quiero un taxi	I'm looking for (want) a taxi

Directions and Locations

Izquierda	Left
Derecha	Right
Adelante	Forward
Atrás	Backward
Arriba	Up
Abajo	Down

Dos cuadras de aquí	Two blocks from here
Lejos	Far/distant
Cerca	Near/close
Recto	Straight (ahead)
Norte	North
Sur	South
Oeste	West
Este	East
Entrada	Entrance
Salida	Exit
Esquina	Corner (exterior)
Rincón	Corner (interior)

Accommodation

Hotel/Posada	Hotel
Hospedaje/Pensión	Guest house
Hay cuartos?	Do you have rooms?
Para una persona	For one person
Para dos (tres) personas	For two (three) people
Cuánto son or A cómo son?	How much are they?
Hay con baño privado?	Are there rooms with private baths
Hay unos con cama matrimonial?	Do you have ones with doule beds?
Con dos camas	With two beds
Hay cuartos más barato?	Do you have cheaper rooms?
Hay agua caliente?	Do you have hot water?
Funcionar	to work/function/be in working order
Está bien	That is good (I accept)
A qué hora hay desayuno?	What time is breakfast?
Hay comida?	Do you have meals/Is there food?
Qué hay para comer?	What do you have to eat?
Tiene (usted) un candado?	Do you have a padlock (for the room)?
Tiene (usted) candelas?	Do you have candles?
Quiero salir muy tetnprano	I wish to leave very early
Jabón	Soap
Toalla	Towel
Papel Higiénico	Toilet paper

Driving

Carro	Car
Moto	Motorbike
Bicicleta	Bicycle
Alquilar	to rent
Gasolinera	Petrol station
Gasolina	Petrol
Garaje	Garage
Carretera	Road
Camino	Path/road
Permiso (Carnet) de conducir	Driving licence
Conductor (Piloto)	Driver
Peligro	Danger

Shopping, Service, Sightseeing

Guia	Guide
Abierto	Open
Cerrado	Closed
A qué hora abre el museo?	What time does the museum open?
A qué hora cierra el museo?	What time does the museum close?
El dinero	Money
Pisto	Money/income (slang)
La tienda	Shop
La golosina/pulperia/sastrería	Shop (Honduras)
El mercado	Market
Barato/Caro	Cheap/Expensive
Cuánto vale eso?	How much is that?
Está demasiado caro	It's too expensive
Hay rebaja?	Is there a discount?
No se puede	It's not possible
No hay	There isn't any
El correo	Post office
El banco	Bank
La oficina de turismo	Tourist office
Agencia de viaje	Travel agent
La fannacia	Chemist

Artesanía	Crafts
La Policia	Police force
Comisaía	Police station
La playa	Beach
El mar	Sea
La iglesia	Church

Maya Clothes and Market Goods

Indigena	Indian/Indigenous person
Traje	Traditional costume
Artesania/Tipica	Crafts
Huipil	Blouse/Top
Corte	Skirt/Wrap
Faja	Belt/Sash
Cinta/Bola/Tzute	Headdress
Cubrecama	Bedspread/Cover
Alfombra	Carpet/Rug
Mantel	Tablecloth
Servilleta	Napkin
Cinturón	Belt
Sombrero	Hat
Joyas	Jewellery
Pulsera	Bracelet
Collar	Necklace
Anillo	Ring
Plata	Silver
Oro	Gold
Máscara	Mask
Carraca	Rattle
Escultura	Carving

Useful Words and Phrases

Cuidado!	Careful
Puedes ayudarme?	Can you help?
Por favor	Please
Gracias	Thank you

Lo siento/disculpe	Sorry
De nada	It's a pleasure
Cómo te llamas?	What's your name?
Mucho gusto conocerte	It's a pleasure meeting you
Con mucho gusto	With pleasure
Si/No	Yes/No
Quizás	Maybe
Por qué?	Why?
No sé	I don't know
No entiendo	I don't understand
D Jame en paz	Leave me alone
Habla despacio	Speak slowly
Qué es esto?	What is that?
Para qué es esto?	What is that for?
Servicio/Bano	Toilet/Bathroom
Aquí	Here
Allá	There
Que	What
Quien	Who
Como	How
Cuando	When
Bueno	Good
Malo	Bad
Tengo hambre	I'm hungry
Tengo sed	I'm thirsty
Estoy cansado (masc.), *cansada* (fem.)	I'm tired
Tiene fuego?	Have you got a light?
No fumo	I don't smoke
Tomar	to drink (slang)
Estoy casado/a	I'm married
Marido	Husband
Esposa	Wife
Niño/a	Child
Novio/a	Boyfriend/Girlfriend
Prometido/a	Engaged

Embarazada	Pregnant
Divorciado/a	Divorced

Time

Qué hora es?	What time is it?
Tiempo	Time
Hace tiempo	A long time ago
Ahora	Now
Después/Más tarde	Later
Temprano	Early
Hoy	Today
Ayer	Yesterday
Mañana	Tomorrow
Mañana	Morning
Tarde	Afternoon (late)
Noche	Evening
Mediodía	Midday
Año	Year
Mes	Month
Semana	Week
Día	Day

Days

Lunes	Monday
Martes	Tuesday
Miércoles	Wednesday
Jueves	Thursday
Viernes	Friday
Sábado	Saturday
Domingo	Sunday
Feria	Bank holiday
Vacaciónes	Holidays

Numbers

Uno/a	One
Dos	Two

Tres	Three
Cuatro	Four
Cinco	Five
Seis	Six
Siete	Seven
Ocho	Eight
Nueve	Nine
Diez	Ten
Once	Eleven
Doce	Twelve
Trece	Thirteen
Catorce	Fourteen
Quince	Fifteen
Dieciséis	Sixteen
Diecisiete	Seventeen
Dieciocho	Eighteen
Diecinueve	Nineteen
Veinte	Twenty
Veintiuno	Twenty-one
Treinta	Thirty
Cuarenta	Forty
Cincuenta	Fifty
Sesenta	sixty
Setenta	Seventy
Ochenta	Eighty
Noventa	Ninety
Cien	One hundred
Ciento uno	One hundred and one
Quinientos	Five hundred
Mil	One thousand

Restaurants and Food

Restaurante	Restaurant
Comedor	Eating place
Comida corriente	Meal of the day
Desayuno	Breakfast

Almuerzo	Lunch
Cena	Dinner
Pan	Bread
Mantequilla	Butter
Queso	Cheese
Jalea	Jam
Miel	Honey
Azúcar	Sugar
Pan tostado	Toast
Huevos (fritos/revueltos)	Eggs (fried/scrambled)
Huevos a la mexicana	with tomato, onion and hot sauce
Huevos rancheros	with hot sauce
Hervir	Boil
Mosh	Porridge
Pastel	Pastry/cake
Mesa	Table
Silla	Chair
Cuchillo	Knife
Tenedor	Fork
Cuchara	Spoon
Sopa	Soup
Condimento	Salt and pepper
Salsa picante	Hot sauce
Mostaza	Mustard
Cenicero	Ashtray
Cuenta	Bill
Anafre	Beanpaste snack (Honduras)
Pinchos	Meat kebabs
Chile relleno	Stuffed pepper
Chuchitos	Stuffed maize dumplings
Enchilada	Crisp tortillas with salad/meat topping
Quesadilla	Flour tortilla stuffed with cheese
Taco	Stuffed tortilla
Tamale	Maize pudding wrapped in palm leaf

Drinks

Bebidas	Drinks
Agua	Water or fizzy drink
Jugo	Fruit juice
Licuado (leche/agua)	Milkshake (with milk or water)
Cenveza	Beer
Vino	Wine
Café negro	Black coffee
Café con leche	White coffee
Té (con limón)	Tea (with lemon)

Meats

Carne	Meat
Lomtto	Meat (usually beef)
Carne de res	Beef
Bistec	Steak
Marano (Cerdo)	Pork
Chorizo	Sausage
Tocino	Bacon
Jamón	Ham
Chuleta	Chop
Guisado	Stew
Milanesa	Breaded meat
Cordero	Lamb
Ternera	Veal
Venado	Venison
Pollo	Chicken
Pato	Duck
Pavo	Turkey
Conejo	Rabbit
Tepezcuintle	A jungle rodent
Higado	Liver
Asado	Roasted
Al horno	Baked
A la parrilla	Grilled

Fish and Shellfish

Pescado entero	Whole fish
Pescado frito	Fried fish
Tiburón	Shark
Bacalao	Cod
Trucha	Trout
Atún	Tuna
Ceviche	Raw fish salad
Mariscos	Shellfish
Camarones	Shrimp
Langosta	Lobster
Calamares	Squid
Cangrejo	Crab

Vegetables

Verduras	Vegetables
Ajo	Garlic
Cebolla	Onion
Papas	Potatoes
Arroz	Rice
Frijoles	Beans
Tomate	Tomato
Hongos	Mushrooms
Aguacate	Avocado
Col	Cabbage
Lechuga	Lettuce
Pepino	Cucumber
Zanahoria	Carrot

Fruit

Coco	Coconut
Plátano	Banana
Papaya	Pawpaw
Melón	Honeymelon
Sandía	Watermelon
Durazno (Melocotón)	Peach

Piña	Pineapple
Pitaya	Guatemalan fruit (purple inside)
Fresas	Strawberries
Guayaba	Guava
Limón	Lemon
Naranja	Orange
Manzana	Apple
Toronja	Grapefruit
Uvas	Grapes

Travel and the Maya

Coe, M. D. *The Maya*, London, Thames & Hudson, 1986

Coe, M. D. *Breaking the Maya Code*, London, Penguin, 1994

Exquemeling, J. *The Buccaneers of America*, London, Routledge & Sons, 1924

Guderjan, T. H. *Ancient Maya Traders of Ambergris Caye*, Belize, Cubola Productions, 1993

Huxley, A. *Beyond the Mexique Bay*, London, Chatto & Windus, 1936

Keenagh, P. *Mosquito Coast*, London, Chatto & Windus, 1937

Squier, E. G. *Adventures on the Mosquito Shore*, New York, Worthington Co., 1891

Stephens, J. L. *Incidents of Travel in Central America*, Chiapas and Yucatán, London, Dover, 1970

Thompson, J. E. S. *The Maya of Belize: Historical Chapters since Columbus*, Belize, Cubola Productions, 1988

Thompson, J. E. S. *The Rise and Fall of Maya Civilisation*, University of Oklahoma Press, 1968

Warlords and Maize Men: A Guide to the Maya Sites of Belize, Belize, Cubola Productions, 1989

Wright, R. *Time Among the Maya*, London, Bodley Head, 1989

History and Analysis

A History of Belize, Belize, Cubola Productions, 1995

Afro-Central Americans: Rediscovering the African Heritage, London, Minority Rights Group Reports, 1996

Barry, T. & Vernon, D. *Inside Belize*, Albuquerque, Resource Centre, 1995

Belize: A Country Guide, Albuquerque, Resource Center, 1990

Bethell, L. (ed.) *Central America Since Independence*, Cambridge, CUP, 1991

Dobson, N. *A History of Belize*, Longman, 1973

Further Reading

Grant, C. H. *The Making of Modern Belize*, Cambridge University Press, 1976

Godfrey, G. D. *Ambergris Caye: Paradise with a Past*, Belize, Cubola Productions, 1996

Hyde, E. *X Communication*, Belize, Angelus Press, 1995

King, E. *Belize 1798: The Road to Glory (a 'novel history')*, Belize, Tropical Books, 1991

Pearce, J. *Under the Eagle: US Intervention in Central America and the Caribbean*, London, Latin America Bureau, 1982

Shoman, A. *Backtalking Belize*, Belize, The Belizean Chronicles Series, 1995

Shoman, A. *Thirteen Chapters of a History of Belize*, Belize, The Belizean Chronicles Series, Angelus Press 1994

Tedlock, D. (trans.) *Popol Vuh*, New York, Simon & Schuster, 1985

Woodward Jr, R.L. *Central America: A Nation Divided*, Oxford, OUP, 1985

Belizean Literature

Ellis, Z. *On Heroes, Lizards and Passion*, Belize, Cubola Productions, 1994

Ruiz Puga, D.N. *Old Benque*, Belize, Cubola Productions, 1994

Snap Shots of Belize (an anthology of short fiction), Belize, Cubola Productions, 1995

Marine Life and Diving

Greenberg, I. *Guide to Corals & Fishes of Florida, the Bahamas and the Caribbean*, Miami/Florida, Seahawk Press, 1986

Middleton, N. *Diving Belize*, New York, Aqua Quest Publications, 1994

Human, P. & Deloach, N. *Reef Fish Identification*, Jacksonville/Florida, New World Publications Inc, 1996

Human, P. & Deloach, N. *Reef Creature Identification and Reef Coral Identification*

Flora and Fauna

A to Z of Belizean Wildlife, Belize, Belize Audubon Society, BRC Printing, 1995

Cockscombe Basin Wildlife Sanctuary, Wisconsin, Hamaca Press & Orang-utan Press, 1996

Emmons, L. *Neotropical Rainforest Mammals*, Chicago, University of Chicago Press, 1990

Howell, S. & Webb S. *The Birds of Mexico and Northern Central America*, Oxford, OUP, 1995

McLeish, N., Pearce, N., Adams, B. & Briggs, J. *Native Orchids of Belize*, Amsterdam, AA Balkema, 1995

Page references to chapter titles and main entries are in **bold**.

Page references to maps are in *italic*.

activities **27–33**
Agressor Fleet 31
agriculture 41–2, 52–3
Agriculture and Trade Show 16
air travel 2, 5
Altun Ha 86–7
Ambergris Caye **92–106**, *93*, *97*
  archaeology 98
  Basil Jones 95
  bird watching 98
  boat trips 101–2
  Chac Balam 94
  diving 28–9, **99–100**
  eating out 94, 105–6
  fishing 100
  getting there 96
  history 94–5
  Marco Gonzalez 94
  marine reserves 101
  San Pedro 92, 94, *97*, 104–5
  shopping 102
  snorkel trips 101–2
  tourist information 97–8
  where to stay 102–5
Anderson, Ian 33, 147
archaeology 27
atolls, *see* Cayes
Audubon Society 32, 37, 57, 66, 86
babies 12–13
Baird's Tapir 127
Balboa, Vasco Nunez de 45
Barrier Reef 28, 90, 91–2
Barton Creek 178
Barton Creek Cave 138
Baymen 49, 72

Belize City **70–88**, *71*
  airline offices 76
  Altun Ha 86–7
  Bermudian Landing 86
  Bliss Institute 80
  bookshops 76
  Cayes 87–8
  colonial houses 80–1
  Community Baboon Sanctuary 59, **85–6**
  crime 70
  directory 76–9
  dive boats 77
  drugs 70
  eating out 83–4
  emergencies 76
  entertainment 84
  Fort George Lighthouse 81
  Fort Street 80–1
  getting around 75
  getting there 72–4
  Government House 78–9
  Haulover Creek 70
  history 72
  Hutson Street 81
  immigration 77
  Marine Museum 80
  Marine Terminal 80
  money 78
  national parks 78
  newspapers 76
  nightlife 84
  post office 78
  St Johns Cathedral 79
  shopping 81
  telephones 79
  tour agencies 79
  tourist information 75
  where to stay 81–3
  Zoo 85

Belize Defence Forces (BDF) 14
Belize Eco-Tourism Association (BETA) 66
Belmopan **124–7**, *125*
  archaeological vault 124
  getting there 125
  National Agricultural Show Weekend 124
  where to stay 126
Ben Loman's Cave 149
Benque Viejo 143
Bermudian Landing 86
BETA (Belize Eco-Tourism Association) 66
bicycles 8
bird watching 27, 56, **57–9**, 122
Black Rock Jungle Lodge 127, **142**
Blackbeard (Edward Teach) 49
Bliss, Baron 80, 81
Blue Creek **171–2**, 179
Blue Hole 29
Blue Hole National Park 147–8
Bluefield Range 119
boats 2–3, 5–6
Boca Ciega 29
bookshops 36
Branch Mouth 131
buccaneers 48–9
Bullet Tree Falls 131, **132–3**
Burdon Canal 148–9
buses 3–4, 7, 12
Butterfly Breeding Centre 59, **183**
Butterfly Fish 62

BDF (Belize Defence Forces) 14

Caesar's Place 127
Cahal Pech 131

Cakchiquel Maya 45
camping 37, **139–40**
Cancún 188
canoeing 33
Caracol 44, 122, 124, 135, **136–7**
cars 3–4, 7–8
Caste Wars 95, 174
caves 134, **138**
   caving tours 129
   potholing 32–3
Caves Branch Jungle River Camp 33, 147
Caye Caulker 29, 90, **106–13**
   bird watching 110
   diving 110–11
   eating out 113–14
   getting there 107–8
   kayaking/sailing 111
   tourist information 108–10
   water taxis 109–10
   where to stay 111–13
Caye Chapel 88
Cayes **90–120**
Cayo District **121–44**
Cerros 186–7
Chaa Creek 59, 137, **141**
Chan Chich Lodge 186
charter boats 6
Chatoyer, Joseph 153
Che Chem Hah 138
Chetumal 186
Chichen Itzá 45
Chiclero Botanical Trail 183
children 12–13
Chiquibul Cave System 134, **137**
cinemas 24
climate 13
Cockscomb Basin Jaguar Reserve 31, 37, 147, **163–4**
Columbia River Forest Reserve 67
Columbus, Christopher 45
Columbus Day 16

Community Baboon Sanctuary 59, 66, **85–6**
conservation areas 66
consulates 15–16
coral 28, 64, 65
Coral Caye Conservation 21
coral reefs, *see* reefs
Corozal 174, **186–8**
credit cards 22
crime 14
crocodiles 63
Crooked Tree Wildlife Sanctuary 57, 58, **175–6**
Crystal Skull mystery 170
Cuadros village culture 43
Cuello 182
currency 5, 21–2
customs formalities 5
cycling 8
Dangriga 123, 146, 148–9, **151–9**, *155*
   boats to the Cayes 156
   eating out 157
   entertainment 157–8
   getting to and from 153–4
   nightlife 157–8
   tour agents 156
   tourist information 154–6
   where to stay 156–7
Dem Dats Doin 172
democracy 51–2
disabled travellers 14–15
diving **28–31**, 90, 92
   boats from Belize City 77
   equipment 64
   reef hazards 64–5
   safety precautions 92
dolphins 63
Douglas da Silva 135, 139
drink 18
eating out 16–18
economy 52–4
ecotourism **65–8**, 165
education 53
El Pilar 132–3
electricity 15

embassies 15–16
emigration 54
English Caye 88
entry formalities 4–5
Esquivel, Manuel 51
ethnic groups 54
exit tax 4
fauna 56–60
   underwater 62–5
ferries, *see* boats
festivals 16
fishing 27–31
Five Blues Lake National Park 67, **148**
flora 61–2
   underwater 62–5
Flores 144
food 16–18
Freetown Sibun 123
Gales Point 123, **149–50**
García sisters 133
Garifuna 17, **146**, 147, **151–3**
gay travellers 18
Glovers Reef 29, 30, 91, 92, **118–19**
Goff's Caye 88
Guanacaste National Park 123–4
Guanaja 45
Guatemala 3, 14, 48, 50–1, 143–4
guest houses 37
Half Moon Caye
   bird watching 57
   diving 29–30
Hawksbill turtle 63
Hawksworth Bridge 127
health 12, **18–19**, 53
hiking 31–2
history **40–54**
   agriculture 41–2, 52–3
   British rule 50–1
   Creole Society 49–50
   early societies 42–3
   economy 52–4
   independence and democracy 51–2

independence from Spain 47–8
Maya 43–5
modern society 54
piracy 48–9
prehistory 40–1
Spanish Conquest 45–7
Hol Chan Marine Reserve 29
holiday homes 37
Honduran Bay Settlement 48, 49
Hopkins 158–9
horse riding 32
hotels 36–7
Hughes, Peter 31
Hummingbird Highway 146, 147
Hurricane Hattie 72
immigration 49–50, 54
Independence Day 16
Indigenous Experience 165
insects 59–60
insurance 19–20
Ixchel Farm 61
jellyfish 63, 65
Jewfish 62
jungle lodges 122, **140–3**
Kaminaljuyú 43–4
kayaking 33
La Milpa 184
Lamanai 180–2
Lighthouse Reef 29, 91, **116–17**
Little Belize 178
living in Belize 20–1
Long Caye 62
Lubaantun 170
Macal, River 122, 131, **137**
Mam Maya 45
mammals 59–60
manatee 150–1
 spotting tours 60–1, 149
maps 21
marijuana cultivation 176
Maya **42–5**
 on Ambergris Caye 94–5
 artefacts 26

Indigenous Experience 165–6
 Kekchi Maya 146–7
 Mopan Maya 146–7
 Santa Cruz Maya 174
media 23–4
Medical Advisory Service for Travellers Abroad (MASTA) 12, **19**
Medicine Trail 61
Melchor de Menchos 144
Mennonites 178–9
Mexico 3–4
 getting to and from 188
Midas Campsite 131
Mitchell Hedges, F.A. 170
money 5, 21–2
Monkey Bay Wildlife Sanctuary 123
Mopan, River 122, 131
Moray eels 64
Morgan, Sir Henry 48
Mosquito Indians 80
motorbikes 7–8
Mount Hope 126
Mountain Equestrian Trails 32, **143**
Mountain Pine Ridge 32, 37, 61, **134–7**
 camping 139
museums 23
Nabitunich Lodge 131, **142**
national holidays 23
natural Belize **56–68**
nature reserves 22–3
New Falls 171
newspapers 23–4
Nim Li Punit 171
Nohmul 182
Northern Belize **173–88**
Olmec 42
opening hours 22–3
Orange Walk 174, **176–80**, *177*
 eating out 180
 getting to 176
 history 176
 tourist information 179

 where to stay 179–80
Orchid Trail 61
Over the Top restaurant 148
Pacbitun 133–4
packing 24–5
PACT tax 4
Pacz Tours 32–3
passports 4
Pedro de Alvarado 46
People's United Party (PUP) 51–2
photography 25
pirates 47, 48
Placencia 146, **159–63**
 eating out 163
 entertainment 163
 getting to 160
 nightlife 163
 sports and activities 161
 tourist information 160–1
 where to stay 161–3
police 14
politics 48, **51–2**
Pook's Hill 126
post offices 25
potholing 32–3
 caves 134, **138**
 caving tours 129
practical A–Z **12–38**
prehistory 40–1
Price, George Cadle 51
privateers 49
Programme for Belize 184
Progreso 179
Protected Areas Conservation Tax 4
Protected Areas Conservation Trust (PACT) 67
Punta Gorda 67, 147, **164–70**, *167*
 eating out 169–70
 getting to and from 166, 168
 tourist information 168
 where to stay 169
Pusilhá 172

Quiché Maya 45
radio stations 24
rail travel 3
Rainforest Medicine Trail 130, **137**
rainy season 13
reefs 62–5
   Barrier Reef 28, 90, 91–2
reptiles 59–60
Rio Bravo Conservation Area 61, **183–6**, *185*
Río Frío Caves 137, **138**
Río On 135, **137**
River Haven 123
river rafting 33
road travel 3–4
   buses 7, 12
   cars 7–8
Roaring River 126
St George's Caye 87–8
St George's Caye, Battle of 50, 72
St Herman's Cave 147
St Margaret's village 148
St Vincent 152–3
San Antonio **133–4**, 170–1
San Ignacio (Cayo) 122, **127–30**, *129*
   archaeology 128–9
   Branch Mouth 131
   Cahal Pech 131
   caving 129
   cycling 129
   eating out 140
   El Pilar 132–3
   fishing 130
   getting to 128
   horse riding 130
   jungle lodges 140–3
   Natural History Centre 130
   nightlife 140
   Rainforest Medicine Trail 130, **137**
   tourist information 128
   where to stay 138–40
   Xunantunich 132

San Pablo 182
San Pedro Columbia 170
Santa Cruz Maya 174
Santa Elena 127
Santa Rita 186
Sargeant's Caye 88
Sarteneja 182
Sayonara 30
scorpionfish 28, 64
sea kayaking 33
sea travel 2–3, 5–6
seafood **17–18**
   closed season 68
Seine Bight 162
self-catering 37
Sepoys 49
sexual attitudes 25–6
Shark Ray Alley 29
sharks 28, 62–3, 64
Shipstern Reserve 182–3
shipwrecks 30
Shipyard 178, **179**, 180
shopping 26–7
Sibun, River 123
slavery 45–6, 49
snakes 60
South Water Caye 29, 158
Spanish Conquest 45–7
Spanish Lookout Caye 88
specialist tour operators 8–10
Spiny Lobster 63
sports **27–3**
Spotted Scorpionfish 64
Stann Creek and Toledo **145–72**
stinging coral 28, 65
stingrays 65
Tanah 133
Tapir Mountain Nature Reserve 127
taxes 4, 35, 37
Teach, Edward 'Blackbeard' 49
Teakettle 126
telephones 33–4
temperature 13

Tikal 44, 45
tipping 34–5
Tobacco Caye **120**, 158
Tobacco Reef 119–20
toilets 35
Toledo District 146
Toledo Eco-Tourism Association 165
Toltecs **42**, 44
tourism industry 53–4
tourist information 35
trains 3
travel **2–10**
   entry formalities 4–5
   getting around 5–8
   getting there 2–4
travel agents 8–10
Trujillo 153
Tuffy Cut 29
Turneffe Islands 29, 30, 90–1, **115–16**
turtles 63, 114
Twin Cayes 62
underwater flora and fauna 62–5
United Democratic Party (UDP) 51–2
United Provinces of Central America **47–8**, 50
Uxbenka 171
Vaca Cave 138
Versaille, Treaty of 50
Victoria Peak 31, 147
village culture 43
visas 4
Wave Dancer 31
whales 63
when to go 13
where to stay 36–7
wildlife 56–61
women travellers 37–8, 70
working in Belize 20–1
wrecks 30
Xunantunich 132
Yo Creek village 182
youth hostels 37
Yurumein 152

From the UK

Reef and Rainforest Tours Ltd, Prospect House, Jubilee Road, Totnes, Devon TQ9 5BP, tel: 01803 866965, fax: 01803 865916, have been offering Belize since 1989. Arrange tailor-made itineraries. Specialising in wildlife and birding. Accommodation in top jungle lodges and small coastal/island resorts. Charter catamaran. Diving/snorkelling. Mayan ruins including Tikal. ATOL bonded.

From the USA

Close Encounters/Belize
PO Box 1320, Detroit Lakes
MN 56502, USA
tel: 218 847 4441
toll free (USA): 888 875 1822
fax: 218 847 4442
e-mail: *belizejq@tek.star*
Web page: *http://www.travelsource.com/close-encounters/*
Specializing in exceptional reef, rainforest and ruins adventures representing over 45 resorts throughout the country. Discounted airfares for US departures.

TRIPS Worldwide
dramatically different

Specialist in Tailor made holidays to..
BELIZE
Holidays with your name on.
Built on your budget, your passions, your dreams.
COSTA RICA, CUBA, DOMINICA, GUATEMALA, HONDURAS, MEXICO, GUYANA, TRINIDAD & TOBAGO.
SPEAK TO SOMEBODY WHO HAS BEEN THERE!
Call for our new brochure and a copy of World Comic, Trips Travel Magazine.
9 BYRON PLACE
CLIFTON, BRISTOL, BS8 1JT, UK
PHONE: 0117 987 2626
FAX: 0117 987 2627
Email enquries@trips.demon.co.uk

ATOL 3150   LATA

BELIZE
CHANCHICH, CORAL CAYES, LAMANAI.
When you book your flights, hotel and ground arrangements with us you can be confident that you are dealing with a professional, first class company where quality of service and value go hand in hand.

South American Experience
Specialist in tailor-made itineraries
● LOW COST FLIGHTS ● HOTELS & TRANSFERS
47 CAUSTON ST, PIMLICO, LONDON SW1P 4AT
TEL: 0171-976 5511. FAX: 0171-976 6908

ATOL 3071

The Series for Food Lovers...

Cadogan's new **Lazy Days** series offers a choice of 20 indulgent days out in selected regions of Europe, focusing on a leisurely lunch in a -memorable restaurant, combined with a little sightseeing.

Detailed maps lead you right to the restaurant door, and recipes from each chef inspire you to cook or simply tempt you to eat.

Titles available:

Lazy Days Out in the Dordogne & Lot
Lazy Days Out Across the Channel
Lazy Days Out in Tuscany
Lazy Days Out in Andalucía
Lazy Days Out in Provence
Lazy Days Out in the Loire

About the Guides...

'Cadogan Guides have a reputation as the outstanding series for the independent traveller who doesn't want to follow the crowd...'

Daily Telegraph

'The quality of writing in this British series is exceptional... The Cadogan Guides can be counted on for interesting detail and informed recommendations.'

Going Places

'The characteristic of all these guides is a heady mix of the eminently practical, a stimulating description of the potentially already familiar, and an astonishing quantity of things we'd never thought of, let alone seen.'

Art Quarterly

'Cadogan Guides are entertaining... They go a little deeper than most guides, and the balance of infectious enthusiasm and solid practicality should appeal to first-timers and experienced travellers alike.'

Michael Palin

'It's difficult to praise the Cadogan books too highly...good writing, amusing comment and invaluable advice.'

The Independent

Also Available...

Country Guides

Antarctica
Central Asia
China: The Silk Routes
Egypt
France: Southwest France;
　Dordogne, Lot & Bordeaux
France: Southwest France;
　Gascony & the Pyrenees
France: Provence
France: Côte d'Azur
France: The South of France
France: The Loire
Germany
Germany: Bavaria
Guatemala
India
India: South India
India: Goa
Ireland
Ireland: Southwest Ireland
Ireland: Northern Ireland
Italy
Italy: The Bay of Naples and Southern Italy
Italy: Lombardy, Milan and the Italian Lakes
Italy: Tuscany
Italy: Three Cities—Rome, Florence and Venice
Japan
Morocco
Portugal
Portugal: The Algarve
Scotland
Scotland's Highlands and Islands
South Africa
Spain
Spain: Southern Spain
Spain: Northern Spain
Syria & Lebanon
Tunisia
Turkey: Western Turkey
Zimbabwe, Botswana and Namibia

City Guides

Amsterdam
Brussels, Bruges, Ghent & Antwerp
Florence, Siena, Pisa & Lucca
London
Moscow & St Petersburg
Paris
Prague
Rome
Venice & the Veneto

Island Guides

Bali
The Caribbean and Bahamas
The Caribbean: NE Caribbean;
　The Leeward Islands
The Caribbean: SE Caribbean;
　The Windward Islands
The Caribbean: Jamaica
Crete
Cyprus
Greece: The Greek Islands
Greece: The Cyclades
Greece: The Dodecanese
Greece: The Ionian Islands
Madeira & Porto Santo
Malta, Comino & Gozo
Sicily

Plus...

Healthy Travel: Bugs, Bites & Bowels
Travel by Cargo Ship
Five Minutes off the Motorway
Henry Kelly in the West of Ireland
London Markets